T0339430

Seven Essentials for Business Success

Successful leaders are great teachers, and successful teachers serve as models of leadership. This book enables both leaders and teachers to understand and use the best practices developed by award-winning professors, each of whom teaches one of the seven areas that are essential for business success.

These professors candidly discuss their successes and failures in the classroom, the mentors who inspired them, how they developed their teaching methods, and their rigorous preparation for class. Through descriptions of the professors in action, readers will gain an insider's perspective on their teaching skills, and witness how they teach the seven essentials for success in a variety of settings—MBA, Executive MBA, and executive education courses. The chapters also describe the daily lives (professional and personal) of the professors, and the impact they have beyond the classroom in improving organizations and society.

If you are a leader or teacher—or if you are interested in the content of a business school education—this book provides an insider's perspective on the best practices used by legendary professors when teaching the seven essentials that represent the core body of knowledge for business success.

George Siedel is the Williamson Family Professor Emeritus of Business Administration and the Arthur F. Thurnau Professor Emeritus of Business Law at the University of Michigan. As a Fulbright Scholar, he held a Distinguished Chair in the Humanities and Social Sciences. He has received the Bernard Teaching Leadership Award from the University of Michigan and the Distinguished Career Achievement Award from the Academy of Legal Studies in Business.

"This book should be required reading for new professors, and experienced professors will also benefit from the rich detail that includes stories, quotes and the pedagogy literature."

— *Professor T. Leigh Anenson, University of Maryland Smith College of Business*

"George Siedel has masterfully captured teaching lessons every business leader can learn from award-winning business school professors. Diligently employ these lessons in your organization and watch your employee engagement and performance soar!"

— *Tom Highley, Managing Partner, Cordis Capital Partners*

Seven Essentials for Business Success

Lessons from
Legendary Professors

George Siedel

Routledge
Taylor & Francis Group

NEW YORK AND LONDON

First published 2022
by Routledge
605 Third Avenue, New York, NY 10158

and by Routledge
2 Park Square, Milton Park, Abingdon, Oxon, OX14 4RN

Routledge is an imprint of the Taylor & Francis Group, an informa business

Library of Congress Cataloging-in-Publication Data
Names: Siedel, George J., author.
Title: Seven essentials for business success : lessons from
legendary professors / George J. Siedel.
Description: New York : Routledge, 2021. | Includes
bibliographical references and index.
Subjects: LCSH: Success in business. | Leadership. |
Employee empowerment. | Business education.
Classification: LCC HF5386 .S4474 2021 (print) |
LCC HF5386 (ebook) | DDC 658.4/09—dc23
LC record available at https://lccn.loc.gov/2021005614
LC ebook record available at https://lccn.loc.gov/2021005615

ISBN: 978-1-032-03445-4 (hbk)
ISBN: 978-1-032-03444-7 (pbk)
ISBN: 978-1-003-18731-8 (ebk)

Typeset in Sabon
by codeMantra

Contents

Dedication   vii
List of Figures   ix
About the Author   xi
Preface   xiii

1 Seven Remarkable Professors Teaching Seven
  Essential Areas for Business Success   1

2 The Seven Essential Areas: The Core Body
  of Knowledge Taught at Business Schools   14

3 Stanford Accounting Professor Charles Lee: Make
  Sound Investment Decisions While Searching for
  Truth in Your Personal Life   29

4 Wharton Legal Studies Professor Richard Shell:
  Understand Your Legal Responsibilities as a
  Leader and Your Personal Motivation for Success   50

5 Chicago Finance Professor Steven Kaplan: Learn
  How to Make Financial Decisions and Start a Business   71

6 Michigan Management Professor Gretchen
  Spreitzer: Design Your Life to Thrive in the New
  World of Work   90

7 Northwestern Marketing Professor Florian
  Zettelmeyer: Understand Data Analytics for
  Business Success   113

8   MIT Operations Professor Georgia Perakis: Learn
How to Improve Business Operations through
Innovative Research and Practice   137

9   Harvard Strategy Professor Jan Rivkin: Develop
Skills to Formulate Strategy and Gain Competitive
Advantage   157

10 Lessons for Leaders and Teachers: The Teaching
Process and the Power of Authenticity   185

Appendix A: Zoom Lessons for Leaders   215
Appendix B: Business School Rankings and the
Methodology for Business School Selection   220
Index   227

Dedication

This book is dedicated to C. Roland "Chris" Christensen, who has been called "the patron saint of teaching" (Schmotter, 1998). According to Russell Edgerton, former president of the American Association for Higher Education, watching Chris in the classroom was like observing "Rostropovich and Bernstein conduct a symphony" (Blagg, 2008).

I first met Chris on January 10, 1992, when he led a seminar on "Developing Discussion Leadership Skills" for faculty at the Ross School of Business at the University of Michigan. I was asked to summarize his key lessons during a faculty workshop that followed the seminar. Inspired by colleagues at the University of Michigan and other universities where I served as a visiting professor, I had earlier considered writing a book about the teaching skills of master professors. Chris' seminar was the catalyst for proceeding with the project.

The project lay dormant for several years when I served as associate dean at Michigan Ross and attended to other professional responsibilities. During that time, I communicated with Chris, who let me know that he was enthusiastic about the project. During our telephone conversations, he recommended a number of readings, and he sent me additional suggestions with a cover note that concluded, "Have a great adventure."

By the time of his death in 1999, when he was the Robert Walmsley University Professor Emeritus at Harvard, Chris had taught for over a half a century. He was well known as a pioneer in the field of business strategy, which he called his "first adventure," and the Academy of Management honored him for his leadership in this area with its first Outstanding Educator Award (Blagg, 2008).

Chris' "second adventure" began when Dean George Baker invited him to lead an initiative to help Harvard Business School professors develop their teaching skills. Harvard President Derek Bok then asked Chris to help improve the quality of teaching throughout the university. This initiative led to the development of seminars that he conducted at universities around the world, including the aforementioned one at the

University of Michigan. Chris was also well known for two books that are cited in the chapters that follow: *Education for Judgment* (Christensen, 1991) and *Teaching and the Case Method* (Christensen, 1987).

In recognition of his leadership in developing high-quality teaching, Harvard Business School established the Christensen Center for Teaching and Learning, and created the C. Roland Christensen Professorship of Business Administration. And the University of Utah named a building at the Eccles School of Business after Chris—the C. Roland Christensen Center. Despite his many accomplishments and honors, Chris was a modest individual. Two days after the seminar at Michigan Ross, he sent participants a note in which he mentioned that "to take two days out of your busy schedule was a 'gift' of major significance to your associates and to your institution." Noting several specific changes that he planned to make in his seminar materials as a result of our feedback, he went on to thank *us* for teaching *him*!

A video of Chris teaching a class captures his modesty and values. With mannerisms not unlike Mr. Rogers, he brought to life the qualities of a great teacher. The video concludes with Chris walking across campus on his way home with a voiceover that refers to his beloved wife, Dorothy Smith, whom he nicknamed "Smitty":

"Every day before I go into the office, if I am teaching, the last thing I do is to hug Smitty, I'll look at her, and she'll say, 'Good luck, Rollie. Do your best.' And when I can come home and say, 'It really worked… something happened,' it's worth it all" (The art of discussion leading, n.d.).

I hope that whether you are a teacher in a traditional classroom or a leader acting in your role as a teacher to improve your organization, this book will enable you to make something happen. When you do so, it will make your teaching "worth it all."

References

Blagg, D. (2008, March). Classroom legend. *HBS Alumni Bulletin*, pp. 22–28.

Christensen, R. et al., Eds. (1991). *Education for judgment*. Boston: Harvard Business School Press.

Christensen, R., Ed. (1987). *Teaching and the case method*. Boston: Harvard Business School.

Schmotter, J. (1998, Spring). An interview with Professor C. Roland Christensen. *Selections*, pp. 2–7.

The art of discussion leading. (n.d.). Retrieved from Vimeo: https://vimeo.com/104311202

Figures

3.1   Professor Charles Lee   31
4.1   Professor Richard Shell   53
5.1   Professor Steven Kaplan   73
6.1   Professor Gretchen Spreitzer   94
7.1   Professor Florian Zettelmeyer   115
8.1   Professor Georgia Perakis   140
9.1   Professor Jan Rivkin   160

About the Author

George Siedel is the Williamson Family Professor Emeritus of Business Administration and Arthur F. Thurnau Professor Emeritus of Business Law at the University of Michigan. He graduated with honors from the College of Wooster and completed his graduate studies at the University of Michigan and at Cambridge University. Professor Siedel worked as an attorney in a professional corporation before joining the faculty at the University of Michigan, where he served as Associate Dean at the Ross School of Business. At Ross, he was also the founding director of the GMAC-AACSB Minority Summer Institute, the Senior Seminar, and the Washington Campus Undergraduate Studies Program.

Professor Siedel was a Visiting Professor at Stanford University and Harvard University, a Visiting Scholar at the University of California, Berkeley, and a Parsons Fellow at the University of Sydney. He has been elected a Visiting Fellow at Cambridge University's Wolfson College and a Life Fellow of the Michigan State Bar Foundation. As a Fulbright Scholar in Eastern Europe, he held a Distinguished Chair in the Humanities and Social Sciences.

The author of numerous books and articles, Professor Siedel is the recipient of research awards from the University of Michigan (the Faculty Recognition Award) and the Academy of Legal Studies in Business (the Hoeber Award, the Ralph Bunche Award, and the Maurer Award). In 2018, the Academy of Legal Studies in Business selected Professor Siedel for its Distinguished Career Achievement Award.

Professor Siedel has also received many teaching awards, including the Bernard Teaching Leadership Award from the University of Michigan and the 2018 Executive Program Professor of the Year Award from a consortium of thirty-six leading universities committed to international education.

Preface

Business schools mirror the university in microcosm, as business professors teach and conduct research in seven key areas—the "seven essentials"—that are based on the foundational disciplines of psychology, economics, and statistics. This mixture of disciplines produces a complex and diverse teaching environment that has led to the development of a variety of teaching methods.

While books have been written on one of these methods, Harvard-style case teaching, this is the first that explores the strategies and skills used by leading professors across the seven key areas. Given the interdisciplinary nature of a business school education, I hope that an understanding of the teaching methods and authenticity exhibited by the master professors profiled in this book will be of interest to professors in all disciplines and will also inspire business leaders whose teaching role is important to the success of their firms.

The book addresses these questions:

- What are the essential areas—the core body of knowledge—necessary for success in business?
- How do leading professors at top-ranked business schools teach these essential areas?
- What lessons can leaders and teachers learn from these master teachers?
- Beyond the teaching process they employ, what is the unique characteristic called "authenticity" that enables these professors to inspire future business leaders and to engage in activities beyond the classroom that improve society?

To answer these questions, *The Seven Essentials* takes you on a road trip to seven top-ranked business schools where you will meet seven award-winning professors. Each teaches one of the seven essential areas that constitute the core body of knowledge—the foundation for business success: accounting, business law, finance, management, marketing, operations, and strategy.

The book opens in Chapter 1 by explaining the process for selecting the professors and why the seven essential areas are critical to the success of businesses ranging from start-ups to giant international firms. Chapter 2 describes the key elements in each area as taught at the seven top-ranked schools. In so doing, the chapter, in effect, provides a checklist of the knowledge necessary for anyone interested in starting a business or becoming a manager.

In Chapters 3–9, you will meet each of the seven professors as they candidly describe the factors that led to their success in the classroom. During a visit to their classrooms, you will gain an insider's perspective on their teaching skills and witness how they teach the seven essentials for success in MBA, Executive MBA, and executive education courses. You will also learn about their daily professional and personal lives, and the impact they have beyond the classroom in improving organizations and society.

Teaching is an important skill for business leaders, just as leadership is the mark of a successful teacher. If you are a leader or a traditional classroom teacher, this book will provide an opportunity to improve your teaching skills by using the menu of options in Chapter 10, which summarizes the teaching process used by the seven professors.

Chapter 10 concludes with discussion of a key factor in the success of these professors beyond their teaching skills: the authenticity they bring to the classroom and to their other activities. While authenticity is an elusive concept, their professional lives include concrete examples in the form of their passion for the material they teach, concern for students, dedication to lifelong learning, and focus on a higher purpose that benefits society. Through their efforts, they inspire students to understand the importance of values and integrity, enable the creation of hundreds of startup companies and thousands of jobs, encourage organizations to create positive work environments that inspire employees to strive for excellence, and support the development of policies designed to enable people at all levels of society to share in a nation's prosperity.

U.S. President James A. Garfield expressed his admiration for one of his professors in this widely-cited quote: "The ideal college is Mark Hopkins on one end of a log and a student on the other." In recent times, the log linking the teacher and student has increasingly become electronic. Appendix A provides lessons on meeting the teaching challenges that video conferencing platforms present. Appendix B describes business school rankings and the methodology used to select the schools depicted in this book.

Chapter I

Seven Remarkable Professors Teaching Seven Essential Areas for Business Success

This book identifies the best practices used by leading MBA professors when they teach the seven essential areas for business success. The formula used in developing this book is simple. Owners of and managers in any business, large or small, must understand seven areas that are essential for its success: accounting, business law, finance, management, marketing, operations, and strategy. To illustrate best practices in teaching these areas, I have selected seven legendary business school professors— one from each area—who have been honored for their exceptional teaching skills at seven top-ranked schools.

Overview of this Book

After introducing the seven professors in the next section, the rest of Chapter 1 describes the goal of this book in detail. Later sections in this chapter focus on (1) why this book is important for leaders, teachers, and individuals interested in the content of a business school education, (2) the process used for selecting the seven professors, and (3) the importance of the seven essentials in achieving business success.

Chapter 2 elaborates on the seven essentials by describing how business schools cover this core body of knowledge. Profiles of each school in this chapter include little-known facts. For example, can you match these individuals with the business school they attended: President John F. Kennedy? Dr. Oz? Jay Berwanger (the first Heisman Trophy winner)? Benjamin Netanyahu? Michael Bloomberg?

Chapters 3–9 profile each of the professors, who are from seven leading business schools. These chapters include summaries of the professors' teaching, research, and other activities (including a "Day in the Life" feature); in-depth interviews; observations of the professors in action while teaching their classes; comments from their students; a discussion of their impact beyond the classroom; and a summary of the lessons learned from them.

Chapter 10 concludes the book with a review of the seven professors' teaching methods, along with an examination of the "authenticity" that makes them extraordinary. The authenticity they bring to their teaching and research extends to the positive impact they have on society. In an interview published in *Poets and Quants* (the leading source of information about business schools), Dean William Boulding of the Fuqua School of Business at Duke University emphasized the importance of this impact when discussing the role of business schools in society:

> If we can't produce the talent and insights that help us tackle the challenges in the world then we are not doing our jobs. So we need to make sure we are responsive to the times we are in and the times we will face in being a positive force in society and helping to improve lives.
>
> (Byrne, 2020)

Meet the Professors

Before turning to the goals of this book in the next section, we will first visit the seven professors to learn how they spend a typical workday. Our trip begins on the East Coast, at Harvard Business School in Boston, Massachusetts, and concludes on the West Coast at the Stanford Graduate School of Business in Palo Alto, California.

Are you familiar with the "Snooze Alarm Test" that determines your level of enthusiasm for life by counting the number of times you hit your snooze alarm before getting up? (Hint: a high number indicates low enthusiasm.) On our chosen day, Harvard Business School (HBS) Strategy Professor **Jan Rivkin** passes the test with flying colors, as he wakes before the alarm. His main event for the day is preparing for and teaching a class on Strategy—a course that all Harvard MBA students are required to take. During the class, he focuses on a case that involved crafting strategy during a leadership change at the ice cream company Ben & Jerry's. However, as a senior leader at HBS, his day is also filled with meetings with corporate recruiters, students, colleagues, and alumni. His leadership responsibilities also include serving as the Co-Director of the US Competitiveness Project, which focuses on making America more competitive while simultaneously enabling the average person to benefit more from the country's resources. It is no surprise that his day ends late in the evening with an email review that includes sending thirty-two messages relating to his widespread responsibilities.

MIT's Sloan School of Management is located down the road (Memorial Drive) from Harvard in Cambridge, a seven-minute subway ride on the Red Line. Sloan Operations Professor **Georgia Perakis**, fueled by Greek iced-coffee, begins her workday with a presentation to a research project sponsor in Spain and a follow-up meeting with PhD students on the project's next steps. As director of the Executive MBA Program (EMBA), she then meets with the program's assistant dean and staff. Next come meetings with PhD students for research updates and with teaching assistants to prepare for her next class. In all these activities, her goal is to have a positive impact by working on important real-life problems that drive her research and provide her students with examples of the models she teaches. Her day ends late in the evening with work on emails and posting materials on her EMBA course website. The course—Data, Models, and Decisions—is considered to be the most challenging in the program.

The Wharton School of the University of Pennsylvania, located in Philadelphia, is a five-hour car ride (or ninety-minute flight) southwest of Cambridge. Here we find Business Law Professor **Richard Shell**, after an early morning breakfast and meditation, opening his workday with a phone discussion about a faculty development program. This is followed by a meeting with the Deputy Dean, emails and calls regarding upcoming programs, helping a student with a midterm paper, preparing and teaching a three-hour class in the Wharton-mandated law course titled "Responsibility in Global Management," and after-dinner work on email. One of his calls relates to a program he co-founded called "Purpose, Passion, and Principles." This program helps students address issues that are not part of the formal MBA curriculum, such as defining how success and happiness relate to the students' life goals—topics covered in Professor Shell's bestselling book *Springboard: Launching Your Personal Search for Success* (Shell, 2014).

Moving northwest nine hours by car (or two hours by air) from Philadelphia to Ann Arbor, Michigan, **Gretchen Spreitzer,** a Management professor at the University of Michigan's Ross School of Business, is already in her office by 7:30 a.m., following an early morning jog with her dog and running partners. Her day includes discussions with colleagues about faculty and teaching matters, listening to a student's thesis defense, teaching a cutting-edge course on the new world of work, meetings with student teams and with the donor who endowed her chair, and attending a StoryLab event, which concludes her twelve-hour workday at 7:30 p.m. In teaching her course, she includes research from a new field called "Positive Organizational Scholarship" that she has pioneered with Ross colleagues. Their research focuses on creating positive work environments designed to enhance employee engagement.

A four-hour car ride west from Ann Arbor to Chicago takes us to the University of Chicago on the south side of the city, where Finance Professor **Steven Kaplan** opens his day by teaching a three-hour course on corporate and entrepreneurial finance at the law school. He then crosses campus to the Chicago Booth School of Business where, after a short break for lunch, he leads an afternoon session in his Special Topics course that is part of the school's New Venture Challenge. During this session, student teams practice presenting their business plans to successful entrepreneurs who serve as judges. By the end of the course, eleven of these teams receive investments totaling over $850,000. Companies created by past teams have made more than $7.5 billion in mergers and exits. Professor Kaplan concludes his afternoon by editing a research paper and, in the evening, reviewing the judges' feedback to the student teams.

A forty-five-minute cab ride from Chicago Booth north along Lake Shore Drive takes us to Northwestern's Kellogg School of Management and into the life of Professor **Florian Zettelmeyer,** who chairs the Marketing Department. Professor Zettelmeyer passes the Snooze Alarm Test by awakening before his alarm sounds. After arriving early at his office, his workday begins with a meeting with the Global Head of Learning for a large consulting company on the design of a new executive program. He then teaches a two-hour session to around fifty executives in a program titled "Leading with Advanced Analytics and Artificial Intelligence." After lunch, he helps a colleague develop a lecture, talks with the CEO of a major travel company who needs help finding a new head of Artificial Intelligence and Data Analytics, meets with a colleague to discuss the Marketing Department's teaching schedule, and teaches another session in the executive program. His day closes with dinner, viola and violin lessons with his sons, cleaning up the kitchen, and a well-deserved glass of wine.

The last trip of the day is a four-hour plane ride from Chicago's O'Hare Airport to the San Francisco International Airport, followed by a short drive to Stanford's Graduate School of Business in Palo Alto. Stanford Accounting Professor **Charles Lee** arrives at Peet's Coffee when it opens at 5:00 a.m. and then heads to his office, where he responds to emails and prepares for back-to-back sections of his course titled "Alphanomics: Active Investing in Equity Markets," which run from 8:00 a.m. to 11:45 a.m. He is highly qualified to teach this course, which won the Innovation in Financial Accounting Education Award from the American Accounting Association. His experience includes serving as the leader of a worldwide active equity research team with joint responsibility for the North American active equity trading business at Barclays (now Blackrock). At the time, Barclays managed over $300 billion in active equity assets. Following class, he attends a long meeting of a university-wide faculty appointments committee, meets with students until 7:00 p.m., and then heads home to watch the Golden State Warriors play basketball.

The Goal of this Book

The leading universities where they work have honored these seven extraordinary professors for their teaching excellence. By sharing their teaching philosophies and inviting us into their classrooms, they have given us a wonderful gift—the opportunity to learn about the best practices they use when teaching the seven essentials necessary for success in business. The profiles of the professors in Chapters 3–9 illustrate how they prepare for teaching, build a learning community, emphasize the big picture, simplify their subject matter, make the learning interactive, and show their students why understanding the course material is essential to business success. This book provides leaders and teachers with a menu of these practices (summarized in Chapter 10) that they can use to improve the learning process in their organizations and classrooms.

This book also provides examples of that rare quality called "authenticity," which is a product of each professor's passion for the course material, concern for their students, and dedication to continuous learning. Authenticity is also characterized by a sense of purpose that leads to an impact beyond the classroom. In the chapters that follow you will learn about

- Jan Rivkin's work on developing the next generation of civic leaders in cities across the country,
- Georgia Perakis' passion for using high-quality research to address pressing problems facing businesses,
- Richard Shell's program that helps MBA graduates find purpose and happiness in life,
- Gretchen Spreitzer's pioneering efforts to develop positive work environments,
- Steven Kaplan's New Venture Challenge that has resulted in the creation of thousands of jobs,
- Florian Zettelmeyer's efforts to enable managers around the world to understand and use analytics, and
- Charles Lee's work with students to help them answer life's most difficult questions: "Who am I? What am I doing here? Where am I going?"

The Teaching Role of Leaders and the Leadership Role of Teachers

This book targets three audiences: leaders playing a teaching role within their organizations, teachers as leaders, and individuals interested in the content of a business school education.

Leaders as Teachers within Their Organizations

Several years ago, an executive development organization approached me about a business coaching opportunity. The CEO of a large company planned to retire in three years, and he was considering three candidates, each from a different functional area, to succeed him. He wanted someone to coach them on the areas where they needed improvement and to advise him on his final selection. I was not interested because of other commitments, but this opportunity did cause me to wonder about the criteria I would use in recommending a final candidate. Of course, knowledge of the seven essential areas and the ability to work across functions is important. However, perhaps more significant is the ability to teach and develop people, the most important resource in today's information-based economy.

As I later learned through the research of experts like Sydney Finkelstein and Noel Tichy, what separates great leaders from average leaders is the ability to teach. As Finkelstein, the director of the Center for Leadership at Dartmouth's Tuck School of Business, notes in the title of his 2018 article in the *Harvard Business Review,* "The best leaders are great teachers." He concludes, "If you're not really teaching, you're not leading" (p. 145).

Tichy, a Michigan Ross professor who headed GE's Leadership Center at Crotonville, put it this way in his book *The Cycle of Leadership: How Great Leaders Teach Their Companies to Win*:

> The essence of leading is not commanding, but teaching. It is opening people's eyes and minds. It is teaching them new ways to see the world and pointing them to new goals. It is giving them the motivation and discipline to achieve those goals. And it is teaching them to share their own knowledge and teach others.
>
> (Tichy, 2004)

Based on years of studying exceptional leaders, Finkelstein addresses the following questions in his *Harvard Business Review* article.

What do exceptional leaders teach? He concludes that they teach skills, tactics, principles (including integrity and ethical standards), and life lessons. One example of life lessons he cites is a meeting of the LinkedIn CEO with a senior vice president that changed the latter's management philosophy following their discussion of Buddhist principles.

How do they teach? Finkelstein concludes that two critical elements are the timing of the instruction and the form of delivery. A key skill is the ability to ask questions. As Finkelstein states: "Star leaders also take a page from Socrates and teach by asking sharp, relevant questions" (p. 145). The answers to these questions are important to a leader's own ability to continue learning.

What do these leaders do beyond their direct teaching? Finkelstein notes the importance of modeling by leaders—that is, serving as role models as they walk the talk.

This book addresses the same questions. First, if you are a leader or aspire to become one, you will learn **what** the seven great teachers teach—the cutting-edge knowledge that constitutes the seven essentials for business success. Second, beyond content, the profiles in Chapters 3–9 take you into classrooms to demonstrate **how** the seven professors teach the seven essentials. Finally, the discussion of authenticity in Chapter 10 illustrates the leadership principles that they **model** for their students.

As this book went to press, a fourth question was added to the list: What can leaders learn from professors who gained substantial experience during the COVID-19 pandemic when teaching courses remotely over video conference platforms like Zoom? Appendix A, "5 Zoom Lessons for Leaders," addresses this question.

Teachers as Leaders

Understanding the best teaching practices used by the seven professors profiled in this book is important to traditional classroom teachers and PhD candidates. Just as leaders play a teaching role, teachers play an important leadership role. Tom DeLong, the Baker Professor of Management Practice at Harvard Business School, has experience as both a teacher and a leader (as chief development officer at Morgan Stanley). In his book *Teaching by Heart* (DeLong, 2020), he concludes that "teachers lead and leaders teach. Again, this may not be obvious, but think about how teachers model behaviors they want students to adopt, how they motivate by telling stories, how they make decisions that affect all students" (Hanna, 2020, p. 49). The seven professors profiled in this book are role models in their ability to combine best practices in the teaching process with the authenticity that lies at the heart of great teaching.

The Content of a Business School Education

If you are interested in the content of a business school education because you are considering applying to an MBA program or starting and managing a business, this book introduces the seven essential areas for business success and describes how professors at seven leading business schools teach these areas. The topics covered in this book relating to business and career success include:

- the importance of thinking beyond your resume when making life decisions (Chapter 3),
- how to personalize your search for success (Chapter 4),
- the most important advice for someone starting a new business venture (Chapter 5),
- strategies for developing a successful career in the new world of work (Chapter 6),

- the key elements you should understand when preparing a presentation (Chapter 7),
- how to use data and models when making business decisions (Chapter 8), and
- factors to consider when creating a business strategy (Chapter 9).

Selection of the Seven Professors and the Research Process

Each of the seven professors we visited on our earlier tour of business schools represents one of the seven areas that are essential for business success (as explained in the next section) and each one is from a leading business school. During the selection process, I first identified the seven schools and then matched each with one of the essential areas. Appendix B describes in detail the methodology for identifying the schools and the matching process. As explained in Appendix B, I used the 2019 *US News* ranking of MBA programs when selecting the schools because it includes the most complete rankings of the essential areas (Ethier, 2018). The *US News* ranking was also the most recent one at the time I started my research, and it is widely followed and highly regarded for its methodology.

I then identified tenured professors at each school who had won awards for teaching in one of the seven essential areas. To ensure that I had not overlooked anyone, I asked deans or associate deans at six of the seven schools for advice on my selection of the professors. I did not contact the Wharton dean because I was familiar with the faculty; the school has invited me on more than one occasion to serve as an outside consultant as part of their Quinquennial (yes, that is a word) Review process. I am grateful to the following business school leaders for their advice. These are the positions they held when I contacted them.

- Chicago Booth: Douglas Skinner, Deputy Dean for Faculty
- Harvard Business School: Lynn Sharp Paine, Senior Associate Dean for International Development
- Michigan Ross: Scott DeRue, Dean
- MIT Sloan: David Schmittlein, Dean
- Northwestern Kellogg: Kathleen Hagerty, Senior Associate Dean for Faculty and Research
- Stanford Graduate School of Business: Maureen McNichols, Senior Associate Dean for Academic Affairs

Finally, from my lists of award-winning professors I selected one representative from each school. Here are the results, which indicate the pairing of each essential area with a school, the professor selected to represent the area, and the chapter that profiles each professor.

- Accounting—Stanford Graduate School of Business: Charles Lee (Chapter 3)
- Business Law—Wharton: Richard Shell (Chapter 4)
- Finance—Chicago Booth: Steven Kaplan (Chapter 5)
- Management—Michigan Ross: Gretchen Spreitzer (Chapter 6)
- Marketing—Northwestern Kellogg: Florian Zettelmeyer (Chapter 7)
- Operations—MIT Sloan: Georgia Perakis (Chapter 8)
- Strategy—Harvard Business School: Jan Rivkin (Chapter 9)

After conducting background research on the seven professors, I sent them questionnaires and scheduled interviews. I followed the interviews with classroom visits. One unanticipated benefit dictated by their teaching schedules is that I had the opportunity to observe the seven professors in a variety of classroom settings described in the following chapters: MBA, Executive MBA, executive education, undergraduate, and law school. Three of the courses (taught by Professors Lee, Spreitzer, and Zettelmeyer) covered advanced topics beyond core course material. During this process, I talked with colleagues of the professors, as well as their students, teaching assistants, and alumni. I also studied videos of presentations by them.

The Seven Essential Areas for Business and Career Success

The seven essential areas that are key to business and career success are known by a variety of names—such as concentrations, departments, functions, and specialties—within business organizations and business schools. Regardless of the nomenclature, these areas cover most of the core body of knowledge that is both taught at business schools and represented in the organization structure of companies. Underlying disciplines such as economics and statistics, while important in business education in laying a foundation for understanding the seven areas, are not included in this book because they are usually not separate departments within companies. We now look at why the seven essential areas are important to both start-up businesses and established companies.

Importance of the Seven Essentials in a Start-Up

To illustrate why the seven essentials are critical to business and career success, consider the challenges faced by an entrepreneur, Taylor, who recently started a business manufacturing plant-based, meatless burgers.

Like most entrepreneurs, Taylor has few resources to meet the key challenges that she faces. If she can afford to pay professionals, she must know enough about the seven essential areas to make informed decisions based on their advice. If she cannot afford professional advice, she must handle the following matters on her own.

Accounting. Taylor must develop and understand a system for record keeping that she will use to make business decisions, pay taxes, and inform investors about how the business is doing. The records are summarized in a balance sheet (reporting the company assets, liabilities, and owner's equity), income statement (reporting the company's revenues and expenses over a set time), and statement of cash flows (reporting the flow of cash into and out of the business).

Business law. Taylor must make decisions relating to a number of legal questions. What is the legal form of the business (partnership, corporation, etc.)? What are her employment law responsibilities when she hires, supervises, and discharges employees? What government regulations govern the way the company manufactures and sells its product? What are the liability risks associated with the product? What types of contracts are necessary for transactions with customers and suppliers? How should the company protect its intellectual property?

Finance. Taylor must decide how to finance her business by borrowing money and/or finding investors. Once she obtains funding, she must decide how to maintain a sensible balance between debt and the investors' equity, and how to invest and use the funds (for example, knowing when to invest in a new manufacturing facility). She must also decide whether to pay dividends to investors. Companies often combine the finance area with accounting because accounting reports are important when making financial decisions.

Management (including HRM). When starting her business Taylor will handle management responsibilities until she can hire lower level managers who will be responsible for each essential area. These managers will also serve as leaders of two company functions that are specifically concerned with management: human resource management (HRM) and strategy (covered below). HRM focuses on hiring and managing the people who are critical to the success of Taylor's business.

Marketing. Taylor must make a number of decisions when marketing her meatless burgers. How should the company promote and advertise the product? What type of sales staff does she need? How can the company coordinate sales with manufacturing? Should it market the product to grocery stores or directly to consumers? How should the company follow up on sales and handle complaints? What type of consumer research is necessary to identify the target market and develop new products? How should the company determine price?

Operations. Operations focuses on efficiently manufacturing and delivering the meatless burgers to customers. How should the company manage its relationship with suppliers? What is the most efficient manufacturing process? What advances in technology should the company use? How can it ensure the highest quality possible? Are the company's facilities appropriate for its manufacturing needs? How would the development of new products affect operational efficiency? How can the company effectively manage its inventory?

Strategy. Strategy, the tie that binds the six other areas, focuses on identifying the goals of the business and deciding how to implement them. In developing a strategic plan, Taylor must consider a variety of questions. How fast does she want to grow the business? What is the best way to achieve this growth? What resources does the company need to achieve her objectives, and how should she allocate these resources to various company activities? Who are her competitors, and how can the company gain competitive advantage over them? How should she measure her company's success?

The Seven Essentials in a Large Organization

Like start-up entrepreneur Taylor, people working in companies around the world must understand the seven essentials that guide their business decisions. Larger, established organizations embed this framework into their structure in the form of functions. As Leinwand and Mainardi note in their article "Beyond Functions" (Leinwand & Mainardi, 2013), "[T]he functional model has become the conceptual core of nearly all organizational structures, public and private. ... Business units come and go with the product life cycle, but finance, HR, marketing, legal, and R&D last forever."

For a real-life example, we now shift from Taylor's start-up to Apple, the perennial leader in *Fortune*'s annual ranking of the world's most-admired companies and the first US company to achieve a $2 trillion market capitalization. (Market capitalization is the total value of a company's stock.)

Apple faces the same concerns as Taylor, although on a grander scale. Unlike Taylor, Apple has abundant resources for addressing these concerns. The organization of these resources into departments generally matches the seven essential areas. Here are the responsibilities of key senior leadership team members who head various departments, as described on the Apple website (Apple Leadership).

Accounting and finance. The company's chief financial officer "oversees the accounting, business support, financial planning and analysis, treasury, real estate, investor relations, internal audit and tax functions at Apple."

Business law. Apple's General Counsel and Senior Vice President of Legal and Global Security "serves on the company's executive team and oversees all legal matters, including corporate governance, intellectual property, litigation and securities compliance, global security and privacy."

Management (HRM). Apple's Senior Vice President of Retail + People "works to help Apple connect, develop and care for its employees—and to help those employees do the best work of their lives. Her teams oversee a broad range of functions, including talent development and Apple University, recruiting, employee relations and experience, business partnership, benefits, compensation, and inclusion and diversity."

Marketing. Apple's Senior Vice President of Worldwide Marketing "has helped the company create the best computers in the world with the Mac, lead the digital music revolution with iPod and iTunes, reinvent mobile phones with iPhone and the App Store, and define the future of mobile computing with iPad." Another key marketing executive, Apple's Vice President of Marketing Communications, "leads a talented and creative team focused on Apple's advertising, internet presence, package design and other consumer-facing marketing."

Operations. The chief operating officer "oversees Apple's entire worldwide operations and customer service and support." Another key operations executive, the Senior Vice President of Operations, "is in charge of Apple's global supply chain, ensuring product quality and overseeing planning, procurement, manufacturing, logistics and product fulfillment functions."

Strategy. Apple's Senior Vice President of Machine Learning and AI Strategy "oversees the strategy for artificial intelligence and machine learning across the company and development of Core ML and Siri technologies." Another key strategy executive, Apple's Vice President of Corporate Development, "is responsible for the company's mergers, acquisitions and strategic investing efforts."

To operate effectively, these Apple leaders must have chameleon-like 360-degree vision and capabilities. They must provide key information and advice upward to Apple's CEO and the Board of Directors, who are responsible for overall leadership at the firm. Because company concerns touch many areas simultaneously, the company leaders must operate horizontally beyond their functional silos when they interact with each other. This requires them to understand enough about the other areas to contribute effectively as members of the leadership team. Finally, they must work with staff at lower levels in their own and other departments. These staff members must also understand the seven essential areas so that they can implement advice received from departments beyond their own.

The Seven Essentials within Business Schools

Business schools use a variety of organizational structures for teaching and research relating to the seven functional areas. Some combine areas, while others have created departments or areas that are similar to the structure of companies like Apple. For example, Michigan Ross has faculty areas that focus on accounting, business law, finance, management, marketing, operations, and strategy. MIT Sloan and Wharton have similar departments, except that both of them combine strategy and management into one area.

The next chapter explains how business schools teach the seven essential areas, the body of knowledge that represents the core of a business education. Chapters 3–9 then profile the seven professors who represent each of these areas.

References

Apple leadership. (n.d.). Retrieved from Apple: https://www.apple.com/leadership/

Byrne, J. (2020, April 15). Why this dean is optimistic about an on-campus start in the fall. Retrieved from POETS&QUANTS: https://poetsandquants.com/2020/04/15/why-a-top-b-school-dean-is-optimistic-about-an-on-campus-start-in-the-fall/3/

DeLong, T. (2020). Teaching by heart: One professor's journey to inspire. Boston: Harvard Business Review Press.

Ethier, M. (2018, March 26). How business schools rank by specialization. Retrieved from Poets&Quants: https://poetsandquants.com/2018/03/26/how-business-schools-rank-by-specialization/

Finkelstein, S. (2018, January-February). The best leaders are great teachers. Harvard Busienss Review, pp. 142–145.

Hanna, J. (2020, March). Teachable moments. HBS Alumni Bulletin, pp. 49–51.

Leinwand, P. & Mainardi, C. (2013, February 13). Beyond functions. Retrieved from strategy+business: https://www.strategy-business.com/article/00161?gko=3b92d

Shell, R. (2014). Springboard: Launching your personal search for success. New York: Portfolio/Penguin.

Tichy, N. (2004). The cycle of leadership: How great leaders teach their companies to win. New York: HarperCollins.

The Seven Essential Areas

The Core Body of Knowledge Taught at Business Schools

The seven legendary professors profiled in Chapters 3–9 teach at leading business schools. This chapter provides background information about these schools and describes the content of their courses in the seven areas that are essential for business and career success. In academic lingo, these are the "core courses" containing the central body of knowledge that everyone needs for a fundamental understanding of business and its environment.

Your Upcoming Lecture to Business School Students

Before we take our tour of specific schools and examine their core courses, let us start with a bird's eye view of all seven schools by assuming that one of them has invited you to guest lecture in a class. You begin your visit to campus with an extended search for parking. This hunt makes you realize why lack of parking is undoubtedly the most-discussed topic in faculty lounges worldwide!

As you walk from the parking lot to the classroom (or perhaps take the escalator if you are at Wharton's Huntsman Hall), you might stop for lunch at a student cafeteria, where you will benefit from first-rate culinary skills at each school. At Harvard Business School's (HBS) Spangler Center, for example, you will find a spacious food court on the main level. For more casual dining, you might stop at the Grille on the lower level to meet your pressing sushi, pizza, and burger needs.

During my visit to HBS, I lunched at the food court. An MBA course on decision making under uncertainty would have been useful as I wandered among various food stations labeled Global New England, Risotto, Salads, Sandwiches, and Stir Fry. I finally landed at the Global New England station, where I sampled root vegetable gratin, beef pot roast with red wine, baked cod with herbs, garlic and thyme mushrooms, and red peppers with scallions. At fifty-six cents an ounce, my bill totaled less than ten dollars. As at other schools, the HBS food court is open to the public.

While enjoying your lunch, you might spot a Nobel Prize winner dining nearby, as I did at Chicago Booth. The probability of such a sighting is highest at Booth, where nine faculty members have received the Nobel Prize in Economic Sciences since it was established in 1968. Three of these Nobel laureates are still active faculty members at the school.

After lunch, you enter the classroom where you will lecture. The seven leading schools I visited configure their classrooms, with some variation, in three styles: case method, traditional lecture, and grouping by table. In a case method classroom, the instructor stands in an open area near the front and center of the room called the "pit," surrounded on three sides by tiered rows of students. This structure enables students to address their comments to each other, as well as to the instructor. In the traditional lecture hall, the instructor stands at the front of the room behind a lectern facing rows of students. The third style, grouping by table of, say, five students per table, facilitates breakout discussions and exercises.

You will be teaching in a case method classroom. Harvard is the leader in case method teaching, using it for 80% of its instruction, according to a *Bloomberg Businessweek* survey reported in *Poets and Quants* (Byrne, 2012). You will learn about this style of teaching in Chapter 9, which profiles Professor Jan Rivkin, a master at case method teaching. The survey indicated that an average of 34% of the courses at the other leading schools profiled in this chapter (except Chicago, which was not included in the survey) use the case method and an average 23% are lecture-oriented. The rest of the reported instruction is based on team projects or experiential learning.

You might feel vulnerable as you stand in the pit with no lectern or table to place your notes. The eighty or so MBA students who surround you on three sides are intimidating for a variety of reasons. Students in the courses I attended at the seven schools were in the graduating classes of 2019 and 2020. Using data for the 2020 class—most of which is from a compilation by *Poets and Quants* (Ethier, 2019)—the average Graduate Management Admission Test scores at the seven schools ranged from 720 to 732, and the average undergraduate grade point average ranged from 3.48 to 3.73.

At an average age in the late twenties, students at these schools bring to class a variety of business experience. If you were to teach in an Executive MBA (EMBA) or executive education class, you would find that the students are around ten years older than the MBAs and have more senior-level experience, which can make them even more intimidating than MBA students. As a colleague once jokingly told me, when he walks into an MBA classroom and says, "Good morning," he receives a rousing "Good morning" in reply. When he greets his PhD class in the same way, the students lower their heads and write down what he says.

But when he says, "Good morning" to his executive education participants, invariably someone sitting near the back of the classroom will lean back in her chair and say, "Well, not in my experience." You will learn more about executive education in Chapter 7, which profiles Florian Zettelmeyer of Northwestern Kellogg, and about the EMBA experience in Chapter 8, which profiles Professor Perakis of MIT Sloan.

You will also find that because they are diverse, students in your MBA class will analyze and comment on your presentation from a variety of angles, and they will enrich the discussion with perspectives that you might not have previously considered. The average percentage of international students at the seven schools ranges from 30% to 42%, and the average percentage of minority students from 22% to 33%. The percentage of female students in the Class of 2020 ranges from 41% to 46%. According to industry information in the seven school profiles that follow (based on Class of 2019 data), upon graduation an average of 29% of the students will go into consulting, 26% into finance, and 23% into technology.

Once you begin your class, you will discover that the students have high expectations. Some schools, such as Chicago Booth, allocate a limited number of points for use in bidding on courses. Commenting on the bidding process, Booth Professor Steven Kaplan (profiled in Chapter 5) noted, "Most students are very serious about getting what they perceive to be value out of the experience" (Harris, 2011).

Students, especially those vying for honors, can be competitive because of a forced curve. At some schools, for example, the average grade point average in each class cannot be higher than a certain number, while others limit the percentage of students who can receive each level of grades—A, B, and so on (Byrne, 2014). If you were to teach in an executive program, grades would not be a factor. However, you will find that even though they are not graded, the executives are intensely concerned about the takeaway value of your class, for which they have paid dearly in terms of money and time away from the office to learn what you have to offer.

Now that you are familiar with your audience, you are ready to teach the bright, experienced, diverse, motivated, and competitive students who surround you and eagerly await your opening words! While I wish you the best, I am afraid that you will soon learn what Richard Elmore observed in the foreword to *Education for Judgment*: "Exposing one's knowledge, personality, and ego to the scrutiny of others in public is not easy work under the best of circumstances" (1991, p. x).

With this big-picture panorama of the schools in mind, we now turn to the core body of knowledge as taught at the seven leading business schools. The sections below open with a background snapshot of each of them. You will learn, for example, why a business degree often serves as a gateway to a variety of careers. Notable alumni of the seven schools include two US presidents (not counting President Kennedy, who enrolled at Stanford but did not graduate), a Secretary-General of the United Nations, the Prime Minister of Israel, a US Supreme Court Associate Justice, and numerous US senators, authors, and leaders of professional sports teams. Following these snapshots, each section explains the seven essential areas necessary for business success as taught at the schools.

Accounting at the Stanford Graduate School of Business

Background

Stanford University established the Graduate School of Business (also known as "GSB") in 1925 after a meeting of business leaders initiated by Herbert Hoover, who began serving as President of the United States four years later. According to Hoover, "A graduate school of business administration is urgently needed upon the Pacific Coast" (Stanford Graduate School of Business, 2015). The mission of the school today is "to create ideas that deepen and advance our understanding of management and with those ideas to develop innovative, principled, and insightful leaders who change the world" (Stanford Graduate School of Business, n.d.).

When I was a visiting professor at Stanford GSB in 1985, I met with then-Dean Robert Jaedicke, who bemoaned the difficulty in revamping the curriculum, noting that at some business schools, it is easier to move a graveyard than it is to change the curriculum. His comment certainly does not apply to GSB, where innovation has been a constant theme over the years.

Location. GSB is located within the 8,100-acre Stanford University campus in the heart of Silicon Valley, thirty-five miles south of San Francisco.

Programs. MBA, MSx (a one-year Master of Science program), PhD, Executive Education

Most popular industries for MBA graduates. Finance (33%), Technology (24%), Consulting (18%)

Notable alumni. Phil Knight (co-founder of Nike, Inc.), Mary Barra (CEO of General Motors Company), Charles Schwab (founder of Charles Schwab Corporation), Jessica Jackley (co-founder of Kiva), Scott Mc-Nealy (co-founder of Sun Microsystems)

Little-known fact. President John F. Kennedy enrolled at GSB shortly after his undergraduate graduation from Harvard but did not earn a degree.

The Accounting Area

The Accounting area at Stanford GSB is a leader in teaching and research. Only three Stanford GSB professors have won the three major teaching awards at GSB, and all are accounting professors: the late William Beaver, Charles Lee (profiled in the next chapter), and retired professor Mary Barth. The fifteen tenured and tenure-track members in the Accounting area conduct research in a number of areas (including securities pricing, incentive systems design, and corporate governance) that extend beyond the accounting silo.

Stanford MBAs must complete two core courses in accounting: Financial Accounting and Managerial Accounting. According to the course description, the Financial Accounting course helps students become "an informed user of financial statement information." To accomplish this, the course learning objectives are:

> (1) understanding accounting rules and terminology and how these are applied to construct financial statements and (2) building an awareness of the judgment involved and the discretion allowed in choosing accounting methods, making estimates, and disclosing information in financial statements.
>
> (Stanford Bulletin, 2020–2021)

The Managerial Accounting course has two parts, as described in the course description:

> The first part of the course covers alternative costing methods and illustrates how the resulting cost information can be used to analyze the profitability of individual products and customers. The second part of the course will examine the role of internal accounting systems in evaluating the performance of individual business segments and divisions of the firm.
>
> (Stanford Bulletin, 2020–2021)

In addition to these core courses, faculty in the Accounting area teach elective courses on a wide variety of topics, such as valuation techniques, financial statement analysis, and global financial reporting. In Chapter 3, you will learn about one of the most important and popular of these courses, Alphanomics, which focuses on how to make successful investment decisions.

Business Law at the Wharton School of the University of Pennsylvania

Background

In an agreement dated June 22, 1881, Joseph Wharton created the first collegiate school of business. His goal was to provide instruction in public and private finance so that graduates would be equipped to serve their communities and maintain "sound financial morality." He directed the faculty to provide teaching that is "clear, sharp, and didactic; not uncertain nor languid. The students must be taught and drilled, not lectured to without care whether or not attention is paid" (Thorpe, 1893).

Today, the original faculty of five has grown to over 200 professors who are paid considerably more than the original professors' salary of $1,500 per year. The Wharton School maintains "a steadfast commitment to our founder's vision of applying unparalleled intellectual resources to prepare young men and women for leadership in the global society" (The Wharton School, n.d.).

Location. Penn Wharton's main campus is located on the University of Pennsylvania campus in Philadelphia.

Programs. Undergraduate, MBA, Executive MBA, PhD, Executive Education

Most popular industries for MBA graduates. Financial Services (36%), Consulting (25%), Technology (16%)

Notable alumni. Elon Musk (CEO of SpaceX and Tesla), Donald Trump (forty-fifth President of the United States), Brian Roberts (CEO of Comcast), Mehmet Oz (TV personality known as Dr. Oz), William Brennan (Associate Justice of the US Supreme Court)

Little-known fact. Joseph Wharton was very concerned about student health. His agreement provided that "sound physical health and high probability of life must be indispensable conditions" for a scholarship. He also specified that for admitted students, "[a]thletic exercises within moderate limits should be encouraged, as tending to vigor and self-reliance" (Thorpe, 1893, pp. 322–323). It is unclear from the Wharton website how the school is currently meeting this obligation!

The Legal Studies and Business Ethics Department

The Legal Studies and Business Ethics Department at Wharton has an international reputation for high-quality teaching and research. The twenty-two tenured and tenure-track faculty (seventeen Business Law professors and five Business Ethics professors) teach a wide variety of courses that include legal aspects of real estate, marketing, entrepreneurship, corporate finance, employment, international transactions, environmental management, blockchain and cryptocurrencies, data protection, securities regulation, the sports industry, and big data.

MBA students at Wharton are required to select one of two core courses: (1) Responsibility in Business, which covers general legal and ethical responsibilities in management, or (2) Responsibility in Global Management, which focuses more on legal and ethical responsibilities at a global level. Among the topics covered in these courses are legal responsibilities to a variety of stakeholders (shareholders, customers, public markets, and society-at-large), corporate law, securities regulation and insider trading, contracting, fiduciary duties, and thinking strategically about the law. Chapter 4's profile of Professor Richard Shell describes The Responsibility in Global Management course in detail.

Finance at the University of Chicago Booth School of Business

Background

In 1890, the University of Chicago opened with funding from John D. Rockefeller and the American Baptist Education Society. Eight years later, the university founded the College of Commerce and Politics, thus laying claim to being the second oldest business school in the United States. Today, Chicago Booth "is dedicated to improving markets and organizations around the world by turning the smartest ideas into meaningful action" (Overview, n.d.).

Location. The main campus of Chicago Booth is located on the University of Chicago campus, a few miles south of the city center.

Programs. MBA (full-time and part-time), Executive MBA, PhD, Executive Education

Most popular industries for MBA graduates. Consulting (34%), Finance (31%), Technology (21%)

Notable alumni. Elizabeth Bradley (eleventh president of Vassar College), Satya Nadella (CEO of Microsoft), Jon Corzine (former US senator), Sara Paretsky (bestselling novelist), David Booth (the school's namesake and co-founder of Dimensional Fund Advisors)

Little-known fact. There were two Chicago Booth firsts in 1935: the school awarded its first MBA, and one of its students, Jay Berwanger, won the first Heisman Trophy. Four years later, the university abolished its football program.

The Finance Area

Two dozen tenured and tenure-track faculty members teach finance at Chicago Booth, including Nobel laureate Eugene Fama (considered the founder of modern finance) and Nobel laureate Lars Peter Hansen.

MBA students at Chicago Booth must take (1) foundation courses on accounting, economics, and statistics that develop analytical skills and (2) courses that cover business functions, management, and the business environment. Within each area, they can select basic or advanced courses. For example, in the business environment category, they can select a basic course or an advanced course such as The Legal Infrastructure of Business or Law, Economics & Business. Students must also take a leadership course in which they develop their management skills.

The three basic courses in the Finance area are Introductory Finance, Corporation Finance, and Investments:

- The Introductory Finance course emphasizes corporate finance, including corporate investment decisions (also known as capital budgeting), corporate valuation, financing decisions (issuance of securities and dividend payouts), and an introduction to asset pricing.
- The Corporation Finance course covers (1) methods used to value investment projects (with a focus on weighted-average cost of capital and adjusted present value) and (2) corporate financial structure (decisions relating to equity and debt financing and dividend payout policies).
- The Investments course develops skills that enable graduates to make solid investment decisions. Topics include portfolio selection, risk and return models, investment performance evaluation, market efficiency, behavioral finance, pricing of derivative securities such as options and swaps, and interest rate structure.

Students can substitute advanced courses for these basic courses. One of the most popular of these advanced courses is Professor Steven Kaplan's course on "Entrepreneurial Finance and Private Equity." Chapter 5 describes a condensed version of this course that he teaches at the University of Chicago Law School.

Management at the University of Michigan Ross School of Business

Background

Established in 1924 with fourteen faculty members, Michigan Ross today has over 150 full-time faculty members. The school's mission is to "build a better world through business and education" (You're a leader, n.d.).

Location. The school is located on the campus of the University of Michigan in Ann Arbor, Michigan.

Programs. Undergraduate, MBA (full-time, part-time, and online), Executive MBA, One-Year Masters (in Accounting, Management, and Supply Chain Management), PhD, Executive Education

Most popular industries for MBA graduates. Consulting (32%), Technology (27%), Financial Services (15%)

Notable alumni. Stephen Ross (school namesake and chairman of The Related Companies), John Fahey (former CEO, National Geographic Society), Richard Snyder (former CEO of Gateway and governor of

Michigan), Terence Davis (former Secretary-General of the Council of Europe), Rob Pelinka (general manager of the Los Angeles Lakers)

Little-known fact. In 2018, Ross Dean Scott DeRue led over thirty Michigan students on a climb of Mount Kilimanjaro, the tallest mountain in Africa. Accompanied by prominent Ross alumni, Dean DeRue used the experience to teach management skills, such as organizing teams to perform effectively and motivating people to accomplish a shared objective. He had earlier summited Mt. Everest (sans students).

The Management and Organizations Area

The Management and Organizations (M&O) area at Ross has over twenty tenured or tenure-track faculty members, several of whom hold joint appointments outside the business school. The area is widely recognized for its teaching and research on a variety of management topics that include change management, cross-cultural management, leadership, and positive organizational scholarship.

Ross MBA students take a core course on Leading People and Organizations, which prepares them for a leadership role. Through this course, they learn analytical frameworks that enable them to diagnose organizational challenges and develop solutions that match their organization's needs. The course also teaches them how to influence others, make decisions in complex environments, build social capital, manage conflict, drive organizational change, and effectively manage the talent necessary for business success.

MBA students have an opportunity to practice their leadership skills and apply other essential areas of business by taking the signature Ross Multidisciplinary Action Project (MAP) course. In this required course, they work with teammates in the US or abroad on a business challenge faced by an organization. M&O faculty members, along with faculty from other areas, advise the teams.

In addition to these core courses, the M&O Area offers a wide variety of electives on topics such as decision management, interpersonal dynamics, creativity and innovation, change management, organizational design, and the science of success. Chapter 6 describes Professor Gretchen Spreitzer's innovative capstone course that helps students design their lives so as to thrive in the rapidly changing professional world they are about to enter.

Marketing at the Northwestern Kellogg School of Management

Background

Northwestern University founded Kellogg in 1908 as The School of Commerce. In 1979, the university named the school the J.L. Kellogg

Graduate School of Management following a gift of $10 million made in honor of the son of the founder of the Kellogg cereal company. The school's mission is "to educate, equip and inspire leaders who build strong organizations and wisely leverage the power of markets to create lasting value" (Home, n.d.).

Location. The main campus is on Lake Michigan, north of Chicago in Evanston.

Programs. MBA (full-time and part-time), Executive MBA, MS in Management Studies, PhD, Executive Education

Most popular industries for MBA graduates. Consulting (31%), Technology (25%), Financial Services (19%)

Notable alumni. Roslyn Brock (chairman, NAACP), Charlie Baker (governor of Massachusetts), Ellen Kullman (former CEO, Dupont), Ted Phillips (CEO, Chicago Bears), Gregg Steinhafel (former CEO, Target)

Little-known fact. The late Don Jacobs, a legendary Kellogg dean, believed that soft skills such as teamwork and collaboration were as important as hard skills like finance and operations acumen, and he encouraged the use of team exercises in every course. According to an article on Dean Jacobs in *Poets and Quants*,

> This was so unusual at the time that at an academic conference devoted to graduate business education in the 1980s, a rival dean was nearly aghast when Jacobs explained that Kellogg students do the majority of their work in teams. 'At our school,' the dean shot back, 'we call that cheating'.
>
> (Byrne, 2017)

Today, team-based education is a staple at business schools worldwide.

The Marketing Department

The renowned Kellogg Marketing Department includes over twenty tenured and tenure-track professors. Over the years, the department has been home to many giants of marketing, including Sidney Levy, Brian Sternthal, Bobby Calder, Louis Stern, Alice Tybout, and Philip Kotler. When I spoke with the now-retired Professor Kotler (who is considered the founder of modern marketing) at a conference in New York City, he endorsed my selection of Florian Zettelmeyer for the marketing profile in Chapter 7.

The marketing core course "focuses on the influence of the marketplace and the marketing environment on marketing decision making; the determination of the organization's products, prices, channels and communication strategies; and the organization's system for planning and controlling its marketing effort" (Course catalog, n.d.). In the Kellogg tradition, the course emphasizes teamwork in the completion of course assignments.

The Marketing Department offers a wide array of electives on topics such as social media marketing, advertising strategy, launching new products, brand management, and customer loyalty. Professor Zettelmeyer teaches a course on "Customer Analytics," and his executive education course on analytics is one of the most popular in the world. Chapter 7 describes this course in detail.

Operations at the MIT Sloan School of Management

Background

The MIT Sloan School of Management originated in 1914 with Course XV, Engineering Management, in the Department of Economics and Statistics. Today, Management courses are still listed under the heading "Course 15," wedged numerically (but not symbolically) between Economics (Course 14) and Aeronautics and Astronautics (Course 16). The school's mission is "to develop principled, innovative leaders who improve the world and to generate ideas that advance management practice" (Why MIT Sloan, n.d.)

Location. The Sloan School of Management is in Cambridge, Massachusetts, across the Charles River from Boston.

Programs. Undergraduate, MBA, Executive MBA, Sloan Fellows MBA, Master of Finance, Master of Business Analytics, Master of Science in Engineering and Management, PhD, Executive Education

Most popular industries for MBA graduates. Consulting (31%), Technology (31%), Finance (20%)

Notable alumni. Kofi Annan (seventh Secretary-General of the United Nations), Carly Fiorina (former CEO of Hewlett-Packard), Benjamin Netanyahu (Prime Minister of Israel), Cressida Pollock (CEO, English National Opera), Nitin Nohria (former Dean, Harvard Business School)

Little-known fact. Although the MIT "Engineers" sports teams compete mainly at the NCAA Division III level, Sloan has produced a number of leaders in the sports industry, including graduates who have served as CEO of the Los Angeles Dodgers, general manager of the Houston Rockets, head of Jaguar Racing, and president of the Korean Football Association. Students organize the annual MIT Sloan Sports Analytics Conference, purportedly the largest student-run conference in the world, which attracts students and representatives from a large number of universities and professional sports teams.

The Operations Area

As described on the MIT Sloan website, the sixteen faculty members in the Operations Management group at MIT conduct research on "efficiencies in planning, organizing, and supervising in production and manufacturing. ... Operations management has firm foundations in supply chain management and logistics" (Operations Management, n.d.). Nineteen faculty members in another group, Operations Research and Statistics, focus on "operations research, statistics, analytics, machine learning, and data science" (Operations Research and Statistics, n.d.). Professor Georgia Perakis, profiled in Chapter 8, is unusual, in that she is a member—and has served as head—of both groups.

MIT Sloan students, often known to each other as "Sloanies," are required to take an operations core course called Data, Models, and Decisions, which focuses on how to use data when making management decisions. The data analytics topics in the course include "introductory probability, decision analysis, basic statistics, regression, simulation, linear and discrete optimization, and introductory machine learning" (MIT subjects, 2020–2021). Chapter 8 describes how Professor Perakis teaches this challenging course.

Strategy at Harvard Business School

Background

Harvard originated the first MBA program in the world in 1908 with fifteen faculty members and thirty-three students. Today, the school has over 85,000 alumni who live in 169 countries. The HBS mission is "to educate leaders who make a difference in the world" (About, n.d.).

Location. Separated from the main Harvard University campus by the Charles River, HBS has an idyllic residential campus large enough to house an entire liberal arts college.

Programs. MBA, PhD, Executive Education

Most popular industries for MBA graduates. Financial Services (29%), Consulting (21%), Technology (20%)

Notable alumni. Michael Bloomberg (former Mayor of New York City), George W. Bush (forty-third President of the United States), Stephen Covey (self-help author), Salman Khan (founder of the Khan Academy), Sheryl Sandberg (COO, Facebook)

Little-known fact. In December 1962, the HBS faculty voted to admit women into the first year of the MBA program. Eight women enrolled the following September. According to one professor, "The Admissions Department was told it had to be pretty sure about them, there shouldn't be more than a 5% chance of their failing" (Building the foundation). A 1970 graduate wrote to women in the Class of 1971 that "it is vital that every woman have a fairly definite reply to the question 'What's a nice girl like you doing in business school?'" (The girls of HBS, 2013). By 2021, women comprised over 40% of the graduating class.

The Strategy Unit

Over twenty tenured and tenure-track professors teach the required MBA strategy course and a number of MBA electives that include advanced competitive strategy, corporate strategy (creating value across markets), global strategy, strategy and technology, strategy execution, healthcare strategy, and competitive dynamics. The faculty also teach strategy in executive education and doctoral courses.

The strategy course that first-year students are required to take enables them to develop the skills necessary for formulating strategy, including the use of analytical tools and the ability to conduct analyses of industries and firms. Through the course, they are able to understand

- A firm's operative environment and how to sustain competitive advantage.
- How to generate superior value for customers by designing the optimum configuration of product mix and functional activities.
- How to balance the opportunities and risks associated with dynamic and uncertain changes in industry attractiveness and competitive position (Strategy, n.d.).

This course is described in greater detail in Chapter 9, which highlights Professor Jan Rivkin.

The Chapters that Follow

Chapter 1 described the seven essential areas for business success and explained how they align with key departments within companies and business schools. That chapter also matched each of the seven areas with a professor at a leading business school. Chapter 2 has provided details on the schools and the core body of knowledge covered by each of the seven areas.

Sometimes the characteristics of these schools are stereotyped—for example, "X school is known for its collegiality" or "Students at Y school are especially competitive." However, as the opening of this chapter revealed, if you parachuted into a random classroom, you would have difficulty identifying the school based on the makeup of students in the class. You *would* find, however, variation in the teaching methods used by the professors. In most cases, the variation results from the professors' personal choice rather than school culture, as they have considerable flexibility in developing their own teaching methods. The one exception is Harvard Business School, known for case method teaching—which professors reinforce by course preparation through a teaching team, as described in Chapter 9.

In the chapters that follow, you will have an opportunity to meet the seven remarkable professors and learn about how they teach the seven essentials for business success. The final chapter, Chapter 10, summarizes their teaching methods and discusses the rare quality called authenticity that results from their work both inside and beyond the classroom.

References

About. (n.d.). Retrieved from Harvard Business School: https://www.hbs.edu/about/Pages/mission.aspx

Building the foundation. (n.d.). Retrieved from Harvard Business School: https://www.library.hbs.edu/hc/wbe/exhibit_mba-program.html

Byrne, J. (2012, November 18). *How the world's top business schools teach their MBAs.* Retrieved from POETS&QUANTS: https://poetsandquants.com/2012/11/18/how-the-worlds-top-business-schools-teach-their-mbas/

Byrne, J. (2014, February 27). *How MBAs are graded at top schools.* Retrieved from POETS&QUANTS: https://poetsandquants.com/2014/02/27/how-mbas-are-graded-at-top-schools/#:~:text=Yale's%20current%20grading%20system%20has, Proficient%2C%20Pass%2C%20and%20Fail.&text=While%20MBA%20students%20in%20general, of%20the%20class%20at%20graduating.

Byrne, J. (2017, October 31). *A tribute to Kellogg's legendary Don Jacobs.* Retrieved from POETS&QUANTS: https://poetsandquants.com/2017/10/31/a-tribute-to-kelloggs-legendary-don-jacobs/

Course catalog. (n.d.). Retrieved from Northwestern Kellogg: https://www4.kellogg.northwestern.edu/coursecatalogschedule/CourseDetail.aspx?CourseID=205493

Elmore, R. (1991). Foreword. In R. G. Christensen et al. (Eds.), *Education for judgment* (pp. ix–xix). Boston: Harvard Business Review Press.

Ethier, M. (2019, December 16). *The M7: Still (mostly) the most magnificent of them all.* Retrieved from POETS&QUANTS: https://poetsandquants.com/2019/12/16/the-m7-still-mostly-the-most-magnificent-of-them-all/

Graduate school of business. (2020–2021). Retrieved from Stanford Bulletin: https://exploredegrees.stanford.edu/graduateschoolofbusiness/#course inventory

Harris, M. (2011, October 13). *At business schools, classes go to highest bidder.* Retrieved from Chicago Tribune: https://www.chicagotribune.com/business/ct-xpm-2011-10-13-ct-biz-1013-confidential-bidding-20111013-story.html

Home. (n.d.). Retrieved from Northwestern Kellogg: https://www.kellogg.northwestern.edu/news-events/conference/marketing-leadership-summit/2016.aspx

MIT subjects. (2020–2021). Retrieved from MIT Course Catalog Bulletin: http://catalog.mit.edu/subjects/15/

Operations management. (n.d.). Retrieved from MIT Management: https://mitsloan.mit.edu/faculty/academic-groups/operations-management/about-u

Operations research and statistics. (n.d.). Retrieved from MIT Management: https://mitsloan.mit.edu/faculty/academic-groups/operations-research-statistics/about-us

Overview. (n.d.). Retrieved from The University of Chicago Booth School of Business: https://www.linkedin.com/school/universityofchicagoboothschoolofbusiness/about/

Stanford graduate school of business. (n.d.). Retrieved from Stanford Business: https://www.gsb.stanford.edu/#:~:text=Our%20mission%20is%20to%20create, leaders%20who%20change%20the%20world.

Stanford graduate school of business. (2015). *90 years of progress and innovation.* Stanford GSB Oral History Program.

Strategy. (n.d.). Retrieved from Harvard Business School: https://www.hbs.edu/faculty/units/strategy/Pages/curriculum.aspx

The girls of HBS. (2013, July-August). Retrieved from Harvard Magazine: https://harvardmagazine.com/2013/07/the-girls-of-hbs

The Wharton School. (n.d.). Retrieved from Penn: https://catalog.upenn.edu/undergraduate/wharton/#missionandphilosophytext

Thorpe, F. (Ed.). (1893). *Benjamin Franklin and the University of Pennsylvania.* Washington: Government Printing Office.

Why MIT Sloan. (n.d.). Retrieved from MIT Management: https://mitsloan.mit.edu/about/why-mit-sloan

You're a leader. (n.d.). Retrieved from BUSINESS+IMPACT: https://businessimpact.umich.edu/about/mission/

Chapter 3

Stanford Accounting Professor Charles Lee

Make Sound Investment Decisions While Searching for Truth in Your Personal Life

In 1995, Robert Coles, a professor of psychiatry and medical humanities at Harvard University, published an essay in *The Chronicle of Higher Education* titled "The Disparity Between Intellect and Character" (Coles, 1995). He wrote the essay after meeting with a student who was distraught after another student propositioned her on more than one occasion. She recounted to Professor Coles that she had "taken two moral-reasoning courses with [the other student], and I'm sure he's gotten As in both of them—and look at how he behaves with me, and I'm sure with others." She went on to note, "I've been taking all these philosophy courses, and we talk about what's true, what's important, what's good. Well, how do you teach people to be good?" After noting his difficulty with responding to this "unnerving" question, Coles decided that in the future he would discuss with his students more explicitly the "disparity between thinking and doing."

Fifteen years later, on March 30, 2010, a Stanford student cited Coles' essay in an article in *The Stanford Daily* titled "Just a Thought: You Are Not Your Resume" (Milanovic, 2010). After acknowledging the difference between moral-reasoning skills and moral conduct, she noted that the accomplishments on a resume do "not necessarily make us good at being people." And what does being good mean? "I have no idea—my bad," she concluded.

Fast forward five more years to April 13, 2015, when Charles Lee, the Moghadam Family Professor at the Stanford Graduate School of Business, and University of Washington President Ana Mari Cauce addressed over 700 UW students and faculty on the topic "You Are Not Your Resume." This event and others like it originated after Professor Lee read the Stanford student's essay and realized that it raised an important question that students around the country should ask: "Who am I beyond my resume?"

Professor Lee is especially well qualified to address this question. Yes, his resume is impressive, with many teaching and research awards and a career in which he has achieved success as measured by "resume" standards in both business and academia. However, he has also been engaged in an odyssey that began when he left a prestigious accounting firm to attend a seminary and eventually complete a PhD. As a result of this odyssey, he has developed a firm understanding of who he is and where he is headed, and he is able to share his faith-based wisdom through his words and example to students well beyond the traditional classroom.

Meet Professor Lee

Professor Lee's Resume

The following resume summarizes Professor Lee's fifteen-page CV.

Professional Experience

- Academic: Stanford University (2008–present); Peking University, Cornell University, University of Michigan.
- Industry: Nijun Capital (Co-Founder), Barclays Global Investors, New York Stock Exchange, KPMG Peat Marwick Thorne. Led a worldwide active equity research team and was jointly responsible for North American active equity business at Barclays (now Blackrock). At the time, Barclays managed over $300 billion in active equity assets.

Educational Background

MBA (1989) and PhD (1990), Cornell University; Cert in Biblical Studies (1986), Ontario Theological Seminary; B. Math (1981), University of Waterloo

Selected Honors and Awards

Numerous honors and awards at Stanford and elsewhere include the following.

- *Teaching*: Distinguished Teaching Excellence Award for the MBA Program, Distinguished Service Award for the PhD Program, Teaching Excellence Award for the MSx Program (Executive MBA), Stanford University Graduate School of Business; similar awards at the Johnson School, Cornell University, and the University of Michigan Ross School of Business.
- *Research*: Roger F. Murray Research Excellence Award, Innovation in Financial Accounting Education Award, Notable Contribution to Accounting Literature Award, Moskowitz Prize for Best Quantitative Study of Socially Responsible Business Investing, Graham and Dodd Award of Excellence

in Financial Writing, many "Best Paper" and "First Prize" awards.

Service

Professional service to American Accounting Association includes selection as Distinguished Visiting Faculty and Presidential Scholar. Service to Stanford University includes University Advisory Board. Co-Editor or Associate Editor of several leading academic journals.

Teaching Experience

- MBA: Alphanomics, Financial Accounting, Applied Portfolio Management, Financial Analysis and Valuation, Financial Statement Analysis, Intermediate Accounting
- PhD Seminars: Market Efficiency and Informational Arbitrage, Market Efficiency, Accounting Research. Served on many PhD thesis committees.

Publications

Over fifty refereed publications in leading accounting, economics, and finance journals that reflect his interest in topics that transcend disciplinary boundaries. Over 27,000 Google Scholar citations.

Figure 3.1 Professor Charles Lee.

An Interview with Professor Lee

The following interview includes content from Professor Lee's presentations on teaching that he has given several times at the annual New Faculty Consortium, sponsored by the American Accounting Association.

1. **What attracted you to teaching?**

   When I was nine, we emigrated from Taiwan to Canada, where my mother was a professor of Mandarin Chinese at the University of Toronto. I saw the impact she had on students. Many of her students didn't know anything about China. They attended a language class and fell in love with the culture. I saw that happen over and over again during her thirty-plus years as a professor.

   But she wasn't the reason I became a professor. I already had an undergraduate degree and was a chartered accountant in Canada. I grew up in a non-religious family and became a Christian around that time. The church sent me to teach a group of so-called "difficult youths" in a Chinese church. These youths were different from their parents and hard for their parents to teach.

   I had a really good time. When I asked them what they wanted to learn, they told me they wanted to learn about marriage and dating—especially dating. I guess they didn't think they were getting the straight story from their parents. I taught a class where I made some of them teach. I assigned different chapters from a book for them to teach. It was so gratifying! It was amazing because I didn't feel like I did very much, but it had such an impact on the kids.

   This experience made me realize that I wanted to be a teacher! I then thought: What degree can I get where they would pay me to teach? I realized that I was pretty good at math, and I decided to apply to a PhD program. I didn't go into the PhD program thinking I knew anything about research. I just knew that if they let me in, I would get to teach.

2. **Before entering the PhD program at Cornell, you obtained a Certificate in Biblical Studies. That seems like an unusual endeavor for a future accounting professor. How did that come about?**

   When working for an accounting firm I decided that I wanted to go to a seminary. When I went in to resign, I ended up having a conversation with my boss, who was a partner [in the firm] and the national director of auditing standards. I was terrified to meet with him. But he invited me out to lunch, where he told me that he had the same exact experience three years before, when he wanted to resign. So we had a long conversation, and I realized that God wanted me to stay in that job and to determine later what I should be.

   So I always wanted to go to a seminary and realized I wouldn't be able to do that once I started the PhD program. My wife also encouraged me to complete the certificate before I entered the PhD program. I took some night classes beforehand and then was in the seminary for a full year before completing the layman's certificate.

3. **Who were your role models in helping you learn how to teach?**
   When I entered the PhD program, I didn't know much about teaching accounting, and I didn't get any teaching experience during the program because we didn't have to teach. I finished my MBA and PhD in only four years, which was good except that I didn't have any experience as a teacher. When I showed up for my first teaching position at the University of Michigan, they assigned me to an MBA class, and I had to learn how to teach on the spot.

   I was terrified about the prospect of teaching, so I sat in on David Wright's [a professor at the University of Michigan] Intermediate Accounting class. To this day I am grateful to him. I started to realize that understanding accounting is very different from teaching accounting. I knew the technical aspects of accounting, but I didn't know how to convey the material in a way that would matter to the students. Sitting in on Professor Wright's class was eye opening.

   Beyond observing him, I didn't receive other formal support. I really didn't realize how incredibly intense it is to teach for the first time to an MBA class. I remember my first day of teaching Intermediate Accounting. I was nervous, and when I'm nervous, I talk really fast. So I went through two days' worth of lectures during my first class! I recall that the students quietly filed out of class. I realized when I returned to my office that if they had videotaped that class, I would not have had a job anymore.

   At the end of the term, I talked with Carlton Griffin. Professor Griffin joined the Michigan Ross faculty after retiring from his position as Chairman of the Board of what is now Deloitte. I asked him, "How do you do this? I don't think I am ready." He said to me, "Charles, it's preparation, preparation." And I realized that although I thought I was prepared and I walked into class with a lot of goodwill, I did not think through every step of every lecture.

   I also realized that understanding the material didn't qualify me to teach. You have to think about why someone really wants to know this material. What does it matter to them? And then you have to think of examples. The examples, to some extent, are more important than the structure because you can find the structure in many places, but it's the examples that bring it to life. At the same time, I was being recruited to teach at a church, and I realized that the sermon structure is easier to develop than illustrations, but it's the illustrations that give life to a sermon. So you spend a lot of time gathering good illustrations. I *lovingly* collect them.

4. **Did you receive teaching advice later in your career at Cornell and Stanford? Did senior professors visit your classroom for observation?**
I might have been terrified if a colleague had visited my classroom. I didn't receive teaching support at Cornell, but by that time, I already had my class preparations in hand. The same at Stanford, but Stanford was challenging because of a culture that is more idiosyncratic than other schools. There are certain undercurrents that would have been helpful to understand in advance.

For example, I teach investing, and a significant percentage of my students already have experience in private equity or asset management. I had to become more aware of their training and attitudes toward particular types of investments. There is a strong culture here based on a history of people graduating and doing well in private equity and venture capital. They have a particular approach to investing, and I didn't know that.

I also didn't know how much I could push the Stanford students. They have so many things to distract them—such as global study opportunities and many visiting speakers like Oprah Winfrey coming to talk. So it took me a while to understand and get a feel for the culture.

The thing that really helped me was going on global study trips with the students. When you spend a few weeks with them, you get to know them. I went to China on a number of trips with the students. In that environment, they organize everything and are steering the ship. I got to observe their interactions and observe the social norms and expectations they have for each other. This made me realize how far you can push them, which is helpful in running the classroom dynamics.

5. **How do you handle classes that mix students with significant investing experience and rookies?**
This is the most difficult part of teaching my Alphanomics course. There are pros and there are newbies on the bus that I drive during the journey of the course. The course is closely aligned to what asset managers do—and I have to keep everyone engaged. I tell them on Day 1 that this is a collective challenge. We are going to make sure the bus delivers. I tell them on the first day that my job is to make sure that the material is comprehensible to the reasonably equipped layman. I do not make magical leaps of logic. I aspire to use no jargon, and I ask the class to hold me accountable for that. I promise the newbies that they will not be lost.

To keep the pros engaged, I give open-ended assignments. We analyze real-life situations. This gives the pros a chance to go to town because no one knows the answer to the question of whether they should buy shares at today's price.

I also form groups of three-to-five people with an "adopt-a-newbie" policy. Each group must have at least one-third newbies. Otherwise, all the former hedge fund managers will cluster into the same group. So while some assignments are completed individually, they also work on teams in completing analyses

6. **What advice would you give to a rookie teacher?**

   I have been asked to speak on effective teaching many times at the annual New Faculty Consortium sponsored by the American Accounting Association. The audience consists essentially of all the newly minted accounting professors from across the country—around 130 per year.

   When I teach these new teachers, I use a framework derived from Aristotle. Three main elements of classical rhetoric are essential to creating an effective learning environment:

   - Logos—the content of the message
   - Pathos—the emotional features of the message, such as the passion, fervor, and feeling a speaker conveys
   - Ethos—the perceived character of a speaker, determined especially by the concern expressed for the listener

   I tell them that the intimidating part about watching good teachers is that you'll say, "I'll never be like that." You might not be able to be someone who starts each class with a joke or someone who walks into the room like a talk show host and interviews students. Maybe *you* can do this, but I can't. But it isn't necessary to imitate the style of another teacher.

   There are, however, the three elements that are essential to good teaching. The first, content development (**logos**), begins with the development of a central theme or idea for each lecture and for the course as a whole. This is akin to the trunk of a tree. A given lecture might convey, say, twenty-seven facts (the leaves and branches of the tree), which might be reduced to seven especially important facts that might be compressed to three essential facts that might be concentrated into one theme—the trunk.

   The half-life of everything I teach is probably fifteen minutes. Too often, I try to get every little detail right when I should be focusing on the trunk of the tree and the key branches. I need to have a very clear sense of hierarchy. One professor at Cornell, Tom Dyckman, once asked me about my teaching. I responded that because I was teaching three consecutive sections, I was having a hard time keeping track of what I said and was concerned that I might have missed something. He responded that I shouldn't test on things that I might forget to talk about, which was great advice.

Content development also involves simplicity. Simplicity does not mean being shallow in covering the material. Instead, it requires what Oliver Wendell Holmes Jr. called "the simplicity on the other side of complexity." This is a simplicity that arises from understanding the material so completely that you are able to simplify it for others to learn. In other words, you can simplify in a manner that is a faithful representation of the complexity. This concept of simplification is like writing a research paper. The paper itself might be quite complex, but then it is first simplified when preparing the abstract and then simplified further when developing the title.

Another key factor in content development is engagement in the form of frequent interactions with students during and between classes. While there is no one checklist of techniques for achieving engagement, some guidelines are helpful. For example, early in the course, share your teaching philosophy with the class. Use a learning contract to let students know about your expectations regarding workload, etc. Give the class some highlights from future lectures. Wrap up each class with a summary of key concepts. Use feedback forms to find out what students have learned and what they find confusing.

The second element in the Aristotelian framework is **pathos**, the passion and love you have for your material, which are key to motivating students. If you are not excited about what you are doing and you cannot see a reason for it, there is no chance that you are going to succeed as a teacher. I don't teach what I am not excited about, and I like sharing things that I feel excited about.

Sometimes I even want to briefly share with students some research I am working on that doesn't have anything to do with our class but that I think is exciting. I started doing this at Michigan because my research related to finance but I was teaching Intermediate Accounting. I told them that one of the reasons you pay high tuition to attend a leading MBA program is that professors are doing research most of the time. It would be a waste of your money if you left the program without knowing about our research. So I told them,

> I will turn my back, and you vote on whether it's okay for us to spend five minutes from time to time discussing an issue that goes beyond Intermediate Accounting but has something to do with markets and how people use information.

Everyone voted "yes." So that was the start.

I am also fortunate in that my research and teaching are very synergistic, so I can apply findings from my papers when I show students how to predict stock returns, etc. I also use research in part to determine the structure of the course and the main underlying theme.

The main thing in terms of passion is that you want students to see why the course is important to them. I once heard that the main goal of teaching is not to feed students but to make them hungry. When we dump everything from our brain into their brain, that's not teaching. Teaching is asking them to look at the world and say, "Isn't that cool? And why is it cool? Why is it like that?" We want to enable them to search for the answers themselves.

The final element is **ethos**, which Aristotle thought was the single most important element in oral communication and persuasion. Ethos is the character of the speaker as determined by the perceived concern the speaker has for the wellbeing of the students. Does it really matter to you who they are and how their life is going? Are they important to you? If you get this one right, everything else follows along.

How can you show concern for your students? Be authentic. (It is okay to be human.) Be prepared for each class. Be humble. Solicit help and feedback from them.

The key takeaway is to love your subject and love your students. Loving your students doesn't mean you have to be mushy. It just means they are important to you. It is really hard to fake it if they are not important to you.

7. **How do you prepare for class?**
It took a while, but I eventually learned that flipped classrooms are much more pedagogically appropriate. For me, the preparation for class is really making sure I am delivering something that is alive and hot instead of something heated up in a microwave. To do this, I have to be engaged and interested. If I taught the same thing in the course year after year, I wouldn't be engaged. So I figured out that if I outsourced some material to the pre-class videos, then I could do other things in class that are more live and that keep me in the moment. Flipping the class helped me do this. [Professor Lee's version of a flipped classroom is explained later in this chapter.]

I try to teach using live cases to keep me engaged. The theory is old and structured and doesn't change much, but the application does change. Because I teach about markets and companies, I use new examples every year because every year there is some company I want to value and there is an unfolding drama with that company. So we don't know what is going to happen to its valuation.

8. **What do you like most about teaching? What do you like least?**
Teaching is incredibly gratifying. I see the impact, the life change. I feel that it is not commensurate with my teaching. I don't deserve to see that type of impact. It is gratifying and humbling to see people get excited about things and do things differently in a way that,

even over a long time, they would say moved their lives in a positive direction.

The thing I like least is managing the left tail of grade distributions. Sometimes only one or two students in that tail can cause me to lose a lot of sleep.

9. **How do you evaluate your success as a teacher?**

This sounds cheesy, but I don't know how to measure it. I think I know when I have done my best. I try not to focus on specific results but on the fact that I have done my best.

10. **What is the biggest challenge you have faced as a teacher?**

Sometimes you are cruising, and then someone reacts negatively. A student might question your motives. Am I teaching the really good stuff or keeping it for myself? Students who don't do the assignments are a problem. Even when I encourage them to complete an assignment, they sometimes become belligerent.

11. **Is teaching important at Stanford?**

Teaching is extremely important. Whenever we hire someone from the outside, we ask for names of a large sample of students and people whom they have advised. Stanford then writes to all of them. Currently, I serve on a university-wide committee that reviews appointments, and in some files there are over twenty letters from former students. We feel that if you cannot teach and are perceived as someone who cannot attract talented colleagues and students, you are imposing negative externalities on the school, and you don't belong here even if you are eligible for a Nobel Prize.

12. **Does the Graduate School of Business provide teaching support for professors?**

Rookie professors can attend talks and workshops, and we also offer individual advice when someone is struggling in the classroom. We don't offer anything systematic for seasoned professors, but this is not a problem. There is a strict standard of acceptable teaching at the tenured level. We have so many amazing teachers that people feel weird if they are here and don't care much about teaching.

13. **What is your proudest achievement?**

Becoming the third person in the history of the school to win teaching awards from students in our three degree programs.

14. **What do you do for fun?**

Fly fishing and photography are my two biggest hobbies, but my wife and I are also active as counselors in a Christian fellowship. We spend a good deal of time with graduate students from China enrolled in schools across the campus. The students are at our place a lot. They are very smart but in a totally new environment. We have seen many generations of them.

15. **If you were not a professor, what other profession would you choose? What profession would you like the least?**

I can't think of another profession, although the ministry is a possibility. I would least like to be a fly-fishing guide because I would be so frustrated.

16. **What three individuals, living or dead, would you most like to have dinner with?**

Jesus of Nazareth ("For now we see through a glass darkly, but then face to face" 1 Corinthians 13:12.) My father, who passed away in his early fifties—regrettably too young for me to have taken a genuine interest in knowing him. Mother Teresa, whose private memoir *Come Be My Light* is fascinating; her journey of faith in the presence of honest doubt is so mesmerizingly human (Teresa, 2009).

17. **If there is a heaven, what would you like God to say to you when you arrive?**

I expect God will not need to say anything. I expect I will cry; perhaps He will cry as well. I think that would be more than enough.

Professor Lee in Action

The Course: Alphanomics: Active Investing in Equity Markets

I visited Professor Lee's classroom, located in the Class of 1966 Building in the Stanford Management Center. He taught back-to-back sections of Alphanomics: Active Investing in Equity Markets, one from 8:00 to 9:45 a.m. and the second (which I attended) from 10:00 to 11:45 a.m. This course received the 2017 Innovation in Financial Accounting Education Award from the American Accounting Association.

The course is open to first-year (class of 2020) and second-year (class of 2019) MBA students. The 419 students in the 2020 class, for example, were selected from 7,797 applicants and had an average GMAT score of 732. Forty-two percent were international students from 62 countries outside the United States. Women comprised 41% of the class. The average pre-MBA work experience was four years, led by students with experience in investment management/private equity/venture capital (21%), consulting (19%), and technology (17%). The most common undergraduate major was humanities/social sciences (48%), followed by engineering (34%), and business (18%).

The Alphanomics course, which includes concepts from economics and finance, illustrates Professor Lee's ability to teach beyond the functional silo of accounting. The course emphasis on how to become an active investor is based on an important premise stated at the beginning of the syllabus: "When information is costly, equilibrium prices cannot fully incorporate all value-relevant information."

An article in *Forbes* (Shao, 2010) provides context for this premise. The article notes Professor Lee's leadership in challenging the notion that the stock market is efficient—that is, the idea that an investor cannot beat the market because all information has already been incorporated into stock prices. As he states in the article, "The naïve view that markets are efficient by fiat is silly. You need to look under the hood. You can't just assume that the engine works." Through a concept he developed called "informational arbitrage," investors can try to profit from market inefficiency through analysis of complex information.

Stated in everyday language, and reflecting his predilection for fly fishing, the *Forbes* article concludes with this quote from Professor Lee:

> When you go to the river, you sit there first and just watch. You see many things you hadn't seen before—dragonflies are floating or damselflies are flying, the way the wind and sun move. Then you hear sounds you never heard before. Then you notice how the fish are doing. What are they eating? Where are they going? The goal is not to say how many fish you catch. The goal is to know and understand the river. That's the way I look at investing and studying markets. If you understand the river, you will catch a lot of fish.

With this premise in mind, the syllabus notes that the "main goals of the course are to develop students' ability to:

- assess the value and worth of individual firms,
- identify attractive investment opportunities with quantitative stock screens, and
- manage a portfolio of publicly traded securities."

To help students develop these skills, Professor Lee divides the course into three parts: (1) conducting an analysis at the firm level, (2) quantitative approaches to selecting stocks, and (3) managing a portfolio and trading in public equity markets.

As noted previously, a significant challenge in teaching the course is that some students have significant investment experience while others are rookies, and some have a professional interest in the subject matter while the interest of others might be personal. Students are required to read three textbooks, and the course materials include a variety of web resources on stock selection and risk management.

Professor Lee bases grades on class participation (25%), six individual assignments (35%), and a final group project (40%). He divides the final project into two parts. First, the group must design a trading system complete with a stock ranking algorithm and a simulation. Second, they must complete a detailed financial analysis of one firm that integrates concepts and tools from the course.

The description of the course concludes with an important tip for students that reveals Professor Lee's concern for them, as well as his sense of humor:

> The material in this class builds up quickly, so *the key to success is to keep up with the weekly assignments.* [Emphasis in syllabus.] This will make for (relatively) painless learning for you, and much better domestic relationships for me. Thank you for your cooperation. Welcome aboard, buckle up, and I hope that you enjoy the ride.

Inside Professor Lee's Classroom

The class I attended, taught near the end of the course, focused on constructing a portfolio and managing risk. I "buckled up" prior to attending the class by watching a forty-minute video-recorded lecture that Professor Lee assigned to the students. By providing them with background material, the video enabled the students to engage in active learning in the classroom.

Although I do not pretend to fully understand the intricacies of the topic (as illustrated by the results of my own stock picks), the pre-class lecture was well structured and easy to follow. Students receive a detailed handout outlining the material. During the lecture, Professor Lee spoke with fast-paced energy and enthusiasm that could have made notetaking difficult. But as he spoke, he wrote comments in the margins of the handout, which set a perfect pace for students to take notes. Having the lecture on video also enables students to slow down the speed and watch the videos more than once. This is especially useful for students whose first language is not English or who may have difficulty understanding the material.

Professor Lee began the video with an overview of what he planned to cover in the lecture: multi-factor models used to explain return and forecast risk, risk analysis, and an equity model called BARRA—software that is widely used worldwide for equity risk modeling. During the lecture, he provided students with the theory behind the BARRA software, using a combination of algebraic formulas, visuals, plain language, and a focus on the big picture.

Professor Lee sprinkled the pre-class lecture with everyday language that helps students visualize the concepts. For example, he talked about portfolio construction using a "can opener" analogy that he had introduced in an earlier class when referring to a book by Richard Grinold and Ronald Kahn titled *Active Portfolio Management* (Grinold, 1999).

In their book, they recount the story of an economist, an engineer, and a philosopher stranded on an island with a lot of canned food but no can opener to open the cans. The engineer develops an engineering solution: boil the cans and then drop them on rocks. The philosopher speculates about the philosophical nature of food and how it relates to life. The economist's solution: "I've got it! Assume you have a can opener" (pp. 109–110).

Grinold and Kahn explain that, within the context of active portfolio management, the can opener is an assumption of success that raises questions that call for rigorous analysis. Especially important in this analysis is the information ratio that active investors can use to look forward at opportunities (ex-ante) or look backward (ex-post) to analyze the success of a portfolio. Grinold and Kahn define the information ratio as "the ratio of the expected annual residual return to the annual volatility of the residual return" (p. 5).

Professor Lee's use of the pre-class video is an example of a "flipped" classroom. Under the traditional teaching model, professors lecture in class and students complete homework assignments outside of class. With a flipped classroom, professors reverse these activities. While there are several variations of flipped classrooms, Professor Lee uses a mixed model where some of his lectures are available outside of class through videos, which frees time for increased student activities in class, although students must also complete assignments outside of class.

Once class starts, Professor Lee uses the following teaching techniques that illustrate why his classes are so engaging.

1. **Warm Welcome and Plan for the Day**

   Professor Lee opened class with a warm welcome and a discussion of a book by Nicola Gennaioli and Andrei Schleifer titled *A Crisis of Beliefs: Investor Psychology and Financial Fragility* (2018). Using the Lehman Brothers collapse in 2008 as a case study, they show that how we form our beliefs plays a role in our continuing financial instability. Professor Lee then provided an agenda for the day, passed out handouts, and commented on what he would cover during the next class.

2. **Reasonable Pace**

   As he did during the pre-class lecture, Professor Lee used an overhead projector (which was sandwiched between two screens projecting his PowerPoint slides) to write notes on slides. This set a measured pace for students to take notes while absorbing the complex material.

3. **Everyday Language**

   As he also did during the pre-class lecture, Professor Lee used everyday language to describe complicated concepts. For example, in an earlier class, he explained that institutional investors increasingly distinguish between an alpha approach to investing (based on a forecast of a stock's potential to appreciate) and a beta approach (which measures the volatility of a stock in relation to the market). He emphasized that a beta approach, like orange juice, is cheap (in that investors can simply invest in a mutual fund with low expenses), while an alpha approach, like vodka, is more expensive. He frequently used the orange juice versus vodka metaphor in explaining investment strategies. For example, he emphasized that paying alpha prices for beta products "would be like paying vodka prices for a drink with 95% orange juice in it."

4. **Energy and Enthusiasm**
   Although he had just finished teaching another long class, Professor Lee brought abundant energy and enthusiasm to the class, with lots of natural hand and arm movement. The energy was contagious, enabling even an interloper like me, with limited knowledge of the course content, to become enthusiastic about the subject matter.

5. **Conversational Style**
   Professor Lee does not use lecture notes when teaching. This resulted in a conversational style that broke down any potential barrier between professor and student and gave the class the feel of a live working session among investment manager colleagues.

6. **Relevant Real-World Examples**
   Professor Lee used many real-world examples that reflected his experience in the financial industry. These examples were interesting and relevant to the topic and gave Professor Lee additional credibility. Despite this experience, he did not pretend to have all the answers and encouraged students to think on their own: "I won't be hurt if you don't do what I recommend. Do it your own way!"

7. **In-Depth Case Study**
   Professor Lee complemented the short examples with an in-depth case study of a student-run hedge fund he started in 1998 when teaching at Cornell University. The fund began with $600,000 in investment from alumni and initially adopted a conservative investment policy. By 2002, the investment philosophy had changed to a combination of quantitative stock selection and fundamental analysis. By 2007, the fund had over $14 million in assets under management.

8. **Interactive Class**
   The class was highly interactive, with many questions from Professor Lee. He listened carefully to student responses, and when replying he even referred to their comments from earlier classes: "Mary, two classes ago, you asked me about _____." He remained positive even when a student's question or comment missed the mark:

"That's a pretty good guess." If students were not able to answer a question initially, he allowed them to keep trying until they developed an appropriate answer.

9. **End-of-Class Summary**

Professor Lee concluded class with a summary of various thoughts on active investing as a science. He emphasized finding new sources of alpha, controlling portfolio risk, and using a combination of academic studies and fundamental analysis tools to develop intuition about stock selection. His closing words were, "Everything still hinges on having a can opener—that is, an investment insight that we can parlay into an 'alpha forecast.'" His final comment was reminiscent of a football coach sending players onto the field: "Now let's go find some alpha!"

10. **After-Class Session**

When class ended, despite having taught for almost three hours, Professor Lee patiently worked with students for another forty-five minutes, although he had an important university meeting scheduled later in the day. During his conversation, he continued his use of simple metaphors, such as "Volume is like vitamin C—you cannot overdose."

He also encourages students to complete a form after each class on which they note "the single most important thing I learned today is ____" and "the muddiest (most confusing) point is ____."

Student Comments about Professor Lee

The following quotations include excerpts from Professor Lee's nomination by doctoral students for his Distinguished Faculty Service Award.

- He straddles and blends academics and practice. He is an expert who has produced mountains of research. Managed funds at Blackrock. Distills material to tangible form that is digestible even for students who are not math geeks. His great energy and enthusiasm are infectious.

- Obsessed with his teaching. He lives with the subject. Great experience, both academic and professional. Many relevant stories. Super prepared. He constantly refreshes material so that it is very up-to-date. Lots of fun.

- I have no experience with investing. Some students like me are base level; others are advanced. His videos help, as does his writing down information on slides during class. No question is too silly.

- Breaks complex material into little steps that you can even apply to personal finance. Makes it simple and easy to follow.
- Complete mastery of material. Makes it useful for newcomers and experts. Learned a lot.
- Makes investing interesting even for students with no background. Covers lots of material in a structured way. Videos and readings are helpful. In class, working through the material forces you to write it down, and this leads to retention.
- His energy is contagious. Friendly, energetic, generally wants best for students. I have no background in investing, but he is very approachable.
- He has a great background. Extremely enthusiastic and positive. Last week I spent two-and-a-half hours in his office. Really engaged if you are willing to put in the effort. Practical experience.
- Students leave his office energized.
- He makes the boring stuff **really** interesting.
- He devotes time and energy to his courses and holds nothing back from the students.
- He is meticulous in course preparation.
- He spends hour after hour incorporating the latest data sources and software to enhance the learning experience.
- He sets aside extra office hours and informal discussion sessions to help the students.
- Many MBA students have built their careers around what Charles teaches.
- He exceeds all reasonable expectations in investing his time and energy in promoting the personal and professional welfare of his students.
- He taught me the importance of integrity, passion for one's work, and maintaining a healthy balance between personal and professional life.
- By the time I graduated from Stanford, there was no one, outside of my family, whose opinion mattered more to me than Charles.
- I can think of no better person to model myself after, both personally and professionally.

Impact Beyond the Classroom

Like other professors, Professor Lee balances teaching with other activities. This was his schedule on the day I visited his class.

A Day in the Life of Charles Lee

4:30 a.m.

Wake up.

5:00 a.m.

At Peet's when it opens for coffee and nibbles. Then to office until class at 8:00 a.m. Prepare, organize handouts. Respond to emails.

8:00 a.m.

In class.

12:30 p.m.

Prepare for University Advisory Board meeting. New appointments, tenure, hundreds of cases. Seven people with three-year terms meet one day per week.

2:30 p.m.

Committee meeting.

4:40 p.m.

Office hours until around 7:00 p.m.

7:00 p.m.

Home in time to watch the Warriors.

Professor Lee's impact extends well beyond the classroom. His service to the accounting profession and the university is exemplary. For instance, he has served on the editorial boards of several leading journals and has engaged in many service activities within the American Accounting Association, such as his session on teaching at the New Faculty Consortium.

His university service includes the University Advisory Board mentioned in the "A Day in the Life" section—a time-consuming three-year commitment. The Board consists of seven people who meet weekly to review all new appointments and promotions from across the university. Preparing for these meetings requires long hours of preparation and reading hundreds of files.

On the research front, Professor Lee is a star. As with his teaching, he does not confine his research to the accounting field, and he has published several articles with leading scholars from other fields such as Andrei Schleifer, a professor at Harvard University, and Nobel Prize winner Richard Thaler, a professor at the University of Chicago. According to Google Scholar, his articles have been cited over 27,000 times.

Professor Lee is also the faculty sponsor of the student-run Veritas Forum at Stanford. The Veritas Forum was founded at Harvard in 1986, and the name is derived from the Harvard motto *Veritas*, meaning "truth." The Forum has spread to campuses across the US and elsewhere. As described on the website, its goal is to consider life's most difficult questions by placing "the historic Christian faith in dialogue with other beliefs" (Home, n.d.). Interfaith campus-wide sessions address broad themes such as justice, morality, faith, and rationality.

In my conversations with him, Professor Lee elaborated on the nature of the questions addressed by the Veritas Forum:

> If we are going to train future leaders, we should role model for them how to have a civil conversation and to disagree without being disagreeable and to ask the same questions human beings have always asked, like what a security guard asks when he sees you late at night: "Who are you? What are you doing here? Where are you going?" These are questions people have pondered since the beginning of mankind, and we come to different decisions.

These questions achieved new meaning during the COVID-19 pandemic, when individuals faced an unusual degree of uncertainty. During a mid-2020 interview, Professor Lee assured students that this was actually a wonderful time to graduate because the pandemic had stripped away the usual "illusion of control." In his words, "Life is never going to be certain. ... It's always decisions under uncertainty that actually elicit out of you who you really are" (Navigating uncertainty, 2020).

In addition to serving as the faculty sponsor for the Forum at Stanford, Professor Lee has participated in dialogs with leading academics from around the country on topics that illustrate the scope of Veritas discussions. These topics and locations include "The American Dream" at Berkeley, Brown University, and Harvard University; "Work Hard, Play Hard, Now What?" at the University of Southern California; and "You Are Not Your Resume" at the University of Washington and Cornell University.

Lessons from Professor Lee

Professor Lee's impact ranges from reshaping the way that investors view the stock market to helping students think about hidden truths at a critical juncture in their lives. Teaching is central to his life, and he continues to ponder the elements of teaching excellence through his national presentations to new faculty members. His teaching embodies the three-part Aristotelean framework that he includes in these presentations: logos, pathos, and ethos.

1. *Content (Logos).* One element of content is the development of a central theme for a lecture or course. This theme is like the trunk of

a tree that is sometimes obscured by branches and leaves. A second element of logos is simplicity, what Oliver Wendell Holmes Jr. called "the simplicity that lies on the other side of complexity." A third key element is engagement that results from frequent interaction with students during and between classes.

Professor Lee is successful on all three fronts. First, while the course content is quite complex, with many branches and leaves, he continually focuses on the goal, which is to understand active investment. Second, he is a master at simplifying, with his constant use of metaphors, such as the vodka and orange juice example. He also simplifies the material through the constant use of real-world examples, which bring his teaching framework to life. He invests a lot of time in finding good examples. In his words, "I lovingly collect them."

Third, he enthusiastically engages students. His warm interaction with them begins with pre-class videos and ends with a willingness to work with them long after the formal class session ends. His engagement with students extends beyond the designated content of the course, as he shares his current research findings with them.

2. *Passion for the Course (Pathos) and Character (Ethos).* Professor Lee's pathos and ethos are closely linked and feed off each other. His pathos is evidenced by the comments from students, who emphasize his passion, energy, and enthusiasm. His passion is driven by his ethos—his concern for his students. His understanding of Stanford students developed in part from global study trips with them, which enabled him to observe student interaction outside the classroom and to understand their expectations and social norms.

Professor Lee's concern for students extends beyond the classroom through his involvement with Veritas on campus and presentations at leading universities around the country. Through these talks, he encourages students to think beyond their resumes and to address central questions in life: Who am I? What am I doing here? Where am I going?

Shortly after observing Professor Lee in the classroom, I spotted an electronic billboard upon deplaning at Chicago's Midway Airport. An ad from a large investment management firm, the billboard read, "Specialized Active Investing in Pursuit of Alpha." Professor Lee's career and life are a curious mixture of teaching his MBA students how to achieve financial success by pursuing alpha while reminding them that financial success will not necessarily bring them happiness. As he noted in one of his Veritas talks, no search for happiness is possible without a search for virtue, goodness, and meaning in life.

One of Professor Lee's comments exemplifies his personal search for meaning: "The key takeaway is to love both your subject and your students." His students reciprocate this love, as reflected by a statement from a student who nominated Professor Lee for one of his teaching awards: "The Graduate School of Business is a better place because of you."

References

Coles, R. (1995, September 22). *The disparity between intellect and character.* Retrieved from The Chronicle of Higher Education: https://www.chronicle.com/article/the-disparity-between-intellect-and-character/?cid2=gen_login_refresh&cid=gen_sign_in

Gennaioli, N. & Shleifer, A. (2018). *A crisis of beliefs: Inverstor psychology and financial fragility.* Princeton: Princeton University Press.

Grinold, R. & Kahn, R. (1999). *Active portfolio management: A quantitative approach for producing superior returns and controlling risk.* New York: McGraw-Hill Education.

Home. (n.d.). Retrieved from The VERITAS FORUM: http://www.veritas.org/

Milanovic, N. (2010, March 30). *Just a thought: You are not your resume.* Retrieved from The Stanford Daily: https://www.stanforddaily.com/2010/03/30/just-a-thought-you-are-not-your-resume/

Navigating uncertainty. (2020, June 26). *YouTube.* Retrieved from https://www.youtube.com/watch?v=VuHnXuAqIqo

Shao, M. (2010, July 13). *Charles Lee on beating the crowd at picking stocks.* Retrieved from Forbes: https://www.forbesindia.com/article/stanford/charles-lee-on-beating-the-crowd-at-picking-stocks/15162/1

Teresa, M. (2009). *Mother Teresa: Come be my light.* New York: Doubleday.

Chapter 4

Wharton Legal Studies Professor Richard Shell

Understand Your Legal Responsibilities as a Leader and Your Personal Motivation for Success

As a college student, Richard Shell seemed to have a preordained career path ahead of him. Both his grandfathers had been in the military. His father was a Marine Corps general who had headed the famous military college Virginia Military Institute. When he enrolled in college, Professor Shell had plans to enter the Navy.

However, his plans went awry when, in his words, he "cut the narrative story" of his life by becoming a pacifist during the Vietnam War. He then began a journey summarized in his bestselling book *Springboard: Launching Your Personal Search for Success* (2014). This journey included painting houses, acting in local theaters, studying transcendental meditation, consulting for a fundraising firm, using his life savings of $3,000 to backpack around the world, suffering a life-threatening illness in Afghanistan, taking up residence in a Buddhist monastery in Sri Lanka, studying with a Zen master in Korea (where he contemplated becoming a monk), and selling insulation door-to-door in his hometown after he returned to the US.

This unusual early life journey led Professor Shell to appreciate the importance of self-understanding. Near the beginning of *Springboard*, he quotes a Stanford commencement address by Apple's co-founder, the late Steve Jobs, who died of pancreatic cancer at the age of fifty-six:

> Your time is limited, so don't waste it living someone else's life. ... Don't let the noise of others' opinions drown out your own inner voice. And, most important, have the courage to follow your heart and intuition. They somehow already know what you truly want to become.
>
> (p. 15)

In Professor Shell's case, the search for self-understanding eventually led him to the Wharton School at the University of Pennsylvania, where today he serves as the Thomas Gerrity Professor and Chair of the Legal Studies and Business Ethics Department.

Meet Professor Shell

Professor Shell's Resume

The following resume condenses Professor Shell's twelve-page CV.

Education

Juris Doctor, 1981, University of Virginia School of Law, where he was an editor of the Virginia Law Review; BA, 1971, cum laude, Princeton University

Academic Employment

The Wharton School, 1986–present; Visiting Scholar, Harvard Law School, 1993–1994; Lecturer, Brandeis University, 1985–1986

Other positions include Associate at Hill & Barlow; Law Clerk for Judge Levin Campbell of the US Court of Appeals; Account Executive and Market Researcher for J.R. Taft Corporation; and social worker in Washington, D.C.

Books

Authored several award-winning and bestselling books published in over fourteen languages. Best known for *Bargaining for Advantage: Negotiation Strategies for Reasonable People* (2006) and *Springboard: Launching Your Personal Search for Success* (2014). The British Library shortlisted the UK version of *Springboard* for the Management Book of the Year Prize.

Articles

Twenty articles in academic journals plus many book chapters, shorter articles, and opinion pieces in the *New York Times, Boston Globe, Wall Street Journal, Philadelphia Inquirer,* and elsewhere

Teaching

Created the following undergraduate, graduate, executive education, and online courses:

- Undergraduate: The Literature of Success: Historical and Ethical Perspectives

- Graduate:
  - Responsibility in Global Management (Wharton required MBA course on law and ethics)
  - Government and Legal Environment of Business
  - Negotiation and Conflict Management
  - Legal Aspects of Entrepreneurship
- Executive Education: Creator and Academic Director of two programs that attract business leaders from around the world: Executive Negotiation Workshop and Strategic Persuasion Workshop
- Massive Open Online Course (MOOC): Success (over 44,000 students enrolled)

Teaching Awards

Over two dozen teaching awards including:

- Undergraduate: Senior Class Teaching Award; David A. Hauck Award (for best tenured teacher in the Undergraduate Division)
- MBA: Class of 1984 Award (for top student evaluations in the MBA Division); Miller-Sherrerd MBA Core Teaching Award for Outstanding Teaching in the MBA Core
- Executive MBA Program: Outstanding Teaching Award

Research Awards

Among many research awards are two CEOREAD prizes (for Best Business Book of the Year and Best Personal Development Book of the Year), the Book Award for Excellence from the Center for Public Resources, and the Hoeber Award from the Academy of Legal Studies in Business.

Service

Serves on numerous university-wide and Wharton committees. Has chaired over a dozen committees, including one that redesigned the entire MBA program. Co-founded the Purpose, Passion and Principles (P3) Initiative at Wharton, which helps students understand how their definitions of success and happiness relate to their goals— both personal and professional. Advisor to business and nonprofit organizations and government agencies around the world.

Figure 4.1 Professor Richard Shell.

An Interview with Professor Shell

1. **What led you to a teaching career?**

   At the age of twenty-seven, I returned from a long journey and lived at home in my parents' basement. At the time, I was selling insulation door-to-door, and I figured out that I couldn't stay in their basement for too much longer. Law school became a good option because I am good with words. So I attended the University of Virginia Law School because it was up the road from where I was living with my parents.

   Early in my law school education, I had an "aha" moment. For quite a significant time, I had been thinking about questions like, *what am I supposed to do with my life* and *who am I*? These questions had produced high anxiety. In my Contracts course in law school, when I and many other students in a class of 150 students had their hands in the air in response to a question from the professor, I suddenly experienced a peculiar feeling. It was as if I had floated out of my seat in the classroom and was looking down from above. And in that moment, I realized that I wanted to be the person in front of the room—the teacher. The excitement in the law school classroom environment was different from any academic environment I had experienced.

During my life before law school, I had done a number of things, including teaching sixth grade and in a daycare center; and touring the United States in a school bus with a theater company called the People's Revolutionary Road Company, where I played the guitar, kazoo, and slide whistle. During that class in law school I realized that, unlike my earlier experiences, teaching is a career that is intellectual, but you also have a great audience of students who are very motivated. I also realized that part of the challenge was keeping their attention, which related to my performance experience.

I had earlier toyed with doing a PhD on Shakespeare but heard that jobs were scarce for Shakespeare scholars. My law school experience made me realize that an academic career in law was possible. When I asked my mentors about how to become a law professor, they counseled that I should be on the Law Review [a research publication edited by the top law students at each law school] and that I should serve as a law clerk for a judge, both of which I did.

I then worked at a Boston law firm, but at the same time I served as a teaching assistant for an undergraduate law course at Brandeis University. Through this experience, it dawned on me that I could teach law outside of law school. Shortly thereafter, I received a call from professors at Wharton who found my resume through a law school placement service. This led to an offer from Wharton, which I accepted over an offer from a law school. I started my teaching career at the age of thirty-seven.

2. **Do you have any role models for your teaching career?**
My brother-in-law, Arthur Kirsch, is a Shakespeare scholar who is now retired from the University of Virginia faculty. He really showed me what the career is like. He loved teaching.

The then-Dean at the University of Virginia Law School, Dick Merrill, gave me good advice that shocked me. He told me that I should not present myself in job interviews as a lawyer with practical experience. I had written an article for a bar journal, and he told me not to put it on my resume. That was my first introduction to the disconnect between academic culture and law practice.

At Princeton, I especially remember Anthony Burgess, author of *A Clockwork Orange* (1986). I had a yearlong seminar with him on creative writing. A very intense guy, he oversaw my senior thesis and induced me to write two plays in iambic pentameter that were based on two short stories by James Joyce. That was quite an intellectual push. In the opening paragraph of a *New York Times* movie review, Burgess mentioned my verse adaptation. I was thrilled! That seminar was very important for me because it radically improved my writing skills even though I learned that I was never going to be much of a creative artist.

3. **Did you have any role models at Wharton?**

   After starting at Wharton, I immediately sought out the best teachers and sat in on Bill Tyson's course. [The late William Tyson was an associate professor emeritus at Wharton.] He was an electrifying teacher, but I realized quite quickly that I could never teach the way he did. But it did give me a sense of how to teach law to business students. Bill was in command of the classroom. He knew the names of all students, and he called on them by name. Bill challenged them to find mistakes in the content, which caused them to be hyper-prepared.

   My biggest role model overall was Tom Dunfee. He was an academic leader who was able to integrate his academic work with his personal life. [The late Thomas Dunfee was an influential Wharton business law scholar and chair of the Legal Studies and Business Ethics Department.]

4. **Did you have any training to become a teacher?**

   No. But I did attend a helpful workshop on how to teach negotiation, taught by Professors Max Bazerman of Harvard and Larry Susskind of MIT. They showed me how to run role-plays, and I had to create a syllabus and present it to the class. The course was especially useful in providing a sense of what it feels like to be a student in a simulation-based course.

   Three years at a law school that cares about teaching provided me with confidence right from the beginning of my teaching career.

5. **Does Wharton provide teacher training?**

   In our department, we require new professors to sit in on classes taught by our best teachers. Professors can also ask the school to video classes, and we have a communication program that provides coaching and mentoring.

6. **How do you prepare for class?**

   When first teaching a course, I prepare a minute-by-minute outline for each class and then refine it as I teach the course. After a couple of years, I feel more confident about the flow. I keep notebooks for each course and outline every reading, which I can review before each class. I walk into class with a one-page, minute-by-minute game plan of exactly what we are going to do, in what order, and how we are going to do it. The class may not always follow that flow, but it gives me a baseline I can go back to.

7. **Are there any philosophies or guidelines that you follow once class begins?**

   Overall, my teaching philosophy closely tracks a Chinese Confucian aphorism: "Tell me and I'll forget, show me and I might remember, involve me and I will learn." This idea appears to come from a Chinese scholar/teacher named Xun Kuang, who (like me) taught the importance of character and morality in everyday life. I have learned nearly everything of importance through practice, so I make the assumption that this is true for my students as well.

I follow this rule of thumb: every moment students are engaged by participation is good. In a class of seventy students, only one person at a time can talk. So I assign students to groups of six that remain intact for the entire course and regularly give them questions to discuss during class. Through this process, more people have a chance to talk, and it gives students who are more introverted a safer space.

I also weave in stories and examples and get students to share their stories with their groups or with the entire class. Some of the most powerful moments in class come from these stories of conflicts at work, with family, in a particular culture, and so on. After they have shared their experiences, we tie the stories to the course themes.

While uncontrolled use of stories might be risky, I want their stories to be true and memorable—and sometimes, that means the stories are far from what you would expect in a graduate school classroom. Basically, I want them to tell the truth to each other about their life experiences. Even in a large class, it is possible to create a trusting atmosphere. I tell stories about myself so they get the idea that it's okay to be truthful and vulnerable. So, for example, students have described sexual assaults in work settings, being pressured by their bosses to defraud clients, and being asked to cover up unsafe conditions on construction sites.

They also share how they have resisted illegal or unethical conduct—for example, by quitting a job because of the corrupt environment they are in. One student (a former lawyer getting an MBA) shared that a senior partner in the law firm where she worked asked her to write a memo on the Foreign Corrupt Practices Act to justify the firm's hiring the nephew of an Asian client as a summer intern. When she concluded that they couldn't legally hire the nephew, the senior partner told her that she hadn't looked hard enough. She repeated the research, with the same answer. Finally, the senior partner screamed at her that the answer had to be "yes" so they could hire the nephew, and she had to figure out how to get to yes. She then left to go on a long walk and never returned to the office.

8. **How does your research relate to your teaching?**
Professors at many leading business schools think of themselves as scholars who teach. I think of myself as a teacher who writes. This is not a part of our common identity in academic life. My books have all been about courses I have taught. Teaching is my source code. This is an indication of my commitment to teaching as my identity.

9. **How can you tell whether you have been successful with your teaching?**

The evaluations are one measure. Students provide a lot of comments that are helpful. The major metric that I have is this: If at the end of the course I feel more energy than at the beginning (instead of feeling depleted and exhausted), I have done a good job. It means that my intrinsic motivation has been operating.

10. **Is teaching important at Wharton in promotion, tenure decisions, and annual salary reviews?**

    In general, bad teaching can count against you, but great teaching does not count for you if you are not producing top-quality research. The school now gives annual bonuses based on teaching evaluations, so teaching does affect your compensation.

11. **What advice would you give to someone who wants to become an effective teacher in a formal classroom setting like yours or in other settings (for instance, when a manager plays a teaching role in leading a team)?**

    Three pieces of advice. First, prepare, prepare, prepare. Second, involve your audience. Third, students do not learn anything except on the foundation of what they already know. So your selection of examples, images, stories, and metaphors is crucial. Don't use a sports example in a class where students are unfamiliar with that sport. Think about your audience's common experience and then seek examples, stories, and images they can identify with. Check frequently to see if they are getting it. Read the group and, if they look distracted or preoccupied, give them a challenge, puzzle, or activity to refocus them.

12. **If you were not a professor, what profession would you select? What profession would you like the least?**

    If I weren't a professor, I probably would have ended up being a high school teacher or maybe a Unitarian minister. I would hate to have any repetitive job that requires only limited or highly constrained contact with people, such as taking tolls on a turnpike.

13. **What do you do for fun outside of work?**

    My wife and I enjoy travel, movies, plays (Shakespeare is my favorite; my wife enjoys more modern dramas), reading, eating out, and helping our two sons in whatever ways they will allow. My wife writes personal essays for the *Wall Street Journal*, and I enjoy helping with editing.

14. **What three individuals, living or dead, would you most like to have dinner with?**

    Marcus Aurelius, William Shakespeare, and Benjamin Franklin

15. **If there is a heaven, what would you like God to say to you when you arrive?**

    "I have an opening at Celestial University for someone to teach comparative religion. Are you available?"

Professor Shell in Action

The Course: Responsibility in Global Management

Professor Shell teaches Wharton courses in the undergraduate, MBA, and executive education programs. The courses vary in size from thirty to seventy students. He has also developed a Massive Open Online Course (MOOC) titled "Success," in which over 44,000 students have enrolled worldwide since its launch in the fall of 2017—more than the total number of undergraduate and graduate students enrolled at the University of Pennsylvania in any one year!

I observed Professor Shell teaching a three-hour class (from 3:00 p.m. to 6:00 p.m.) in the school-mandated MBA course titled "Responsibility in Global Management." The class was populated by Wharton first-year (Class of 2020) and second-year (Class of 2019) MBA students. The 862 students in the class of 2020 were selected from 6,245 applicants and had an average Graduate Management Admission Test (GMAT) score of 732. Women accounted for 43% of the class. Approximately one-third of the class were international students and one-third were minority students. The average pre-MBA work experience was five years, and among the fields they came from, consulting led the way with 27%, followed by private equity and venture capital (13%) and technology (10%). Forty-five percent of the class majored in humanities and social sciences as undergraduates, followed by science, technology, engineering, and math (STEM) at 29% and business at 26%.

The fifty-eight students (thirty-five male and twenty-three female) from North and South America, Europe, Asia, and Africa occupied almost every seat in the classroom. The packed classroom is part of Professor Shell's teaching strategy. Early in his career, he taught a low-enrollment course in a large classroom and discovered that it was difficult to engage the students. Cognizant of the work of Italian physician and educator Maria Montessori, who founded the first Montessori School, he recognized the importance of the learning environment and realized that a lot of "social energy" is lost when the size of the classroom dwarfs the number of students. This social energy is important in achieving one of his underlying goals, which is to establish a communal relationship among the students by the end of the course.

Professor Shell's explicit objective in the course is to make students aware of the legal and ethical concerns that arise in business and to understand how they can protect themselves and their organizations from being victimized by these concerns. Course grading has three components: (1) the overall contribution to the course, (2) a short-answer quiz based on course readings, and (3) a final paper. Courses in the Wharton MBA program have a mandatory average grade of B+ and professors are required to give the bottom 10% of the class a "low pass" grade.

The course contribution component includes a Peer Rating, in which students have an opportunity to confidentially rate the contributions of other students by assigning numbers indicating whether their peers enhanced or reduced the value of the course. The final paper requires students to develop their own definition of what responsibility means in a professional setting by conducting original research as well as illustrating their theories using the life and practice of a personal role model.

In its broadest terms, Professor Shell frames the course content generally in terms of three levels of understanding: doing things right, doing the right thing, and being the right kind of person. He emphasizes these elements in every class. For example, the course covers a number of legal guidelines based on areas of law that every business leader should understand, such as fiduciary duties, contracts, regulatory law, and so on. When covering these areas, he emphasizes that they help business leaders *do things right* by providing a set of standards for them to follow. Understanding the legal areas enables leaders to *do the right thing* because of their desire to avoid violating the law. And the law enables them to *be the right kind of person* by providing an opportunity to become authentic and respected leaders when they encourage people within their organizations to follow the letter and spirit of the law.

In covering the legal and ethical context for leadership decisions, Professor Shell makes it clear that he is not trying to teach the details of legal rules and regulations. Instead, he focuses on these broader goals that are likely to have a more enduring impact on the careers of his students: (1) issue identification, (2) understanding legal analysis, and (3) thinking strategically about the law.

The first theme, issue identification, is important because business leaders must be able to identify legal issues that arise in day-to-day decision making to avoid disastrous consequences for themselves and their businesses. For example, Professor Shell asked the class to conduct an "exit interview" negotiation between a managing director of a small consulting firm and an employee who is leaving the firm for personal reasons. The firm required departing employees to sell company stock (acquired as compensation during their employment) back to the company, and the two parties had to negotiate the price of this stock.

Unknown to the departing employee, secret negotiations were in progress for sale of the firm, and these negotiations would result in a dramatic increase in the stock price that the employee would receive if he or she decided to remain with the firm. During the negotiation, many students playing the role of the managing director failed to disclose the sale negotiations. During the debrief of the negotiation, they were shocked to learn that their failure to disclose was an illegal breach of fiduciary duty by the managing director (who was also a majority shareholder in the company). Through this exercise, they learned a valuable lesson that might help them avoid destruction of their careers later.

Professor Shell emphasizes the second theme, legal analysis, because legal advice is an essential component of sound business decision making, and business students must be able to blend legal and economic analysis. While it is not necessary for business leaders to think like a lawyer, they should at least understand how lawyers think.

When teaching the analytical process, Professor Shell explains a sequence that begins when clients explain their stories to lawyers. Lawyers use these stories to develop legal claims. They then identify specific elements associated with each claim and determine whether the facts in the client's story match these elements. Professor Shell reviews this story-legal claims-elements-facts sequence several times using examples from the law of contracts and fraud. By the time he is finished the students have internalized a mantra that will guide them in their future interaction with legal counsel and, along the way, they also have developed a fundamental understanding of the law of contracts and fraud.

Reasoning by analogy and logic is also an important part of a lawyer's thought process that business leaders should understand. To illustrate, Professor Shell asks the class how a baseball might be like a whale. After obtaining a few responses from students, he shows a short video of Barry Bonds hitting his record-setting seventy-third home run. Two fans who fought over the ball in the stands both claimed ownership, which could have been worth millions. During subsequent litigation, one of the party's attorneys argued that his client should get the ball because, like the whalers of the nineteenth century, his man had "harpooned" the ball first and should be entitled to keep it. In the end, the judge said baseballs were not enough like whales for that argument to work, and ordered the two spectators to sell the ball and split the profits.

The third and final course theme is the importance of law in developing and implementing business strategy. To launch this theme, Professor Shell asked students for examples from their pre-Wharton business experience. This led to a lively discussion that he orchestrated, which included topics such as using intellectual property to achieve competitive advantage, the importance of import-export laws, and the use of lobbying for greater regulation by companies that already have high product standards in place.

Inside Professor Shell's Classroom

Professor Shell arrived in the classroom early to work on a technology concern with a technician. Whether working on a technical problem minutes before class or addressing challenging questions from his students, he remained calm and thoughtful, using an occasional raised eyebrow for emphasis. When engaged in dialog with students, he was an active listener and gave them his complete attention.

Professor Shell used a number of well-planned techniques during the class I attended. Here are some examples.

1. **Big-Picture Perspective**

   Professor Shell opened the class with a big-picture review of the agenda for the day and made continuing reference to key course themes. His opening review included comments designed to trigger student curiosity, such as, "Why is a baseball like a whale?"

2. **Use of Relevant and Interesting Examples**

   Near the beginning of class he illustrated the relevancy of the law to business by referring to the day's *Wall Street Journal*. The front page alone had nine articles or news summaries relating to regulations, a proxy fight, settlement of a lawsuit, an arrest for extortion, the legislative process, and claims of fraud. Students were intrigued as Professor Shell reviewed these examples; he had clearly gained their attention.

   After class, he mentioned to me a series of lectures given by William James, the nineteenth-century philosopher known as the "Father of American Psychology" and the brother of novelist Henry James. Professor Shell concluded that, in simple terms, James emphasized motivating students by first getting their attention and then by directing their attention to what is important. His teaching is replete with interesting stories that gain the students' attention, ranging from someone losing a job to a fight over a baseball.

3. **Active Learning**

   As noted previously, Professor Shell's teaching philosophy follows the Confucian aphorism: "Tell me and I'll forget, show me and I might remember, involve me and I will learn." Student involvement started near the beginning of class when two students designated as "TAs-for-the-day" (volunteer teaching assistants who were taking the course) summarized the prior class. The students enthusiastically presented a model they created that provided a 360-degree perspective of the material. Professor Shell praised them for their summary before asking for volunteers to present a summary during the next class. He later told me that these summaries provide continuity from session to session, insights into how students process the information, and a recap for students who miss class—such as one student who missed the class I visited because she was playing violin at Carnegie Hall that afternoon.

Later in the class, Professor Shell divided the class into small groups of around six students for discussion of a legal dilemma faced by an MBA student when a firm pulled a job offer just before she was to begin work. The lively discussion among students in these groups illustrates this aspect of Professor Shell's teaching philosophy mentioned earlier: "Every moment students are engaged by participation is good."

The "exit interview" negotiation described earlier provides another example of Professor Shell's goal of engaging students. Students participated in this negotiation near the beginning of class, but he delayed the negotiation debrief until later, when he moved it seamlessly into a discussion of the law governing contracts and fiduciary duties.

4. **Balance between Call and Response and Deeper Discussion**
Perhaps drawing on his musical background when he toured with the People's Revolutionary Road Company, Professor Shell occasionally used a "call-and-response" technique when covering the elements necessary for a legal analysis of a business opportunity or challenge. For example, during the analysis of a contract dispute, he would say something like, "Your initial meeting with a lawyer starts with..." and would then ask the class to respond. He would follow this with "The lawyer then..." and so on. This was a clever way to imprint the mantra of how a lawyer thinks, enabling students to easily recall the thought process long after the completion of their MBA studies.

At the opposite end of the teaching spectrum, Professor Shell balanced the simple call-and-response technique with deeper theoretical discussions of puzzles or paradoxes that are difficult to grasp and that stretched the students' thinking beyond the subject matter immediately at hand. For example, he asked the class, in what appeared to be a casual aside, "What is ownership?" This triggered a philosophical debate that eventually led to issues relating to property rights in a capitalist society. Through this discussion, his students, whose future careers will be inextricably entwined with the successful functioning of capitalism, gained a broad perspective on the tight integration of law with the economic system.

5. **Preparation of His Own Teaching Material**
Professor Shell distributed several handouts during the session. These included the dilemma involving the pulled offer ("A Wharton Grad Gets an Unpleasant Surprise," which is based on a true story), the "exit interview" negotiation, and a list of questions called "Legal Puzzles and Problems about Fraud and Fiduciary Duties." Professor Shell wrote these handouts, which added credibility

when he discussed the origins of the material when responding to questions in class.

Student Comments about Professor Shell

As the following quotations attest, Professor Shell's students speak of his teaching in glowing terms.

- Made me reevaluate and think about who I am as a person.
- I find that the way he illustrates key concepts of the course with personal stories and challenges as original as it is inspiring.
- Most impactful class. Really changed how I think about things.
- Students admire him for his honesty and transparency.
- Professor Shell is amazing; his experiences bring so much gravitas to the course.
- I love this class; very useful introduction to the legal topics … and a great class to help me better understand myself.
- I appreciated him sharing some of his personal life-pivoting experiences, something that I think required effort and commitment.
- [He is a] fantastic instructor. Theory and real life intertwined.
- Professor Shell is an absolute gem. One of those rare people you meet who appears to walk the talk.
- Professor Shell is a great tutor; this course has proved invaluable to my career and life.
- Love that the professor cares about the course.
- [He is a proponent of getting] students to identify their values and to stick by them; he provides compelling rationales for why this is important to do. Additionally, he shares his personal story with students—building trust by trusting the students first.
- Professor Shell is an amazing instructor. He has an uncanny ability to make everyone's values and opinions seem relevant and valuable. His legal knowledge and care for his students are unrivaled.
- He is good at making the classroom a safe space to share deep personal stories and ethical dilemmas. I'll remember stories and lessons when I face such dilemmas in the future.
- Professor Shell made us think and kept the class engaged with many breakout activities.
- Shell is an incredible instructor who has designed a whole experience that conveys not just the core legal concepts (the process of legal analysis and basics of insider trading, fraud, contract, etc.) but a larger inspirational message about how to be responsible beyond strict legal constraints. … Overall, it was a privilege to be part of this class—this is a Wharton experience that will stick with me for a long time.

- He forced us to come to our own plan of what it means to be a responsible professional. ... I'm glad I got to take his class. I'll remember it forever.
- The course made me think and reflect on who I am as a leader. I loved it. It challenged me and made me stretch my creative thinking.
- The three-hour class went by quickly with him, and he was genuinely interested in making sure each of us took something away from his course.

Impact Beyond the Classroom

Professor Shell has a long record of service to the University of Pennsylvania, the Wharton School, and the Legal Studies and Business Ethics Department. Beyond the university, his public service includes having testified before Congress on securities arbitration reform. To illustrate the breadth of his current activities, I asked him to keep a detailed record of his activities on the day I visited his class.

A Day in the Life of Richard Shell

7:00 a.m.

Wake up. Read *New York Times*, *Wall Street Journal*, and the sports page of the *Philadelphia Inquirer*. Drink Taster's Choice Instant Coffee, some green tea; eat two eggs (over-easy), some blueberries, and two strawberries.

8:30 a.m.

Ablutions and meditation.

9:15 a.m.

Telephone conversation with head of Penn Medicine's new junior faculty leadership development program. Will I teach in it? The director was referred to me by the leader of a Penn School of Arts and Sciences STEM program for junior faculty, which I teach in already.

10:00 a.m.

Telephone call to Social Security Administration with my wife, who will be collecting her full benefit later this year. Setting up direct deposit to our checking account.

10:30 a.m.

Begin my drive to my office at Wharton (around thirty minutes—I will listen to Steve Dubner's *Freakonomics* podcast).

11:00 a.m.

Confer with departmental business administrator on various priorities and issues related to my being department chair. Faculty reappointments, visiting appointments, logistical issues for departmental outside speakers. Random managing by walking around to ask how faculty are doing.

11:30 a.m.

Meeting with Wharton School Deputy Dean. He called regarding some personnel matter, but I have no idea what the conversation entails. We have already gotten our two big promotions through this year—one tenure case and one full professor case. So I am not sure what is on his mind. Perhaps someone from outside the school he is trying to recruit?

12:30 p.m.

Eat Cobb salad for lunch in my office. Read *Daily Pennsylvanian* (student newspaper) and field emails from students, faculty, Wharton Executive Education (I am teaching negotiation in a program for Credit Union CEOs on Wednesday afternoon), outside world (I am setting up a negotiation program in July in Washington, D.C. for the United Food and Commercial Workers as part of their annual collective bargaining meeting for negotiators). Telephone call with Wharton Leadership Office regarding my role in a lunch meeting the next day for student facilitators in the "Purpose, Passion, and Principles" peer-coaching program, which I helped launch and for which I serve as Faculty Advisor.

1:30 p.m.

Meet with undergraduate student about her midterm paper in my Literature of Success class. The paper topic is: "What is Luck and what, if anything, does Luck have to do with your emerging ideas about Success?" With the midterm paper (ten pages) done, students are seeking guidance on how to do better with their final, twenty-page paper on the theme, "What is my 2019 Theory of Success and How Do I Plan to Achieve It?"

2:00 p.m.

Prepare for MBA Responsibility class. Worry about whether AV system will work in class. It was a problem last week when I wanted to show a YouTube video of Barry Bonds hitting his record-breaking home run and two fans fighting over the ball just over the center-field fence. They sued each other, which is one of the cases I'll talk about in class.

3:00 p.m.

Teach MBA Responsibility class.

6:00 p.m.

Drive home.

6:30 p.m.

Dinner with spouse. Talk about why we are still talking about the Robert Mueller investigation.

7:00 p.m.

Back to email.

8:00 p.m.

Watch new Netflix show with spouse.

Thereafter—wind down, read mystery book, sleep.

One of the activities mentioned in the daily schedule provides an example of Professor Shell's impact beyond the classroom: the Purpose, Passion, and Principles (P3) program. He co-founded this eight-week, student-run program and serves as its faculty advisor. During the program, students reflect on the questions they often overlook while in the MBA program, such as how they define success and happiness, and how these definitions relate to their life goals.

Ninety-eight percent of past participants concluded that the program was a valuable experience. Here is an example that an MBA student posted at the P3 website: "At a crossroads in my life, P3 has proven to be an important forum to slow down for introspection, to reflect on my values, to recalibrate my compass, and to anchor my actions with integrity" (P3: Purpose, Passion, and Principles at Wharton, n.d.).

Occasionally, Professor Shell's teaching in class even impacts students who haven't taken his course. For example, the core Responsibility in

Global Management course includes a discussion of the importance of commitments in achieving success. Recognizing that MBA students, unlike professionals in some other careers like medicine, do not take an oath, a student in the course initiated the Wharton Commitment Project. Graduating students who joined the project could volunteer to develop a commitment by answering this question: "What are your personal commitments as you think about your life beyond Wharton?" Thirty-five percent of the graduating class responded. Here are the top ten common themes from the responses of these future leaders:

1. Care for my family
2. Invest in personal relationships
3. Do good/serve others/give back
4. Take care of my health
5. Continue to learn/grow/stay curious
6. Treat others with respect/kindness
7. Act with integrity
8. Pursue passion/meaning
9. Keep challenging myself
10. Enjoy life/do what makes me happy (MBA Program, n.d.)

Professor Shell's impact extends beyond the Wharton campus through his teaching in executive programs, his online course, and his research. The executive programs are challenging to teach because they attract a diverse audience that includes business leaders from a variety of industries, job functions, and regions of the world. His executive teaching extends beyond Wharton programs; for example, he has taught negotiation at the World Economic Forum at Davos.

As noted earlier, over 44,000 learners worldwide have enrolled in Professor Shell's online course on "Success." Course reviews indicate that 44% of the participants start a new career after completing the course. Among the many positive comments on the course website: "The course altered my perspective of success and gave me a better sense of how to live a more fulfilling life based on my personal values" (Success, n.d.).

Although Professor Shell's research includes the publication of a book directly related to law and regulation, *Make the Rules or Your Rivals Will* (2004), his other books extend beyond disciplinary boundaries. His negotiation book *Bargaining for Advantage* (2006) and his book on achieving success, *Springboard* (2014), have had an impact on readers throughout the world. These books combine an amazing breadth of sources with a clear writing style that reflects Professor Shell's early interest in creative writing. Customer reviews express the impact of his books on readers—for example, "Sage advice to all ages. For my children, grandchildren, and for me, the grandfather, as I approach my seventieth birthday this month. You have changed my life" (Springboard: Launching Your Personal Search, n.d.).

Lessons from Professor Shell

While Professor Shell's publications and service to Wharton have had a huge impact, his work in the classroom is his core activity. Why is he so successful in the classroom? Are there lessons for teachers and for business leaders in their role as teachers within their companies? Here is a distillation of the key elements that have led to his success.

1. *Thoughtful Organization of Content.* Professor Shell has a clear agenda regarding the content of his teaching. The topics he covers in his required MBA course—law and ethics—are sometimes considered to be dry, technical, and complex. There is also a risk that students will memorize legal rules for an exam and forget them shortly thereafter. Professor Shell mitigates this risk by focusing on the importance of understanding legal analysis and how a lawyer thinks. Using a four-step process, he uses the law of contracts and fraud to illustrate how students can maximize the value of legal advice.

   He also emphasizes that future leaders must be able to reason logically through analogy and to identify legal issues that can create success or lead to failure in business. Students will probably be unable to recite the details of contract law a few months after the course, but their ability to understand the legal analyses of their business decisions will likely remain with them throughout their careers, as they use legal principles to develop and implement their business strategies in an ethical manner.

2. *Preparation.* Preparation is a key factor in the success of these techniques. Professor Shell's first piece of advice to someone who wants to become an effective teacher is: "Prepare, prepare, prepare." The minute-by-minute game plan he brings to class exemplifies his attention to detail during the preparation process.

3. *Active Learning.* Through years of experience in teaching at Wharton, Professor Shell has developed several techniques for achieving his goals. When using these techniques, he uses a rule of thumb mentioned earlier: "Every moment students are engaged by participation is good." He brings a number of tools to the classroom to facilitate student participation and active learning. These include the use of negotiation exercises, riveting stories to illustrate the subject matter, small group discussions, "teaching assistant" volunteers to review the content of the prior class, and a "call-and-response" technique to emphasize key learning points.

   Other approaches that he uses to engage students include referring to key course themes throughout the class, relating the course material to current events, and authoring course materials rather than relying on material prepared by others.

4. *Transparency in Sharing Experiences.* Professor Shell has a soft-spoken, low-key style in the classroom. Although his sense of humor emerged during interaction with students, he did not tell one joke in the class I attended. Having observed other outstanding professors early in his career, he realized that he could not copy their style. What he brings to class, instead, is an authenticity that arises from his transparency. As he weaves stories and examples into his teaching, he is willing to share his professional and life experiences in a sincere and honest manner that encourages students to reciprocate when discussing their experiences. A story from the introduction to his book *Springboard* illustrates this transparency. In this excerpt he describes collapsing in Kabul, Afghanistan after contracting hepatitis:

> Before I had gone more than fifty yards, I blacked out, collapsing on the side of a street. When I came to, I was lying on my back in some mud and looking up at a ring of dark-complexioned, curious faces forming a tight circle around me. A man in a dirty Afghan army uniform bent over, hands on knees, and peered into my face. A young boy offered his hand to pull me up. I was sure I was going to be sick, but I managed to get to my feet. It isn't often that you know exactly—to the second—when you have hit the bottom of your life.

5. *Learning from Students.* The dedication in the book *Springboard* illustrates another aspect of Professor Shell's authenticity—his appreciation of what students bring to the learning experience: "For my students, past, present, and future. In gratitude for teaching me so much" (p. ix). He reciprocates by sharing with them his wisdom accrued through a series of interesting life experiences and his understanding of the importance of law and ethics. In this endeavor, he treats students as colleagues in the learning process by listening carefully to their comments and treating them with respect.

6. *Holistic Approach to Teaching and Research.* Professor Shell's teaching and research are holistic, feeding off each other. As he stated in an article in *The Pennsylvania Gazette*, "A lot of professors write books and then devise courses. But I actually devise courses and then write books" (Zeitlin, 2013).

Professor Shell's writing provides some important clues to his success as a teacher. In his books on success and strategic persuasion, he emphasizes the importance of credibility. As he states in *Springboard*, "What matters most in your overall success is your ability to exert influence through credibility and authentic relationships" (p. 14). He observes that others will conclude that you are credible when you show that, in addition to your expertise, you are competent and trustworthy. Professor Shell's emphasis on course content that will endure throughout the lives of his students and his use of well-tested teaching techniques illustrate his own expertise.

While trustworthiness is a more elusive concept, in his book on strategic persuasion (*The Art of Woo*), Professor Shell emphasizes the *"consistency between what you say and what you do* [his emphasis]" (p. 107). In his own life, he walks the talk by achieving balanced excellence in his myriad activities—an excellence that is driven by his devotion to teaching.

After leaving Professor Shell's classroom in Huntsman Hall, I walked down a path called Benjamin Franklin Way. Franklin's essay titled "Proposals Relating to the Education of Youth in Pennsylvania" (1749) led to the founding of the University of Pennsylvania. His essay begins: "The good Education of Youth has been esteemed by wise Men in all Ages, as the surest Foundation of the Happiness both of private Families and of Common-wealths." Franklin's proposals included teaching morality, government, law, and justice. Franklin would be delighted to know that over two-and-a-half centuries after writing his essay, Richard Shell is faithfully and successfully implementing these proposals.

References

Burgess, A. (1986). *A clockwork orange*. New York: Norton.

Franklin, B. (1749, October). *Proposals relating to the education of youth in Pennsylvania*. Retrieved from National Archives: https://founders.archives. gov/documents/Franklin/01-03-02-0166

MBA program. (n.d.). Retrieved from Wharton: https://mba.wharton.upenn. edu/story/student-led-wharton-commitment-project-takes-personal-approach-concept-professional-oath/

P3: Purpose, passion, and principles at Wharton. (n.d.). Retrieved from Wharton: https://www.wharton.upenn.edu/story/p3-purpose-passion-principles-wharton/

Shell, R. (2004). *Make the rules or your rivals will*. New York: Crown Business.

Shell, R. (2006). *Bargaining for advantage: Negotiation strategies for reasonable people*. New York: Penguin Books.

Shell, R. (2014). *Springboard: Launching your personal search for success*. New York: Portfolio/Penguin.

Springboard: Launching Your Personal Search. (n.d.). Retrieved from Amazon: https://www.amazon.com/Springboard-Launching-Personal-Search-Success/ dp/1591847001

Success. (n.d.). Retrieved from Coursera: https://www.coursera.org/learn/ wharton-success

Zeitlin, D. (2013, September 6). Shell's odyssey. *The Pennsylvania Gazette*. Retrieved from The Pennsylvania Gazette: https://thepenngazette.com/ shells-odyssey/

Chapter 5

Chicago Finance Professor Steven Kaplan

Learn How to Make Financial Decisions and Start a Business

In June 2008, Professor Steven Kaplan of the Booth School of Business at the University of Chicago gave a convocation address to graduating MBAs. The Neubauer Family Distinguished Service Professor of Entrepreneurship and Finance, Professor Kaplan has won many teaching awards at Chicago Booth, where he started a business plan competition that has resulted in the formation of startup companies that have created thousands of jobs and billions of dollars in value.

Professor Kaplan also has an international reputation for high-quality research. An article in *Fortune* magazine called him "probably the foremost private equity scholar in the galaxy" and a JP Morgan report referred to him as "the patron saint of private equity research" (Professor Steven Kaplan, n.d.). However, in the convocation address, he distilled another aspect of his research that was of special interest to the graduates: the characteristics that lead to being a successful business leader.

He became involved in this area after recognizing that previous research by others was mainly anecdotal and focused on after-the-fact stories about qualities in CEOs who had become successful. What if, he asked, *most* CEOs with the same qualities were failures? With this research question in mind, he and two colleagues obtained detailed assessments of over three hundred individuals who were candidates for CEO positions in firms funded by private equity investors. In analyzing this data, they classified abilities into three categories:

- "hard" or execution-related, such as being efficient, aggressive, persistent, and proactive
- "soft" or interpersonal, such as being flexible, a good listener, open to criticism, and a team player
- Neither hard nor soft, such as being persuasive, organized, analytical, and calm

Which of these characteristics are associated with CEO success (as measured by evaluations of performance and financial return to investors)? The research concluded that the soft skills were not a factor in success.

Some of the "in-between" abilities, like being organized, do make a difference. However, the hard characteristics are most closely related to success. In Professor Kaplan's words, these findings make sense:

> CEOs who are persistent, efficient, and proactive get things done. CEOs who are not, do not get things done, even if they are good listeners, team players, etc. And if you do not get things done, the people working for you get frustrated or even leave, particularly the better ones.
>
> (Kaplan, 2008)

In many ways Professor Kaplan is a poster child for his own research in that he exhibits several traits of a successful CEO. Like successful business leaders, he exhibits hard characteristics such as being proactive— that is, he is self-directed and creative in his research and in developing the entrepreneurship program at Chicago. He is also efficient, as I witnessed during our email exchanges. He immediately replied to my email requests, and his responses were always on point and refreshingly brief (averaging twelve words per message, including one wordless reply with a "thumbs-up" emoji). When I interviewed Professor Kaplan while he was on vacation in Mexico, he called me precisely at the appointed time.

Professor Kaplan is also "hard" in terms of being a tough professor. However, he is an enigma in that in the classroom he exhibits listening skills and a warm concern for his students that are more characteristic of someone with strong interpersonal characteristics.

Meet Professor Kaplan

Professor Kaplan's Resume

The following resume summarizes Professor Kaplan's seven-page CV.

Experience

University of Chicago Booth School of Business, 1988–present; Faculty Director, Polsky Center for Entrepreneurship and Innovation, 1997–present; University of Chicago Law School, Thomas Cole Distinguished Visiting Professor, 2014–present; INSEAD, Visiting Professor, 2001; Kidder, Peabody & Co., 1981–1983, Analyst

Education

PhD in Business Economics, 1988, Harvard University; AM in Business Economics, Harvard University, 1987; AB in Applied Mathematics, summa cum laude, Harvard College, 1981

Professional Activities

National Bureau of Economic Research, Research Associate, 1995–present; Associate Editor, several leading Finance journals; business and nonprofit board of directors

Honors

- Teaching: Named as one of top twelve business school teachers and as one of the top four entrepreneurship professors in US by Business Week; McKinsey Award for Excellence in Teaching; Phoenix Award (for exceptional dedication to the graduating MBA classes, four times)
- Research: Smith Breeden Prize; Nasdaq Award; Roger Murray Prize for Excellence in Quantitative Research in Finance; Markowitz Award Prize
- Service: Richard J. Daley Medal, Illinois Venture Capital Association; Arthur L. Kelley Faculty Prize (for exceptional service beyond teaching and research, two times)

Research

Over forty articles in leading journals; ranked among top 100 in citations out of over 400,000 Social Sciences Research Network (SSRN) authors; over 40,000 Google Scholar citations

Figure 5.1 Professor Steven Kaplan.

An Interview with Professor Kaplan

1. **What attracted you to an academic career?**

   I am from Danbury, Connecticut, where my mother was a real estate broker and my father was a rocket scientist. He designed spy satellites, but he couldn't tell us at the time because it was all classified. He helped build the spy satellites that went over the Soviet Union and took pictures.

   I was always academically motivated. In college, I became really excited about economic research. But I was also attracted to the business world. During my summers I sampled different jobs, such as medical research and working on the Hubble telescope. But it was after I became an investment banker in New York City for two years after college that I decided to marry my interest in research and my interest in business and become a business school professor.

   The motivation wasn't so much to teach. It was really to do research in economics and business. I didn't teach as a graduate student. My wife used to think that was funny: "You are going to be a professor, and you've never taught." I thought that I would figure it out when it actually happened.

   So I was initially attracted to research on economics and finance. I fell into teaching and turned out to enjoy teaching quite a bit.

2. **You have three degrees from Harvard. Were there any people there, or later at Chicago, who were role models for you?**

   Three people at Harvard were big influences. Marty Feldstein [former president of the National Bureau of Economic Research and Chief Economic Advisor to President Reagan] was my undergraduate thesis advisor. Mike Jensen [Jesse Isidor Straus Professor of Business Administration at Harvard] was my dissertation advisor. They were very serious researchers, and their research has had an influence on practice. They both cared about teaching. Paul Asquith [the Gordon Y. Billard Professor of Finance at MIT] was on my dissertation committee. In addition to being a strong researcher, he was a very serious teacher. One person at Chicago who has been a mentor and friend is Rob Vishny [the Myron S. Scholes Distinguished Service Professor of Finance]. He is a superstar researcher and also a very talented teacher.

3. **What teaching training did you have as a PhD student or at Booth?**

   Although I had no training in the PhD program, I did complete the first year of the MBA program at Harvard Business School. So I sat through a year of case studies and understood what it was like to be an MBA student in a case class. While at Harvard, I also sat in on an executive program taught by Paul Asquith and others. He was very generous in giving me a lot of his teaching materials. So I started at Chicago with a good understanding of what it's like to teach an MBA class.

One of the things I picked up at Harvard is to memorize the names and faces of every student before class starts. When I walk into class, I can say, "Hi George. How are you doing?" The students are shocked that I know who they are. Every fall, I have 205 students in three sections. I will start memorizing their names at the beginning of September, and by the time class begins at the end of the month I will know them all.

The thing I decided to do differently from Harvard Business School was a suggestion from my wife, who had been at Harvard's Kennedy School. One of her professors, after teaching a case, would take five or ten minutes to say, "Here's why we did this case." I find that students appreciate when I consolidate what we have covered during the case discussion.

Booth didn't have training programs. The view at that time, but maybe not quite the view now, was to do your research because you will receive tenure based on your research. Make sure your teaching is good enough to keep the students happy. While the teaching quality actually turns out to be pretty good overall at Chicago, the focus has always been on research. You learned how to teach, and you still do, by talking to people who have already taught the course. But since I taught a case course that no one else had taught, I was on my own.

I did videotape my classes two or three years after I started teaching. It was useful to see my quirks so that I could try to correct them. I would talk with a cup of coffee in my mouth. I decided that I needed to stop doing that!

4. **How did you start teaching your courses on entrepreneurial finance, private equity, and new venture development?**
I started teaching in the winter of 1989, when I taught cases in corporate finance. In 1995, Dean Bob Hamada approached me and said, "Look, I want to do entrepreneurship, and I need somebody to teach entrepreneurial finance. I'd like you to do it." I had just gotten tenure and had been teaching the same thing for seven or eight years, so I agreed to try it.

I had done a lot of research on private equity, and the class was basically half private equity and half venture capital. So I viewed it as a way to teach more closely to my research. Because of that class I ended up doing research on venture capital, and one of the papers that came out of the teaching is one of my most cited papers, which Oliver Hart mentioned in his Nobel Prize lecture. [In his Nobel Prize lecture, Professor Hart also cited another one of Professor Kaplan's articles.]

5. **Is your teaching mainly to MBA students, or do you teach to different audiences? Do you notice any differences in the audiences?**
I teach executive education in addition to my MBA courses. I teach in a program for members of boards of directors, one on private wealth management, and one on corporate finance.

The executives have more experience, so in some sense their comments on the institutional details are more sophisticated. On the other hand, they are less analytically schooled than MBA students. So, on the margin, those are the differences.

I also teach a course in the law school every spring. The course is a combination of corporate and entrepreneurial finance. Students in the course are, for the most part, going into corporate law, and they find it helpful to understand the financial aspects of large companies and entrepreneurial companies.

6. **How do you prepare for class? Are you nervous when you walk into class for the first time?**
I am a little bit nervous. But I walk into class thinking that it will be fun for me and for the students. In terms of preparation, the big thing is memorizing all of the students' names and faces.

At the end of each year I evaluate all the cases I've used. Not only do the students complete their course evaluations of me, but I also hand out a supplementary evaluation form in which I ask them to rate all the cases. Based on that evaluation, I can determine which cases are getting old or are not working, and I will usually replace one or two of them. I write almost all of the fifteen cases I use in the class. None of the cases I use today are the same as the cases I used when I started.

7. **In reading about your teaching, I see the word "tough." Why do people refer to you as a tough teacher? Do you cold call students?**
That would be because 40% of the grade is class participation, which is high in all places except Harvard. So the students know that class participation matters. I run the classroom by asking questions, and if the students go off topic or they say something that doesn't make sense, instead of nodding my head, I will say, "No, that's wrong" or, "No, that's not what I asked."

I also am very clear that I start right on time and I end right on time. If you arrive late, it is at your own peril. I am very serious about the class. If students are not serious about the class, I will let them know.

I cold call a little. Because so much of the grade is class participation, plenty of students raise their hands. But I use a cold call if someone has not spoken after the first two or three weeks of the course. After that, some of them start participating more. Others don't. If they want 40% of the grade to be an "F," that is their decision.

8. **How do you evaluate the quality of class participation?**

   After class, I go through the class spreadsheet. If someone didn't talk, I remember that, so the zeros are easy. If someone spoke, I remember whether the comment was just okay or really good and grade them on a scale of one to ten. I am not perfect every time, but after twenty classes, any mistakes tend to even out. At the end of the quarter, very few students complain about their grades. Out of over two hundred students, only three to five will ask about their grade, and in every case, they were on the border between, say, "A–" and "A" or "B+" and "A–."

9. **Do you use a flipped classroom experience?**

   To some extent, I flip the classroom when a guest is present. I usually invite from five to eight guests to my course. My guests sit in the front with me, and we have a conversation. I will ask questions to the students based on the case, and then I will ask the guests for their opinions, so it is very interactive. And I then invite the students to ask questions to the guest. So I'm not sure whether to call this flipped, but the students must think on their feet; it is in real time, and they are encouraged to ask questions and to figure out what they want to learn.

10. **You mentioned earlier that your teaching has spawned some research. What about the reverse? Are you able to bring your research into your teaching?**

    Absolutely. Virtually every paper I write is of interest to both academics and practitioners. If research isn't relevant, why do it? So my research is about private equity and venture capital, and when I do that research, I immediately teach it to the MBAs, along with other people's research.

11. **You base 40% of the students' grade on class participation. What is the rest of the grade based on? Do you use a grading curve?**

    Fifty percent of the grade is the final exam. The remaining 10% is based on a two-page write-up that students complete for each case. They can do the write-ups in groups of three. If they hand in the write-ups, they receive the 10%. This ensures that they are thinking about the case before coming to class, which is important to have a good discussion. It also encourages them to work in groups, which is useful to obtain the perspectives of other students. In the law school, where much of the work is individual, my students tell me that they enjoy the opportunity to work in groups.

    At the law school, I am forced to use a curve, which I don't love. At Booth, there is a maximum grade point average we can give, but I tend not to hit it because of the natural grade distribution.

12. **What do you like most about teaching?**

    The students at Booth and the law school are really talented, and it is really a pleasure to be able to teach them and to give them frameworks and tools that will make them more successful. Over time, it's been great seeing the success of my former students like Satya Nadella, the CEO at Microsoft, and Tom Ricketts, a co-owner of the Chicago Cubs.

13. **What do you like least about teaching?**
Grading 205 final exams. I grade all my own exams. I don't farm grading out to teaching assistants because these are case exams. This takes one week of my life each year. After reading the first fifty exams, it becomes increasingly hard, but it needs to be done.

14. **Have you faced any significant challenges with your teaching?**
The challenge for me, and this has gotten harder over time, is that I am very quick when responding to students. What I most worry about in teaching is that if someone says something that is wrong, I must be careful not to come down too hard. This becomes a bigger problem the older and more senior I become. When I was thirty I was less scary to students. Now I am a little more scary, even though I don't feel that I am. So my biggest challenge is to be careful not to come down too hard and to be more encouraging rather than discouraging. I must navigate between being too nice (where the class doesn't go anywhere) and being too tough (where students become discouraged).

    [In an interview for the Booth student newspaper, *Chicago Business*, Professor Kaplan noted, "One quarter, when I was a little too tough in class, someone wrote on the evaluation form, 'If Prof. Kaplan won the Nobel Prize, it wouldn't justify his arrogance.' That was a little tough" (Kapoor, 2016).]

15. **How do you know whether you have been successful as a teacher?**
There are three ways. First, there are teacher ratings at the end of each quarter. The students are pretty blunt because the ratings are anonymous. Second, we have a system where the students bid for classes. If my course is expensive, I know that I am doing something right. Third, over the medium-to-long term, students stay in touch and let me know how they are doing.

16. **Is teaching important at Booth for purposes of annual reviews or promotion and tenure decisions?**
While teaching is secondary to research, it is problematic if you are a bad teacher. If your research is good but not spectacular, being a strong teacher might help you get tenure.

17. **Does Booth currently provide teaching training to rookie professors? What advice would you give to a rookie professor?**
When people arrive, there are talks about how to teach, but most of the learning is from colleague to colleague. People are very good about sharing material. You can also be videotaped.

    This is my advice to rookies: do your research because research is the number one factor to get tenure. But your life will be much better if you are a good teacher because you will have a better time with your students, you will learn something from them, the Dean's Office will be happier, and, on the margin, teaching does help for tenure. So I recommend putting in extra work the first time that you teach to make yourself a better teacher. Some people are innately better teachers than others, but there are tools that you can implement that will make you a more successful teacher. The first time you teach, you will be spending a lot of time anyway, which will take you somewhat away from your research. So you should go all in to develop these tools. This will pay dividends for a long time.

18. **What is your proudest professional achievement?**

First, receiving tenure in Finance at the University of Chicago.

Second, building the New Venture Challenge, which is rated the number one university accelerator in the country. Basically, that model is something I created, and it has been unbelievably powerful. Grubhub came out of that model and is now worth billions. Other companies that came out of that model are Braintree Venmo, which is now owned by PayPal and would be valued in the billions, and Simple Mills, the second largest natural baker in the country. So we have had unbelievable successes that came from creating a process that is very special.

19. **What do you do for fun outside of your professional life?**

[The following response is from a *Chicago Business* interview with Professor Kaplan.] "I spend a lot of time with family. I have two kids—one is a sophomore in college and the other in junior high school. I support my wife, who is on the senior leadership team at Chicago Public Schools. My wife was the chief administrative officer at CTA and is now a senior person with Chicago Public Schools, and I support her to help her fix the city. I am on a couple of boards, which keeps me busy. I run. In fifteen years, I have run a half marathon thirteen times, and my best time is 1:43, and I usually hit 1:50. I like to go to good restaurants and travel. I am very fortunate in that the stuff I do for work I do for pleasure too. I read about business and the economy, politics, and political economy. (Kapoor, 2016).

20. **If you were not a professor, what profession would you choose?**

I was torn between going to Wall Street and getting a PhD. So if I weren't a professor, I am guessing that I would be on Wall Street at a hedge fund or private equity fund doing things that are similar to my teaching and research.

21. **What profession would you least like to be in?**

Anything in a large bureaucracy. I thought about becoming a doctor, and I didn't particularly care for the clinical side of detecting things and cutting things. I liked the analysis a lot more.

22. **What advice do you have for your graduates?**

I have two pieces of advice. First, "aim high." Our students are very talented. If they aim high, some of them will actually attain things they may never have believed they could attain. Even if they do not reach their high goals, they do well. If, instead, they aim low, that is the best they can do. So, aim high.

Second, "don't ask, don't get." It is very important to be assertive. I find that many students hesitate to ask for advice, help, favors, etc. I tell them that they should ask. The worst off they can be is where they would be if they had not asked. But a surprising amount of the time, people actually are willing to help.

23. **What three individuals, living or dead, would you most like to have dinner with?**

Shakespeare, Moses, and Alexander the Great. While all three are extremely famous, there is much about all three that is unknown.

Professor Kaplan in Action

The Course: Corporate and Entrepreneurial Finance

Professor Kaplan's course titled "Corporate and Entrepreneurial Finance," which he teaches at the law school, is a condensed version of a similar course he teaches at Booth. Commenting on the Booth version of the course in *MetroMBA*, Microsoft CEO Satya Nadella noted that Professor Kaplan "can take a situation and analyze and articulate the issues involved. He can both write well and understand the case quantitatively" (Pfeffer, 2017).

The four parts of the course summarized in the syllabus are: "(1) financing decisions, (2) investment decisions, (3) private equity finance, and (4) entrepreneurial and venture capital finance." The course is a so-called "case course" in that it is based on cases describing real-world scenarios.

In preparing for class, students read the cases and answer study questions. They also submit a short memorandum with recommendations to a CEO or other person making decisions regarding the case. Professor Kaplan assigns readings on the latest corporate finance research to provide students with background information. He also creates Excel worksheets for them. These worksheets include exhibits from the cases so that students can focus on analysis instead of spreadsheet preparation.

Professor Kaplan assigned two cases that he authored for the class I attended. The first one, "Paramount Communications Inc.—1993," is a twenty-five-page case (including fifteen pages of exhibits containing financial and other information) that describes Viacom's attempt to acquire Paramount. The second one, "NetSuite and Oracle," is a thirty-two-page case (including seventeen pages of exhibits) on Oracle's attempted acquisition of NetSuite.

These are the study questions that Professor Kaplan asked students to consider when reading the Paramount case:

- Why do you think Paramount is a takeover target?
- Which of the two firms—Viacom or QVC—would make a better fit with Paramount? Which would Paramount management, i.e., Martin Davis, prefer, if it had to choose?
- What is Paramount's worth as is? In valuing Paramount as is, you should assume that Paramount will have a debt to total capital ratio of 20%.
- How should Redstone proceed? What price should he offer? Should the offer be a cash offer, a stock offer, or some combination? What should he do about the lockout option and the termination fees? Should he bother trying to buy Paramount at all?

While Professor Kaplan has a reputation for being a tough professor, he sees his role as important in preparing students for the real world. As he noted in the *Chicago Business* article:

> I'm pretty tough, and some students are scared of me and think I'm too tough and that really annoys me. In the real world, they are going to run into people much tougher than I am and the right response is to push back and argue. So I would encourage people to be more aggressive.
>
> (Kapoor, 2016)

Perhaps because of Professor Kaplan's reputation for toughness, students take class preparation seriously. One sitting next to me in class mentioned that although she had worked for several years in finance before attending graduate school, it took her six hours to answer the study questions.

In the syllabus, Professor Kaplan emphasizes the importance of attending every class. Arriving on time is also important. In the *Chicago Business* article, he mentioned, "In the old classrooms, I used to lock the door, and this one guy showed up two minutes late and knocked on the door and said I'm sorry. And I said you're late. Go back" (Kapoor, 2016).

Inside Professor Kaplan's Classroom

During the class I attended in the Corporate and Entrepreneurial Finance course, it was apparent that Professor Kaplan is not a showman. He does not tell jokes or "perform" for students (although at one point he did a realistic rendition of the *Beavis and Butthead* laugh during a discussion of Viacom's ownership of MTV, which owned the TV series). Instead, he manifests a genuine concern for students through a number of teaching strategies and techniques.

1. **Personal Interest in Students**

   Professor Kaplan arrived early for class and greeted the few students who were already there with a warm, "Good morning" and, "Hope you survived the weather." (The campus had experienced an unseasonal April snowfall the night before.) He greeted other students (thirty-one total) as they arrived. His warmth is reflected in the course syllabus, where he lists his office hours and notes that "I enjoy talking with students. I am happy to talk about the course, your career, current events, etc." This was apparent during his conversations with them during the break and after class. He smiled frequently during the class, which had a calming effect as his students struggled with the complex material.

   Even during the COVID-19 pandemic, Professor Kaplan was able to connect with students. As he explained to me, "The more connection you can create ahead of time, the better. I met in small zoom groups—5 or 6 students—for a breakfast or lunch with most of the students in my course. With 200 students, this meant 35 of these sessions. I found them very valuable in getting to know the students and showing the students that I was a person and not just a face on a screen."

2. **Emphasis on Relevant Content**

   Professor Kaplan invited to the class a prominent corporate attorney who specializes in corporate financing and mergers and acquisitions. Some guest speakers make presentations to the class. However, in this class, instead of a formal presentation, the attorney sat in the front row and provided candid and unscripted answers to questions posed by Professor Kaplan throughout the class, such as: "Does anyone do this type of valuation in practice? Would this feature be important to your client?" This interactive approach emphasized the relevance of the class discussion to the business world.

   By comparing the 1993 Paramount case with the 2016 NetSuite case, Professor Kaplan was able to show that approaches to valuation that were used several years ago are still useful today: (1) a discounted cash flow analysis, (2) an analysis based on the value of comparable publicly-traded companies, and (3) a private market valuation based on comparable transactions. This reinforced the relevance of the course material.

3. **Interactive Teaching Style**

   Professor Kaplan began class by peppering the students with questions about the Paramount case. He used their first names while calling on volunteers or cold calling them with questions like, "Who is the target?" and "Why is Paramount the target?" He listened carefully to their responses and followed up their answers with other questions. For example, when a student noted that Paramount was the target because it is undermanaged, he asked the student to explain why he thought so. He also called out students when their analyses were suspect: "You are now giving me a different argument."

This give and take required intense concentration by the students. Although most of them used laptops, from my perch at the back of the room I observed that no one was checking emails or shopping online. Their attention did not diminish even though this was a three-hour class (with a ten-minute break in the middle).

4. **Teaching Students to Deal with Ambiguity**
   When discussing calculations, Professor Kaplan did not jump to his conclusions. Instead, he patiently worked through the calculations with the students, relying on a series of questions. He emphasized that there are different ways to analyze the questions, and often there are no right answers. For this reason, the syllabus emphasizes that he does not distribute case solutions after class. Instead, he encourages students to "learn to distinguish between sensible and senseless arguments" rather than obsessing over the ambiguity in the cases. As he warns them: "If you are uncomfortable with ambiguity, this class may not be for you."

5. **Simplification of Complex Subject Matter and Big-Picture Focus**
   Professor Kaplan occasionally used simple diagrams to explain complex material. For example, he diagramed Viacom and Paramount as separate and combined entities to launch a discussion of the difference between the cost and revenue synergies that might arise from a combination of the companies. He also used simple analogies that students could easily understand, such as comparing the valuation of a company with the sale of a house.

   The discussion of synergies illustrates another facet of Professor Kaplan's teaching. In a course like his it is easy to become lost in the trees—that is, the analytical details. To prevent this, he frequently emphasized the big picture, such as Viacom's strategic rationale for the acquisition.

6. **Blending Rigor with Support**
   Professor Kaplan embodies the ability to provide support to students while demanding intellectual rigor. For example, when he asked the class to complete a valuation of Paramount, students produced a wide range of values. He kindly reminded them that this was their first experience with valuation and that their disparate results were normal. He assured them that the analysis would feel natural by the end of the course.

7. **Reference to Business Experience and Research**

   As a result of his business experience (such as serving as a member of the Board of Directors at Morningstar and the Zayo Group) and stellar research record, Professor Kaplan was able to use frequent examples drawn from the business world and recent academic research. For example, he discussed research that provides empirical evidence about what happens to the stock price of targets and acquirers in a variety of circumstances. His reference to this research and use of examples, coupled with his authorship of the cases and course readings, adds additional credibility to his already solid reputation for excellence in the classroom.

8. **End-of Class Summary**

   Professor Kaplan concluded the session with a summary of the key learning points. These included the strategic rationale for an acquisition, motivations and incentives of the parties, implementation concerns, valuation methods, and negotiation tactics. At the end of class he also reminded them of the topic (private equity) and readings (a case and five readings, four of which he authored) for the next class.

Student Comments about Professor Kaplan

In an interview published in *Poets and Quants*, Booth graduate Joanna Si described why Professor Kaplan was her favorite professor:

> I have never been so afraid to show up late to a class! On day one of class, Kaplan showed up having memorized everyone's names and random facts about our backgrounds. I will also likely never forget the time I was cold called to explain my model to the class and subsequently never showed up to his class unprepared. I learned so much as a result and discovered I liked the subject enough to pursue a VC internship. As intimidating as he may appear in the classroom, he made time to meet with students to go over concepts or discuss their career interests and business ideas.
>
> (Schmitt, 2017)

Students in the class I attended echoed these thoughts in the following quotations.

- Brilliant.
- Makes time for you.
- Has a ton of experience.
- Very thorough.
- Doesn't make us feel dumb when we ask stupid questions.

- Comprehensive presentation slides.
- Very clear.
- Reading a textbook would take four times as long as his lectures to internalize the material.
- No nonsense.
- Goes at warp speed.
- Doesn't cut students down on our comments but will cut us down if we are late for class.
- Clear slides.
- Enthusiasm is infectious.
- Responds to emails.
- Willing to answer all questions during office hours.

Impact Beyond the Classroom

Professor Kaplan's training as a half-marathon runner was undoubtedly useful on the day of my visit, as he moved from the law school, where he taught the three-hour class in the morning, to Booth, where he led a four-hour afternoon session in which student teams pitched their startup ideas to seasoned entrepreneurs. Between and after these two marathon sessions, he handled matters beyond class, including editing a research paper.

A Day in the Life of Steven Kaplan

6:00 a.m.

Wake up

7:00 a.m.

Go to office

7:45 a.m.

Meet class speaker for breakfast

8:30 a.m.

Teach Law School class: Corporate and Entrepreneurial Finance

11:40 a.m.

Record grades from class, make phone calls, clear email, get ready for class

---

1:00 p.m.

Teach class: Special Topics in Entrepreneurship: Developing a New Business Venture

5:00 p.m.

Edit research paper to meet paper deadline

6:00 p.m.

Eat dinner

8:00 p.m.

Review the judges' feedback from the Special Topics class

Beyond his teaching, Professor Kaplan is well known for his research on private equity and for his leadership of the entrepreneurship program at Chicago Booth. His research has garnered over 40,000 Google Scholar citations, and he ranks among the top 100 in citations out of over 400,000 authors on the Social Sciences Research Network. He has testified during committee hearings in both the US Senate and House of Representatives. Among his research awards are the Smith Breeden Prize, the Roger Murray Prize for Excellence in Quantitative Research in Finance, and the Markowitz Award. With MIT Professor Antoinette Schoar, he created the Kaplan-Schoar Public Market Equivalent (PME)—an approach for benchmarking private equity funds.

Professor Kaplan had an opportunity to merge his teaching and research interests in 1995 when Dean Robert Hamada asked him to develop an entrepreneurship program at Booth. At the time, Booth offered only three entrepreneurship courses, none taught by regular faculty. Professor Kaplan accepted the challenge. As quoted in *Chicago Business*, "I didn't know any better, so I said 'yes'" (Kapoor, 2016).

Professor Kaplan proceeded to develop a course on Entrepreneurial Finance, became Faculty Director of the Polsky Center for Entrepreneurship and Innovation, and started the Edward L. Kaplan, '71, New Venture Challenge (NVC). (The names for the Center and the Challenge have evolved over time. Professor Kaplan is not related to Edward Kaplan.) Today there are over twenty Booth courses on entrepreneurship. Professor Kaplan's leadership and willingness to listen to students played an important role in this growth. As he put it in *Chicago Business*,

> We make sure that what we do, we are doing well. It is very student driven. Most of the things that we do are because the students come

and tell us they want it. And if we hear enough from the students that they want a certain new program, we figure out that there is probably demand and we should be doing it.

The NVC plays a key role in entrepreneurship education at Booth. During a year-long process, students do the following:

- Generate and validate their ideas, form teams, and apply to the Challenge by submitting an eight-page feasibility study.
- Have an opportunity to take Professor Kaplan's Special Topics course. During the course, teams present their business plans and receive feedback from venture capitalists and entrepreneurs who serve as judges.
- Following an end-of-course presentation in the class, certain teams are selected to present their final plans to judges. The top teams receive cash prizes along with various goods and services. Winning teams must provide Booth with equity in their company.

I attended a 2019 session of the Special Topics course during which students presented their business plans to the judges. Students had initially formed over ninety teams, and thirty-three teams were invited to take the course. Twelve of these teams were selected to pitch their final plans to the judges. Eleven finalists shared over $850,000 in investments in their businesses. The top team, which garnered $365,000 in investment, is creating a business that allows art dealers to bypass intermediaries by selling valuable works of art directly to buyers. Other finalists planned development of

- an eSports league designed to promote a sense of community among gamers;
- AI software that identifies public safety threats in security cameras and feeds this information to law enforcement;
- a platform that uses analytics to enhance the workplace experience of employees;
- a company that wants to create healthy snacks using local super-foods, such as chips made with cricket powder; and
- a company whose goal is to create cosmetic prescription products through imaging technology.

The impact of Professor Kaplan's NVC is impressive. As summarized on the Challenge website, the program has resulted in "more than 330 startup companies and created thousands of jobs for the economy. NVC startups have ... achieved more than $7.5 billion in mergers and exits" (Edward L. Kaplan, '71, New Venture Challenge). For example, Grubhub won a prize of $17,000 when it tied for first place in the 2006 competition. The market value of the company later grew to billions of dollars.

Given his record as a pioneer in entrepreneurship education, what advice does Professor Kaplan give to students involved in NVC? In a quote from a *Chicago Tribune* article, he emphasized the importance of customers: "Convince us you're going to get customers; convince us that what you're developing solves a problem and that people will buy it" (Sharma, 2017). He later provided more general advice that was summarized in *The Booth Experience*: "Be ambitious. You have to think big to be successful in the program. Being ambitious pushes you to be bolder in your presentation, put more into growing the idea, and excites you about the possibilities that [lie] ahead" (Nwabudike, 2017).

Lessons from Professor Kaplan

A lengthy interview with Professor Kaplan, observation of his work in the classroom (while he taught the Corporate and Entrepreneurial Finance course and led a four-hour NVC session in which student teams pitched their business plans to judges), and discussions with his students reveal the following elements that are key to his success as a teacher:

1. *Personal Interest in Students.* Professor Kaplan memorizes the names and faces of his 205 students every fall so that he can address them on a first-name basis when they enter class for the first time.
2. *Synergies between Teaching and Research.* Professor Kaplan's teaching occasionally generates research ideas, and he brings his research into teaching. His leadership of entrepreneurship initiatives at Booth has enabled him to integrate his teaching and research interests.
3. *Preparation of His Own Teaching Material.* Professor Kaplan has written almost all the cases that he uses in class. He then uses student evaluations at the end of each course to improve or replace certain cases.
4. *Highly Interactive Classroom.* His methodology includes rigorous questioning rather than lectures. Students also have frequent opportunities to interact with guests who are leaders in their field.
5. *Listening Skills.* Professor Kaplan listens carefully to student comments during class. Outside class, his ability to listen to students' concerns has led to the creation of a leading entrepreneurship program. As he put it, "Most of the things that we do are because the students come and tell us they want it."
6. *Emphasis on Relevant Content.* In his teaching, as well as his research, Professor Kaplan emphasizes material that is relevant to the future careers of his students. The presence of prominent practitioners in his classes reinforces the relevance of the content.

7. *Simplification of Complex Material and Big-Picture Focus.* He occasionally uses simple diagrams and analogies to explain complex material. He uses simplification to help students understand, rather than skirt, the inherent ambiguity in the course material.

8. *End of Class Summary.* Unlike some case teachers, he summarizes the key learning points at the end of each class.

9. *Big-Picture Focus.* Professor Kaplan often moves beyond the analytical details to emphasize the big-picture questions that firms face when making financial decisions.

These specific elements are dominated by a balancing act that exemplifies Professor Kaplan's concerns about teaching success. On the one hand, he feels the need to be tough and to provide students with a rigorous classroom experience that prepares them for the real world. On the other hand, he recognizes the importance of providing support to students and being more encouraging than discouraging. In his words, "I must navigate between being too nice (where the class doesn't go anywhere) and being too tough (where students become discouraged)." Based on his tremendous success in (and outside) the classroom, he clearly has achieved this balance.

References

Edward L. Kaplan, '71, New Venture Challenge. (n.d.). Retrieved from Polsky: https://polsky.uchicago.edu/programs-events/new-venture-challenge/nvc/

Kaplan, S. (2008, June 15). A PEP talk: What can your learn from successful CEOs? *Convocation ceremony at University of Chicago.*

Kapoor, S. (2016, January 16). Coffee on the third floor. *Chicago Business.* Retrieved from Chicago Business: http://www.chibus.com/people/2016/1/25/coffee-on-the-third-floor

Nwabudike, O. (2017, April 6). *NVC series.* Retrieved from The Booth Experience: http://theboothexp.com/2017/04/nvc-series-a-few-words-with-professor-kaplan/

Pfeffer, J. (2017, October 23). Alumnni spotlight. *MetroMBA.* Retrieved from https://www.metromba.com/2017/10/microsoft-ceo-sayta-nadella/

Professor Steven Kaplan. (n.d.). Retrieved from Miami Herbert Business School: https://news.miami.edu/miamiherbert/stories/2020/01/kaplan.html

Schmitt, J. (2017, May 3). *2017 best MBAs.* Retrieved from POETS&QUANTS: https://poetsandquants.com/2017/05/03/2017-best-mbas-joanna-h-si-university-chicago-booth/?pq-category=students/

Sharma, J. (2017, January 10). Startups prep pitches for shot at New Venture Challenge. *Chicago Tribune.* Retrieved from https://www.chicagotribune.com/business/blue-sky/ct-new-venture-challenge-quick-pitch-bsi-20170110-story.html

Chapter 6

Michigan Management Professor Gretchen Spreitzer

Design Your Life to Thrive in the New World of Work

During a sabbatical leave from the University of Michigan in the first half of 2008, Professor Gretchen Spreitzer (the Keith E. and Valerie J. Alessi Professor of Business Administration at the Ross School of Business, University of Michigan) accepted a position as a visiting professor at the University of New South Wales in Sydney, Australia. The leave provided her with an opportunity to give several lectures and conduct research abroad. Her husband, Professor Robert "Bob" Schoeni, a University of Michigan economist, and their two daughters, aged eleven and nine, joined her during the leave.

The trip started and ended on an ominous note. At the start, during a stop in New Zealand on the way to Australia, the couple's oldest daughter suffered a ruptured appendix. Thankfully, she recovered after a lengthy surgery and hospitalization in an intensive care unit.

Upon arriving in Australia, Professor Spreitzer settled into her new academic environment, and the family enjoyed the Down Under experience, which they shared in a blog. There were trips to the Great Barrier Reef and the Blue Mountains, and they explored Sydney with visits to its legendary beaches, the Opera House, and elsewhere. The daughters quickly adapted to their new school, although they reported that the required uniforms with floppy hats felt "weird." In Ann Arbor, Professor Schoeni was known as "Coach Bob" when serving as coach for his daughters' teams, and he soon volunteered for a similar role in Sydney.

But as the end of the leave approached, Professor Schoeni's right hand began to feel cold, and he later experienced spasms in the hand that were followed by a feeling of weakness. After returning to Michigan, he underwent a series of tests that revealed he had Amyotrophic Lateral Sclerosis (ALS), commonly known as Lou Gehrig's disease. ALS is a degenerative disorder that results in an inability to control one's body, voice, and respiratory system. Over 350,000 people have ALS worldwide, and they live two to five years on average after being diagnosed. There is no cure.

Both husband and wife responded to the news with a positive attitude. In 2012, the graduating MBA students at Ross asked Professor Spreitzer to give a "Last Lecture." In the lecture, she discussed what it means to thrive at work and recounted her husband's reaction to the diagnosis in a quote that reflects her own sense of meaning and purpose:

> Almost four years ago, my husband Bob (age forty-four) was diagnosed with ALS or Lou Gehrig's disease—a disease with no treatment or cure. Many who are diagnosed begin to think about their bucket list, turning their attention to things they most want to accomplish in their limited time remaining. But after a lot of careful thought and many conversations, Bob realized that rather than racing around the world ticking off a bucket list, he most wanted to enjoy coaching our daughters' field hockey and softball teams and continue to do his work as a public policy economist because both have such meaning and purpose to him.
>
> (Spreitzer, 2012)

After the couple received the diagnosis, their neighbors and friends quickly mobilized and, within a few months, they formed a nonprofit called "Ann Arbor Active Against ALS" to raise funds for research on treatment and a cure for the disease. The organization has tapped into some unusual fundraising sources. For instance, Lou Gehrig, the legendary baseball player who succumbed to ALS and who was its namesake, was a member of the Phi Delta Theta fraternity. The Ann Arbor nonprofit partnered with the University of Michigan chapter of that fraternity to raise $75,000 through a series of boxcar derbies.

Another funding source was a team of six women, aged from their early thirties to early forties, who decided to raise $100,000 by swimming the English Channel from England to France and back—a total of forty-two miles. In so doing, they broke the world record for a women's relay time. The inspiring video "One Step Ahead" recounts their adventure (Berg, 2013).

In a 2020 newsletter, the organization reported that it had donated $787,000 for ALS research. In a column titled "From Bob & Gretchen," the two professors mentioned one research product: "Bob quickly adapted to using Eyegaze to interface with the computer, which has been life changing—incredible technology" (Let's go, 2020).

Meet Professor Spreitzer

Professor Spreitzer's Resume

The following resume condenses Professor Spreitzer's thirty-five-page CV.

Education

PhD in Business Administration, 1992, University of Michigan; BS cum laude, 1987, Miami University

Academic Experience

University of Michigan, 2001–present; University of Southern California, 1992–2001; Visiting Professor, University of New South Wales, 2008

Awards and Honors

Research and teaching awards include:

- Organization Development and Change Distinguished Scholar Award, Academy of Management
- Researcher of the Year Award, Ross School of Business
- Impact Award for Executive Education teaching, Ross School of Business
- Keynote address, Organizational Studies graduation ceremony, University of Michigan
- Outstanding Scholar Award, Journal of Management Inquiry
- Distinguished PhD Alumni Award, Ross School of Business
- Selected to give "Last Lecture" by graduating MBA students, Ross School of Business
- "Top Gun" Award (for excellence in research, teaching, and service), Marshall School of Business, University of Southern California

Books

Co-authored or co-edited seven books. One of these books, *The Best Teacher in You: Accelerating Learning and Changing Lives* (Quinn et al., 2014), received the Benjamin Franklin Award from the Independent Book Publisher Association. Another book, *The*

Future of Leadership (Bennis et al., 2001), has been translated into five languages.

Journal Articles and Book Chapters

Over fifty journal articles and over forty book chapters. Main research streams are empowerment, leadership, positive organizations, and downsizing. According to Google Scholar, this research has been cited over 35,000 times.

Invited Presentations and Keynote Addresses

Over 150 presentations to audiences ranging from a leadership program for US Army Generals to conferences on sustainable peace

Teaching at Ross School of Business

- Undergraduate: Thriving in the New World of Work; Managing Change; Positively Leading People and Organizations
- MBA: Navigating Change: Skills for Consultants, Managers & Change Agents; Human Behavior and Organizations (MBA required course); Business Leadership (online MBA program)
- PhD: Professional Development Series: Becoming a Professional. Has served on over thirty-five doctoral dissertation committees, including eight as Chair or Co-Chair
- Executive Education: Emerging Leaders Program and several other open enrollment and customized programs
- Massive Open Online Course (MOOC): Leading Ambitious Teaching and Learning (over 25,000 students enrolled)

Professional Service

Professional service includes eight editorial boards and the Academy of Management Board of Governors

University Service

University Service includes Associate Dean for Engaged Learning and Professional Development; Co-Director, Center for Positive Organizations; Management and Organizations Department Chair; and service on numerous advisory boards, task forces, and committees.

Figure 6.1 Professor Gretchen Spreitzer.

An Interview with Professor Spreitzer

I interviewed Professor Spreitzer shortly after she and her husband resolved a difficult dilemma. They had just become empty nesters with the
departure of their youngest daughter to Tufts University. Their other
daughter is a student at Colby College. Both daughters play field hockey
at the collegiate level, and they attended the first field hockey match of
the season: Colby vs. Tufts. Whom to root for? They used different approaches in resolving the dilemma: her husband wore a Tufts hat and a
Colby shirt; Professor Spreitzer wore neutral clothing.

1. **What attracted you to teaching?**
   I grew up in Bowling Green, Ohio, where my dad was a professor of
   sociology at Bowling Green State University. He thought that teaching was a wonderful career because it provided autonomy and the
   ability to choose the topics you care about. The ability to mentor students was also a big attraction. He talked about the academic year
   cycle and how nice it is to have the busy school year and then the
   summer with more thinking time. He also encouraged me because
   he thought it was a great career when you have a family; although
   you work very hard, you have some flexibility in your schedule. For
   me it was kind of a no brainer, as I always had becoming a professor
   at the back of my mind.

   I had two relatively short summer jobs in Washington, DC that
   confirmed my interest in teaching. One was with an urban planning nonprofit organization. I had an interest in how cities and

communities can become great places to live. The work was interesting but it was challenging because of the need for constant fundraising in addition to the work I cared about. The second job was
with PwC in its government services consulting arm. I found that,
for me, consulting was more interesting in theory than in practice.

2. **Did you have any other encouragement to become an academic?**
I was in the Honors Program at Miami University, which was headed
by Dick Nault. He had a deep interest in helping students identify
and play to their strengths rather than having a cookie-cutter model
of success. He saw in individuals what their own greatness was and
allowed them ways to manifest that in their career choices and in
their involvement at Miami. When I told Dr. Nault that I didn't
know what I want to do, he was a good listener and told me that
was okay; I did not have to have it all figured out immediately. He
encouraged me to think about academia.

At that time the AACSB International [The Association to Advance Collegiate Schools of Business] offered scholarships to women
and underrepresented minorities who might not have considered
business school. That made me open to looking at management instead of psychology and sociology.

3. **Did you have any mentors after you enrolled in the PhD program?**
During my first year, I did not have a very good connection to a faculty member. Like me, a lot of students during the first year think,
*"What have I gotten myself into? This isn't at all what I thought it
was going to be."* Bob Quinn [Professor Emeritus of Management
and Organizations at Michigan Ross] invited me to talk about common research interests. At that time, he was developing the Compet-
ing Values Model, and his team of researchers had access to a lot of
data.

His invitation to participate in the research opened doors on
the research side but also on the teaching side because around that
time Bob and Kim Cameron [Professor Emeritus of Management
and Organizations at Michigan Ross] were developing a leadership
program for a major US corporation, and a big piece of that program was the empowerment of middle managers. The company kept
saying, "We are empowering you," and the middle managers kept
saying, "We don't feel very empowered and if you keep telling us
we are empowered when we don't feel that way, it's worse than not
saying anything." Bob encouraged me to study this issue, which was
more practice-based than theory-based. At first, it felt scary because
a more problem-focused dissertation was not common. Now more
people do applied research, but back then it was questionable.

As I did the research, Bob encouraged me to present my findings
to the participants in the program to get their insights. It was "out

of the box" for a PhD student to be talking with managers during executive education programs. This built a lot of confidence, as I realized that I had something worth sharing with them. And through that process I observed the different teaching styles of the faculty in the program. It was neat to see how different instructors were finding ways to connect with managers around very topical questions and issues.

4. **As a PhD student, did you have any formal teacher training?**
   In those days there was no training apart from my executive education experience. For example, my department chair needed someone to cover two sections of the Human Resources course and told another PhD student and me to "just do it." We each had one section and figured it out ourselves, trying to stay one lesson ahead of the students. We had no special expertise in HR, so it was sink or swim.

5. **What teacher training do you provide to PhD students today?**
   Today our students have a year-long developmental experience. In the second year of the program, they teach in a core course that is coordinated with faculty. They have assignments where they have to observe faculty and report their insights. And during the term when they are teaching, the coordinator observes them and provides feedback. So it is much more structured. But when you are learning to teach at that level, you still must find your own way forward to a certain extent.

6. **What types of courses have you taught at Ross?**
   I teach traditional courses in our undergraduate, MBA, and PhD degree programs. In our MBA program I also serve as faculty advisor for our MAP (Multidisciplinary Action Projects) program—a required course where our students work in teams to address business challenges faced by companies around the world. I teach in executive education programs (such as the Emerging Leaders Program: Becoming a Transformational Leader) where enrollment is open to participants in all organizations and in other programs that are customized for specific organizations. I also worked with professors at the University of Michigan's School of Education to develop a MOOC [Massive Open Online Course] on Leading Ambitious Teaching and Learning. Over 20,000 students worldwide enrolled in the course during its first two years. I have also just developed the first residency course for our new online MBA students. This course enables these online students to meet face-to-face with each other and with their professors.

7. **Do you adjust your teaching style when teaching different types of students?**
   I don't do that much adjustment. My teaching style is pretty similar across all venues. I try to be interactive in all of them. I find it much

more interesting as a way to teach, and I also learn from what the students share with me. I would say that I probably am a little more probing with the executives: "Tell me more. Can you give me an example of that?" I don't do as much of that with undergraduates because they have less work experience.

Teaching a MOOC is challenging because you have to find ways to transmit your energy through the videos to students in a way that normally happens through classroom interaction. So I felt like I really had to pump myself up before taping the lectures and felt more depleted afterward because there wasn't that natural energy that comes from the live interaction. I was glad I tried it; it was a good experience. But if that were the primary mode, teaching would be a lot less fun and less interesting.

8. **How do you prepare for class?**

I try to find out from colleagues at Michigan and elsewhere whether there are some best practices. When I taught my course Navigating Change: Skills for Consultants, Managers & Change Agents for the first time, someone had taught the class before, but they had taught it quite differently from my approach to teaching. I went to people in the field whom I respected and who taught change. I asked them about the most powerful exercises, cases, readings, and modules they used. I used some of these resources as a starting point. I have never used a textbook. There is great knowledge out there, and I like to be able to learn from it.

Once I begin thinking about a two-hour time block, or whatever the class period, I try to break it up into several different parts— some parts lecture, some parts group discussion, some parts that use an exercise so that students do something active and I am not a talking head. I walk into class with the times all plotted out.

After I have taught a course for a while—for example, my course on change management—I probably change 20%–30% of the material each year. And I update the slides and the statistics. As I have become a more seasoned teacher, I don't have to do as much prep for material I have taught before, but I would never go into a class without reviewing the slides and readings and thinking about how I can improve them.

9. **Do you get butterflies walking into the first class?**

Of course, of course! Every time. To reduce the butterflies, I look at the students' pictures before the course begins. But most times they don't look like their glamour shots. In class they might be wearing a hat or glasses, which aren't in their pictures. I also review all of their LinkedIn profiles so I can see their employment history, which I use if we have a case involving a company where someone has worked. I used to ask them to fill out a survey about what they hoped to learn in the class, their work experience, and whether they have any special needs or involvements that might intrude on class.

So I feel that I know the students as human beings rather than just a name on a piece of paper. I also use LinkedIn to connect with them, and they realize that I am doing my homework. This pre-class connection with the students reduces the butterflies.

10. **What resources and teaching tools do you use in class?**
In each course around 20%–25% of the material is based on cases. I also use tools that have a solid research basis and that will engage students and give them insights. One is the Positive Leadership Game that Bob Quinn and I developed, which uses a structured brainstorming approach to help students and leaders develop innovative solutions to the challenges they face.

Another tool is the Reflected Best Self Exercise that I developed with Bob Quinn, Jane Dutton [the Robert L. Kahn Distinguished University Professor Emerita at Michigan Ross], and Laura Roberts [from the Darden School at the University of Virginia]. This development tool, which has been used by over 25,000 individuals at universities and Fortune 500 companies, is based on research that shows that understanding our strengths and talents depends to a large extent on how we perceive that others see us. Through the tool, people are able to identify how others see us when we are at our best.

11. **Do you use cold calls?**
When teaching the required MBA course, I used cold calling—not in an aggressive way but to make sure everyone was prepared for class. In my elective courses, where the students are more motivated by the material, I also use cold calling, but not in a traditional manner. For example, I might cold call when I notice that a student is not participating, as a way to draw them into the discussion. Or I use it when I know that a student has a connection to the material, and they haven't shared it with the class. For example, if we are talking about management consulting, I will say something like, "Jim, I know that you did this before you returned to school. How does this match your experience?" Or if we are talking about a company, I might say, "Sue, I know that you worked at this company. Is this similar to your experience?"

12. **Is class participation part of the grade?**
Class participation is usually 25% of the grade. I have a teaching assistant in the classroom to help me do an initial tally of the students. After each class, everyone receives a score: zero if you missed class, one if you attended but didn't participate, two if you participated in some way, and a three if your comments seemed to change the

direction of the discussion or if you bring an insight that was beyond the norm. There might be one or two threes in each session.

13. **How do you handle gunners who want to dominate the discussion?**
If I see the same hands going up again and again, I'll say, "Hey, we have heard from all of these people. What about the rest of you? I'd like to hear from someone we haven't heard from today." Sometimes I ignore gunners or, if I call on them and they go on and on, I'll interrupt and say, "That's helpful. Let's pause for a second and get a different point of view."

14. **Do you bring your research into teaching?**
When I first started teaching I didn't bring my own research into my courses because I wanted to be objective and didn't want to be biased. But I changed over time, especially because my research is relevant to my teaching. I realized that if I have been doing research on downsizing and I am teaching a module on downsizing, it makes sense to talk about my own work. Or because I teach change management and study change management, I should share my findings. Over time I have become much more comfortable bringing my own research into my courses. For example, I might assign some of my own readings. As a result, I feel that my students feel that they are receiving more personalized learning.

When I publish my research in an academic journal, I often try to publish a companion piece in a journal that is more accessible to the business community like the *Harvard Business Review* or the *Sloan Management Review*. Those companion articles are especially useful for class assignments.

15. **What do you like most about teaching?**
I like learning from the students. Sometimes I have not thought about some of the questions that students raise or the insights that they bring to the classroom, and their questions might stimulate a research idea or a better approach to the learning in the classroom. If I were only lecturing that wouldn't happen. Because the class is interactive, I have an opportunity to learn from them.

I also love having a chance to mentor the students and hearing from them after graduation about the impact of the learning.

16. **How do you evaluate your success as a teacher?**
An important measure of my success is having former students come back and tell me that the course was impactful, useful, and worthwhile in their careers.

17. **What do you like least about teaching?**
Probably everyone says this: grading. The required grade distribution is very hard. It is also difficult when I encounter a student who

doesn't care that much about the course. I wish there were a way to reach every student.

18. **How are rookie professors trained to teach?**

When teaching the required course, they work with experienced teachers who coordinate the course. I also encourage them to observe different faculty with the intention of determining their own style. If I tried to be a Bob Quinn, I would be a pretty mediocre Bob Quinn. If I try to adopt the style of Jane Dutton, it wouldn't work. But I can observe pieces from each of them that I can use.

19. **What would you advise rookie professors who are preparing to teach their first class?**

Try to love your students. Look for the bright spots. Try to see the best in them as learners and future leaders. Assume good intent. Be as organized as possible. Be clear in your expectations. Be yourself. Don't try to be something that you are not.

20. **What is your proudest professional achievement?**

This question stumps me. It's hard to toot your own horn. One achievement that means a lot to me was being offered a teaching position at the University of Michigan (especially since we normally don't hire our own PhD students). Winning the Organizational Development and Change Distinguished Scholar Award from the Academy of Management was a nice honor because it came from peers in my research area.

21. **What do you do for fun?**

Women faculty members used to get together to share our favorite non-professional books they read over the past year. This was a challenge because I didn't have time for this type of reading! Chasing my kids around when they were younger with all of their athletic activities was fun. I was their biggest cheerleader and supporter. I am a runner and have running partners. We run around 5K three mornings a week at 6:00 a.m. with our dogs. That's the only time that works because I am usually in my office at school by 7:30 a.m. When it is dark out and kind of scary, it's good to have a partner while running. We even go out in the winter when the temperature drops to twenty degrees.

22. **What profession would you choose if you were not a professor?**

When I was growing up I wanted to be a marine biologist. I love nature and the ocean and being outdoors. I also wanted to be a social worker, but my dad said that I would be the worst social worker in the world because "You are such a softie. You would be bringing your clients home to live with you."

23. **What profession would you least like?**

Any job where there is no flexibility or where you are resolving a lot of conflict. I would be a terrible salesperson, and I probably wouldn't be a very good investment banker where you don't have any control over your time or schedule. I work really hard, but I also like to have some freedom to figure out the pace of my day. I might want to do something during the day to help a friend. I'll work late at night or very early in the morning if necessary, but I'd like that freedom.

24. **What three individuals, living or dead, would you most like to have dinner with?**

My dad (a retired sociology professor and life philosopher who died in 2017), Pope Francis, and Warren Bennis (a leadership guru who was always generous company).

25. **If there is a heaven, what would you like God to say to you when you arrive?**

"You lived to the ripe old age of one hundred because we wanted you to keep doing such good work on earth."

Professor Spreitzer in Action

The Course: The Art and Science of Designing Your Life to Thrive in the New World of Work

The course I visited, The Art and Science of Designing Your Life to Thrive in the New World of Work, is unique in two respects. First, it is the only undergraduate course I observed when visiting the seven professors' classrooms for this volume. Second, it is a Michigan Ross "Capstone" course—a senior-level course that represents the culmination of the students' undergraduate education by drawing on learnings from previous courses.

The forty undergraduate students in the course were bright and experienced. They were part of a class of 506 students (selected from 6,408 applicants) who entered the Bachelor of Business Administration (BBA) program with high average SAT (1450) and ACT (33) scores. Although they were undergraduates, the students brought business experience to the course. During internships the summer before their senior year, members of their class had worked in a variety of functions led by finance (49% of reported internships, mostly in investment banking and corporate finance), marketing/sales (18%), and consulting (13%). The highest percentage of internships were in the tristate area of New York, New Jersey, and Connecticut, followed by the Midwest (where Chicago was the most popular city) and the West Coast (where San Francisco was the most popular destination).

The goal of the course is to help students create a bridge from their academic work to the changing world of work they are about to enter. As the course description notes: "The new world of work might be characterized by more flexibility and uncertainty" (Professional capstone, n.d.). This world results in more job and career changes—both voluntary and involuntary—than in the past. The course relies on the latest management research to enable students to craft "a meaningful career and life" (Professional capstone, n.d.).

The course is divided into four modules. Module I provides a foundation with an introduction to what it means to thrive (and not merely survive) in the new world of work, where technology and other factors have disrupted the traditional job market. Module I introduces a theme that is explored more fully in Module II: the importance of developing knowledge, tools, and resources to thrive in the new world of work. Topics include the power of mindful engagement, the importance of self-reflection, how to understand and leverage strengths, developing mastery, and understanding one's identity.

Module III examines more closely the resources for successfully thriving at work. Topics include how to conduct a diagnostic interview, becoming a better listener, teamwork skills, positive deviancy, reciprocity rings, positive leadership, and finding purpose in life. For example, a Ross graduate who is currently a senior strategy consultant for an international consulting firm gave a presentation on the importance of "side hustles" in developing a career. Side hustles are the development of skills and opportunities on the side that are separate from a core job.

The closing Module IV provides students with practical tools for using resources for success. These included energy management, mindfulness, reflection on positive aspects of work, moving from multitasking to uni-tasking, and the power of helping others. This module included the session I attended, on "Gratitude," which provided additional examples that are described later in this chapter.

In the business school world, courses like this are sometimes considered to be soft or "touchy-feely" by professors who are more quantitatively oriented. In fact, however, these courses are especially challenging because they raise unsettling questions that cannot be answered by quantitative analyses and that have a high impact on company and individual success. When I served as Associate Dean for Executive Education at Michigan Ross, I analyzed program evaluations provided by hundreds of senior managers who were attending our executive programs. The results indicated that these leaders felt that courses on management and organizational behavior like this one provided especially high value.

The course website was well designed, and included a Teaching Team Commitment. The teaching team consisted of Professor Spreitzer, co-teacher Betsy Erwin (the Senior Associate Director at the Center for Positive Organizations, who shares responsibility for the course design with Professor Spreitzer), and Teaching Assistant Tala Taleb, a graduate student at Ross. On the website (The art and science of thriving in the new world of work, 2018), this team made a commitment to the students to:

- [make] this course a valuable learning experience for you,
- [introduce] action-learning experiences that bring your learning to life, and
- [equip] you with the skills and tools necessary for you to create a valuable resource for thriving personally and professionally in the new world of work.

The teaching team used the website for frequent communications with the class. The website also included detailed information about each session and many readings, such as book chapters and articles from a number of sources (academic publications, business journals, and newspapers). Additional academic research and other resources were recommended during class, which enabled the students to develop a large reference library for use after graduation.

Sixty percent of the grade is based on individual assignments that included a reflection journal and a report on "Crowdsourcing a Launch Plan." The reflection journal assignment encouraged students to reflect on how to apply learning from the course to their current life and future plans. The crowdsourcing assignment required students to conduct seven interviews (one hour each) of people at different career stages and to use the interview results to develop a plan to jump start their careers.

The remaining 40% of the grade consisted of a team-based contribution to a resource called the "Thriving in the New World of Work Field Guide." Each team completed a module on topics ranging from developing grit to mindfulness. The combined results were made available digitally to students at the conclusion of the course.

Inside Professor Spreitzer's Classroom

Although I arrived twenty minutes early for the class session on "Gratitude," the teaching team was already busy with setup, placing materials on eight tables scattered throughout the classroom. Professor Spreitzer led the session, while co-teacher Betsy Erwin, sitting near the back of the classroom, occasionally added comments to the discussion. (They took turns serving as lead teacher for each class session.)

Professor Spreitzer used the following approaches in teaching the class.

1. **Warm, Inviting Classroom**
   ABBA's "Dancing Queen" greeted the students on their arrival, which gave the room a warm, new age feel. Later during the class, other music (Santana's "Smooth" featuring Rob Thomas and Billy Joel's "Miami 2017") was occasionally played from a list developed by the students. Professor Spreitzer apparently realizes that today's students are comfortable working with music in the background!

Professor Spreitzer instructed the students to sit at tables arranged by birth order (for example, those who were the oldest children in their families sat at tables 2–4, youngest at tables 5–6, and so on). The seating shifted for each class; in earlier sessions, it had been based on the first letter of the students' names, the last number of their cell phones, the first number of their street addresses, and so on. This approach enabled students to engage in active learning with a different set of individuals each time, throughout the course.

2. **Student Co-Creation of the Learning Experience**
   Students played a role in co-creating the learning experience—for example, their selection of the music for the playlist and the theme for the day: Gratitude. The prior year's class had selected this theme when asked for their topic of choice, and it proved to be so relevant to their careers that it was also added to the current offering of the course.

3. **Review of Prior Session**
   Near the beginning of class, Professor Spreitzer provided a big-picture perspective by reminding the students of the remaining sessions in the course and reviewing lessons learned from a speaker in the preceding class—someone who had graduated from Ross five years earlier.

   Unlike many business school speakers who talk about their success in business, this individual had described a failure early in his career. He had discussed the wide range of emotions experienced when he was blindsided by a layoff two years after starting his first job as a consultant with a leading national firm, and he had shared several lessons learned while in the process of relocating with a global consumer goods company. Framed as a "gift of feedback" to the speaker, Professor Spreitzer encouraged the students to think about how the experience of losing their first job might affect their future decisions.

4. **Blending Academic Research with Real-Life Experience**
   Throughout the session, Professor Spreitzer incorporated real-life experiences, including her personal ones, those of the business leaders with whom she works in executive education programs, and some drawn from students in the class. She was then able to match these experiences with the latest research.

   For example, in reviewing the speaker's presentation during the preceding class, she asked whether the students or their relatives had ever been fired. The many hands that were raised caused students to realize that they should plan for what has become a common experience. Following this survey of their experience, she commented on the following takeaways and provided many citations of the latest research:
   - Continually look for opportunities to connect with people. Build a community of support before the need arises.

- You have control over how to respond, even when faced with forces beyond your control—referring to an earlier class discussion of Viktor Frankl's *Man's Search for Meaning* (Frankl, 2006).
- When you bounce back from something like a job loss, try to "bounce better" by developing a toolbox for making job decisions.
- Plan ahead. Live below your means to develop financial reserves to cover emergencies.

5. **Active Learning**

   True to the Teaching Team Commitment, Professor Spreitzer filled the session with active learning exercises that enabled students to develop their skills in a risk-free environment. In one segment, called "30 Second Celebrations," students talked with others at their table about recent events in their lives that had a positive impact. For example, one student mentioned that she had just attended a symposium on impact investing and had a chance to pitch the valuation aspects of affordable housing. She later told me that she enjoyed events like this because she wanted to "squeeze every drop of learning" out of her remaining days at Ross.

   Professor Spreitzer added her personal cause for celebration—an upcoming long weekend (Thursday to Monday) visit to her daughter in Copenhagen. She also mentioned the positive impact that emerges when her faculty colleagues at Ross begin meetings by noting their celebrations, although she wryly noted the challenge of limiting their comments to thirty seconds!

   In another active learning exercise, she asked students to send a text or email to someone expressing gratitude. She then instructed them to put away their phones until the end of class, at which time she asked them to share the replies they received. These replies, ranging from "made my day" to a return expression of gratitude, illustrated the power of expressing gratitude.

   In another exercise, students reflected in their journals (to the sound of Santana's "Smooth" in the background) on the best gratitude or thank you they had ever received and gratitude that did not work well. These last two exercises served as a springboard for a general discussion of gratitude.

6. **Interactive Teaching Style**

   Professor Spreitzer's coverage of gratitude illustrates her teaching style. Rather than remaining in a stationary position in front of the class, she wandered the classroom while exploring questions about gratitude. What is gratitude? What are the benefits of gratitude? How can one show gratitude to others? How might gratitude be counterproductive? Through her warm, conversational style, she created an environment where students seemed to be comfortable sharing their perspectives and personal experiences relating to gratitude. I estimated that 90% of the students participated in the class discussions during the session.

Professor Spreitzer has a special talent for encouraging participation while keeping the class on track. While at times the session had the feel of jazz improvisation, when students spontaneously discussed experiences that might have been tangential to the main theme, she also orchestrated class discussion toward her learning goals.

Two leadership traits were especially apparent in Professor Spreitzer's teaching style. First, she exhibited exceptional active listening skills by paying close attention to what students said and summarizing their comments to make sure she had understood them correctly. Second, she was non-confrontational and supportive, with comments such as, "I think you are on to something, but I want you to take one more step." She also effortlessly wove academic research into the discussion when, for example, she summarized the benefits of gratitude—such as reduced stress, less conflict, stronger relationships, and reduced employee turnover.

As noted previously, she blended this research with real-life examples. One example involved the Michigan basketball team. Her colleagues from the Center for Positive Organizations had conducted a retreat for the coaches and team at the beginning of the prior season (2017–2018), when the team played in the national championship game. She mentioned that the coach, John Beilein, had kept a gratitude journal, and she showed a film clip illustrating how he had expressed his gratitude to the team and staff in the locker-room following one of their victories.

The class concluded with coverage of gratitude practices for the students to consider for the future. These practices included giving someone a "gratitude artifact" that reminds the recipient of gratitude and keeping a gratitude journal to record things to be grateful for. To illustrate, she gave everyone in the class an artifact in the form of a blank gratitude journal and gave them time to make their initial entries.

Student Comments about Professor Spreitzer

The following quotations from her students illustrate the impact Professor Spreitzer has on their lives.

- Gretchen genuinely cares about students way beyond the class. When I saw her at a Ross event, she asked what I thought about the event and about how my life was going.

- She wants to make sure you are okay every day. It's nice to know someone is on your side.
- I left every single class feeling energized and empowered.
- This has been an unusually stressful semester, but she made the classroom environment so enjoyable that it not only helped me (and I believe other students as well) in class but also throughout my entire life.
- She has the ability to connect with students and share her personal experiences in a way that motivates students to excel in their work.
- Gretchen brings realism to the class.
- Professor Spreitzer was a very kind, engaging professor. She created a warm learning space, always sharing personal tidbits that humanized her. ... It was also always clear that she was genuinely passionate about the material.
- She brings being a professor to another level. One morning she gave two random students a ride to class during a rainstorm.
- I also really enjoyed the community in the class. It is rare for me to get to know all of my classmates by name and truly feel like I know them. I have frequently seen people from this class outside of the classroom and spent time talking to them. This ability is amazing, and I am so grateful for the community Professor Spreitzer [has] created.
- Compassionate, genuine, caring.
- Professor Spreitzer is obviously passionate about the course and understands very intimately the topic of "Change Management."
- It was apparent she worked very hard to give us the best in-class experience and pushed us to think about our lives and how we would behave if faced with potential change in the future.
- She integrates all aspects of life.
- Professor Spreitzer is such a compassionate teacher who truly cares about each one of her students.
- Coming to class every morning to such a positive environment was so beneficial not only for this class but for feeling supported in Ross overall. I'm so grateful to have had the opportunity to learn from her.
- Gretchen was an invaluable resource and a huge reason for the success of the course. She was vulnerable and honest with us and welcomed us into her life as a person beyond the classroom as well.
- She challenged us to think beyond our own perspectives and to dig deeper, all while exhibiting immense trust and respect. Gretchen exemplifies the transformative leader and is a teacher of good people, not just "good students."

Impact Beyond the Classroom

The following "Day in the Life" segment illustrates the breadth of Professor Spreitzer's activities, which include class preparation, faculty discussions about various matters, a thesis defense, teaching, student meetings, and a Ross event in the evening. In mid-2020, her life became even more complex when she was named Associate Dean for Engaged Learning and Professional Development at the school.

A Day in the Life of Gretchen Spreitzer

5:45 a.m.

Alarm goes off, and I take my younger dog on a 2.5-mile jog with my running partners of fifteen years and one of their dogs.

7:00 a.m.

Prepare breakfast (and lunch to go) for my husband and myself. We are now empty nesters, so no school lunches to pack.

7:30 a.m.

At office, processing email and prepping for meetings and class. Impromptu discussions with various faculty members about the faculty review process, team dynamics challenges in MAP teams, and an upcoming department retreat.

9:30 a.m.

Walk across campus for an honors thesis defense for an undergraduate psychology student mentor.

11:30 a.m.

Teach my senior capstone class—today's topic is on "The Power of Gratitude at Work and In Life."

1:00 p.m.

Eat lunch while meeting with my MAP team of four women who have been in India for the past three weeks studying women's empowerment in rural Indian villages.

2:00 p.m.

Meet with my MAP team of six students from four different continents who are developing a distributor scouting and selection process for a large multinational in Europe.

4:00 p.m.

Meet with the person who endowed my faculty chair. So grateful for his generosity!

5:00 p.m.

Early dinner with husband and then back to campus for the Sanger Leadership Center's StoryLab finale for the semester. Proud to hear a couple of my students speak.

7:30 p.m.

Walk both dogs, talk with neighbors about recent neighborhood events, review more emails, and prepare for trip to Copenhagen in two days to visit older daughter for a long weekend. She is spending a semester abroad in Denmark.

9:30 p.m.

Read the paper and head to bed.

Two of Professor Spreitzer's activities outside the classroom are especially noteworthy. First, her exceptional research across several domains has generated over 35,000 Google Scholar citations. Her work on empowerment is especially noteworthy. Through studying employees across industries at all levels at times when they felt empowered or disempowered, she has identified four dimensions that define empowered employees.

- *Sense of meaning*: They have a purpose and are passionate about what they are doing.
- *Sense of competence*: They are confident about their abilities and have the skills necessary to do their work.
- *Sense of self-determination*: They are free to choose how to do their work and have the power to make decisions without being micro-managed.
- *Sense of Impact*: They can make a difference because of their influence.

The second example of Professor Spreitzer's impact beyond the classroom is her work on positive organizations. Michigan Ross is the home of the Center for Positive Organizations, which is grounded in a management research field called "positive organizational scholarship."

This high-impact research "empowers leaders to create positive work environments" that enables them to "enhance engagement and performance, and inspire their employees to innovate, find opportunity, and strive for excellence" (Positive organizational scholarship, n.d.).

Faculty at the Center have published rigorous research in the form of books and articles, produced videos in which researchers explain the field, and developed teaching cases and tools. In 2010, the Center received the Joanne Martin Trailblazer Award from the Academy of Management for creating a new field in management. This was followed, in 2012, by the Academy's Research Center Impact Award in honor of "its extensive influence on management practices" (Recognized for innovation and excellence, n.d.).

Professor Spreitzer is at the forefront in the field of positive organizations. She has served as Co-Director of the Center, has published over fifteen articles in leading journals and book chapters on positive organizations, and is the co-editor of *The Oxford Handbook of Positive Organizational Scholarship* (Cameron & Spreitzer, 2011). She has also taught positive leadership principles in degree and executive education programs.

Lessons from Professor Spreitzer

Professor Spreitzer's approach to teaching provides a checklist of best practices for teachers and business leaders. Among the key elements described earlier are co-creating courses with students, moving seamlessly from specific issues to the big picture, blending research with business experience, developing engaging active learning exercises, creating an interactive learning environment, and getting to know students and their backgrounds.

In addition to serving as a model of excellence in the classroom, Professor Spreitzer has conducted research and has co-authored a book on outstanding teachers titled *The Best Teacher in You: How to Accelerate Learning and Change Lives* (Quinn et al., 2014). In 2015, she was invited to give a speech to graduates of the Michigan Organizational Studies program. In that speech, she shared four key lessons from her research. Professor Spreitzer's own career exemplifies each of these lessons.

1. *Great Teachers Find Meaning in Their Everyday Work.* Professor Spreitzer has found meaning in her work through the powerful impact of her teaching on degree students and business leaders, through her research that provides insights to leaders on empowerment and positive organizations, and through her own leadership roles at Michigan Ross. In commenting on meaning during her speech, she observed:

> When my daughters were young, I realized that too often, I was giving the best of my energy to my colleagues and students and

not to my family. I was coming home exhausted at the end of the workday. I began a quest to be sure that each day at work I did something meaningful or with impact—might be something as small as having coffee with a student who was struggling or helping a colleague with a theoretical puzzle. I found it was rare that I come home depleted at the end of the workday.

(Spreitzer, 2015)

2. *Great Teachers "Keep Their Hearts Open."* In her talk Professor Spreitzer mentioned the two types of virtues that David Brooks noted in his book *The Road to Character* (Brooks, 2015): the "resume" virtues that lead to success at work and the "eulogy" virtues that are important to leading a good life. While Professor Spreitzer has many resume virtues, she also has an abundance of eulogy virtues. Her students mention her interest in them beyond the classroom and her concern for the needs of others, such as offering a ride during a rainstorm to two students. A colleague who has worked closely with her on teaching and research projects introduced her to an audience as follows: "There never has been a moment that she didn't live what she researches and teaches. As a result, my life and the lives of all my colleagues have been continually lifted. She is a generative force in our lives" (Pasick, 2015).

3. *Great Teachers "Find Their Own Path."* When developing her teaching skills, Professor Spreitzer learned from established professors, but she realized that she could not copy them. She found her own path by doing research that was more practice-based and less theory-based than the norm at the time and by presenting her research findings to managers to gauge their reactions. In her graduation address she quoted Steve Jobs, who noted that "our time is limited, so don't waste it living someone else's life. Don't let the noise of others' opinions drown out your own inner voice. And most importantly, have the courage to follow your heart" (News, 2005).

4. *Great Teachers Are "Purposeful in Building a Support Network BEFORE They Need It."* Through her teaching, her many research collaborations with colleagues at Michigan Ross and elsewhere, and her many service responsibilities, Professor Spreitzer has an unusually large support network. This network extends to her personal life, as illustrated by the neighbors and friends who created Ann Arbor Active Against ALS after her husband was diagnosed with the disease.

Professor Spreitzer closed her address with a quote from Ralph Waldo Emerson that embodies the philosophy that has enabled her to become a wonderful teacher and role model: "To be yourself in a world that is constantly trying to make you something else is the greatest accomplishment" (Spreitzer, 2015).

References

Bennis, W. et al. (2001). *The future of leadership*. San Francisco: Jossey-Bass.

Berg, M. (Director). (2013). *One step ahead* [Motion Picture]. Retrieved from https://vimeo.com/64463913

Brooks, D. (2015). *The road to character*. New York: Random House.

Cameron, K. S. & Spreitzer, G. M. (2011). *The Oxford handbook of positive organizational scholarship*. Oxford: Oxford University Press.

Frankl, V. (2006). *Man's search for meaning*. Boston: Beacon.

Let's go. (2020, Fall). Retrieved from Active against ALS: https://www.activeagainstals.org/wp-content/uploads/2020/09/Fall-2020.9.4.pdf

News. (2005, June 14). Retrieved from Stanford: https://news.stanford.edu/2005/06/14/jobs-061505/#:~:text=Your%20time%20is%20limited%2C%20so, follow%20your%20heart%20and%20intuition.

Pasick, R. (2015, April 17). *The best teachers*. YouTube. Retrieved from https://www.youtube.com/watch?v=lOGwHlUBUhA

Positive organizational scholarship. (n.d.). Retrieved from Center for Positive Organizations: https://positiveorgs.bus.umich.edu/an-introduction/

Professional capstone. (n.d.). Retrieved from Michigan Ross: https://michiganross.umich.edu/courses/professional-capstone-designing-your-life-thrive-new-world-work-11205

Quinn, R. et al. (2014). *The best teacher in you*. San Francisco: Berrett-Koehler.

Recognized for innovation and excellence. (n.d.). Retrieved from Center for Positive Organizations: https://positiveorgs.bus.umich.edu/center-awards/

Spreitzer, G. (2012). Thriving. *Unpublished graduation address to MBA students*, University of Michigan.

Spreitzer, G. (2015, May 1). Becoming the best in you. *Unpublished organizational studies graduation address*, University of Michigan.

The art and science of thriving in the new world of work. (2018, Winter). Retrieved from Center for Positive Organizations: https://positiveorgs.bus.umich.edu/wp-content/uploads/MO468-The-Art-Science-of-Thriving-in-the-New-World-of-Work-Syllabus.pdf

Chapter 7

Northwestern Marketing Professor Florian Zettelmeyer

Understand Data Analytics for Business Success

By 2013, Professor Florian Zettelmeyer's career was already exceptional. The Kellogg School of Management had recently named him the Nancy L. Ertle Chair in Marketing. His MBA course on customer analytics was wildly popular with students, resulting in his winning the Lavengood Outstanding Professor of the Year Award, along with many other teaching awards. Before arriving at Kellogg in 2008, he taught at the Haas School of Business at UC Berkeley, where he was the Chair of the Marketing Group and won the Earl F. Cheit Outstanding Teaching Award in both the MBA and PhD programs. He also received the Paul E. Green Award for best article in the *Journal of Marketing Research.*

Despite his accomplishments, Professor Zettelmeyer was restless. There was considerable buzz in the business community and in the press about Big Data. With a background in analytics, he was concerned that business schools were not doing enough to incorporate Big Data issues into the curriculum. When he talked with then-dean Sally Blount about his concerns, she was receptive, and he soon became director of a new program on data analytics.

As a pioneer in teaching data analytics in a business school environment, Professor Zettelmeyer developed a guiding principle that would govern the creation of new courses at Kellogg. Based on the example of Billy Beane, the General Manager of the Oakland Athletics who used analytical insights when signing overlooked players, he realized that understanding data analytics is a leadership issue, not just a technology problem. While they do not need to become technical geeks, he concluded, leaders do need to be able to distinguish between good and bad analytics and understand where analytics have potential to add value to a business.

Developing a guiding principle that analytics is a leadership concern is one thing; selling business leaders on the notion that they should gain a working knowledge of data analytics is another. Teaching data science to seasoned executives could prove to be either sadistic or masochistic—or both. However, Professor Zettelmeyer persevered and soon created one of the most popular executive education programs in the world. In an article in *Kellogg Magazine,* he stated the mantra that he uses to disarm business leaders in this program who suffer from data avoidance: "What very few people understand is that the most important skills in analytics are not technical skills at all. They are thinking skills" (Farrell, 2017).

Meet Professor Zettelmeyer

Professor Zettelmeyer's Resume

The following resume summarizes Professor Zettelmeyer's seventeen-page CV.

Leadership at Kellogg (current)

- Chair, Marketing Department at Kellogg
- Director, Program on Data Analytics
- Various committee, working group, and advisory board memberships

Education

PhD in Management Science, 1986, MIT; MSc in Economics, 1991, University of Warwick; Vordiplom in Business Engineering, 1990, University of Karlsruhe

Work Experience

Kellogg School of Management, Northwestern University, 2008–present; Haas School of Business, UC Berkeley, 1998–2010; Simon Graduate School of Business Administration, University of Rochester, 1996–1997; McKinsey & Company, Inc., 1989–1991

Honors

Over ten teaching awards including the

- Impact Award for teaching excellence at Kellogg (five times)
- Sidney J. Levy Teaching Award for teaching excellence in elective classes at Kellogg (three times)
- Lavengood Outstanding Professor of the Year for teaching excellence at Kellogg
- Earl F. Cheit Outstanding Teaching Award at the Haas School of Business, UC Berkeley (twice)

Selected to give the Commencement Address at Kellogg, 2011

Paul E. Green Award for best article in the *Journal of Marketing Research*

Professional Activities

Co-Editor-in-Chief, *Quantitative Marketing and Economics*; Associate Editor, *Management Science*; several editorial boards

Research

Twenty articles in refereed journals. Research interests include big data and analytics, marketing implications of consumer search and uncertainty, and implications of the internet on traditional industries.

Teaching **(current)**

- MBA: Customer Analytics
- Executive MBA: Marketing Analytics
- Executive Education: Leading with Advanced Analytics and Artificial Intelligence
- Massive Open Online Course (MOOC): Leadership Through Marketing (over 17,000 students enrolled during first four years)

Figure 7.1 Professor Florian Zettelmeyer.

An Interview with Professor Zettelmeyer

1. **Are you from an academic background?**

   My father worked in the development area for the United Nations and for the German government. As a result of his work, I grew up in several countries before attending boarding school. I then attended the University of Karlsruhe, the "MIT of Germany," where I majored in business engineering.

   Both of my parents have PhDs. However, I have an academic background through my mother, although on the research rather than the teaching side of academia. She was Spanish and an art historian who took several years off while traveling with my dad. Later on, she was widely published. She had an incredibly successful academic career without ever having an academic job. She wrote biographies, organized exhibitions at the Prado, and was one of the world's leading experts on painting in the era of Philip II. Occasionally she did valuation work for Christie's and Sotheby's.

2. **Why did you want to become a professor?**

   What attracted me initially was research. Before I got my PhD, I worked as an intern in Germany and Brazil at McKinsey. The most important thing I learned was how to give presentations. That was a core skill at McKinsey. They gave me a roadmap for how to think about communicating and how to think about how everything is a story even though it doesn't necessarily feel like a story.

   I was very influenced by the legendary Gene Zelazny, McKinsey's Director of Visual Communications. I learned a lot from him on how to present, how to structure a story, and how to put together visual aids. My teaching materials still reflect the McKinsey style and format. I received really good training on how to think about visual material. The core idea was using the structure of slides to force yourself to be very systematic about generating the story you are telling and in uncovering the weaknesses in that story. This discipline has been very helpful.

   [In a presentation on "Some Pointers for Preparing Presentations," prepared when he was a professor at Berkeley, Professor Zettelmeyer explained the importance of using a disciplined approach when preparing a presentation. Here are his conclusions.

   - Think of the presentation as a story.
   - Slide structure helps you figure out the story.
   - Slides are not there to remind you what to say.
   - Slides help your audience follow along with you.
   - Much of the preparation is in the transitions (Zettelmeyer, n.d.).

He elaborated in his commencement address to the Kellogg Class of 2011:

> Great communication is always built around a story. ... I literally mean that everything you communicate has to take the form of a story. Every presentation, every speech, every memo, every pitch you make has to be a story in which you key ideas are embedded.
>
> (Zettelmeyer, 2011)]

So at McKinsey I developed a general fascination with presentation. My interest in teaching is an outgrowth of a longstanding interest in doing a good job of presenting. I honed my ability starting at McKinsey and then throughout my PhD years, when I started to enjoy giving academic presentations. I continued putting a lot of effort into academic presentations, and it was only later that I started translating some of those principles into teaching. So it was really research and the presentation of research that got me started with the whole issue of how to communicate.

3. **Did you have any role models when you were in the PhD program at MIT?**

   In my PhD training at MIT, there were people I admired for their clarity. Ricardo Caballero, a famous macroeconomist, had an incredible ability to take complicated macro models and make them seem simple. There was another famous professor who was not easy to understand and very confusing, causing me to wonder whether this person was a bad professor or I was an admissions error. I was intimidated and not willing to raise my hand and ask for clarification. I later learned that this person *was* a bad teacher, and this led me to develop the confidence to raise my hand and say, "I don't get it. Could you please explain?"

   I loved people who had unbelievable clarity of thought when taking very technical material and making it simple and logical. The core of what I have been trying to do in my courses is to combine transparency in explaining something that is quite technical with a storytelling aspect. That combination has worked quite well. I credit the storytelling aspect to my McKinsey training, and I had very good role models for explaining the technical material.

   It came naturally to me to try to deconstruct the material in a way that would be understandable for a person who has never seen it. When I teach in executive education, I tell people that they need a working knowledge of data science so that they will not be intimidated (as I initially was as a PhD student who thought he might be an admissions error) when asking questions and admitting that they don't understand. By "working knowledge," I mean an ability to know the difference between good and bad data, and understanding where analytics can add value.

4. **Did you have any training as a teacher in the PhD program or as a rookie professor at Berkeley?**

I did not receive teacher training, but there were people I admired. For example, Steve Tadelis [who holds the Sarin Chair in Leadership and Strategy at Berkeley] had an incredible ability of being very clear and putting himself into the minds of MBA students.

Another person I admire is my wife, Meghan Busse, who has the ability to be clear in teaching microeconomics in a way that people find relevant and interesting. [Professor Busse is an award-winning strategy professor at Kellogg.] She had an interesting experience once when teaching microeconomics. Students asked her three years in a row whether she could give an example of the "income substitution effect," a concept that is important in microeconomics. When she could not think of a good example of what it was useful for, she chucked it from her course.

I love that story because it illustrates the difference between what students *ought* to know (for example, a topic that is true and beautiful like the income substitution effect) as opposed to what they *need* to know for their lives, their work, and their careers. Having the discipline to teach what is important and useful to students as opposed to what oneself finds appealing and interesting takes discipline, and not everybody does it.

5. **What challenges did you face when learning how to teach?**

Learning how to teach wasn't very fast for me. I was distinctly mediocre for a number of years. The big problem that I had was that I knew how to prep and deliver research presentations but I didn't know how to translate that skill into the classroom. In a 1.5-hour research presentation, I was talking a fair bit, unlike a classroom environment, and had vastly more time to prepare than for a classroom session. I would work on a paper for six to eight months, and in addition to that, I would spend a solid three or four weeks prepping and rehearsing my talk.

In teaching an MBA course with twenty to thirty sessions of 1.5 hours each for the first time, you don't have time to prepare like that. For me, the core skill consisted of developing the instincts to translate what I knew to do in the presentation world into the teaching world in a way that was more feasible from a time aspect.

At some point, I realized that I should tell a story in an arc that would span the whole semester. The process of repeating the course made an enormous difference in my ability to get the course right.

I would make improvements from year to year by writing down in great detail what worked and what didn't. I don't think of myself as a particularly good teacher; I think of myself as a good teacher of the materials I am teaching. And the materials I am teaching have been developed and improved in meticulous ways over a long period of time.

6. **It appears that you have taught a variety of students in the full-time MBA, Executive MBA, and executive education programs. What courses do you currently teach?**

In the MBA program, I teach a course called Customer Analytics. This is my main course, and it has been my mainstay for a long time. Then I went on a completely different journey starting about four years ago. I talked with our dean about how the topic of data analytics was exploding. She put me in charge of our Program on Data Analytics, so I ended up coordinating a curriculum around that topic.

I then began to talk with executives about data analytics. I did this a few times and found it very challenging because the basic approach in the MBA classroom didn't translate into executive education. My idea in the MBA classroom was to be technical but also clear; to be demanding of the students but also to provide them with whatever tools they needed to succeed. So in the end, there is a little bit of a boot camp atmosphere.

This is an experience you can't replicate in an executive classroom. So I ended up trying to figure out very slowly and painfully how to teach and communicate with the executives. I started with a lecture on why analytics is their problem, then one lecture on distinguishing good from bad analytics, then one on discerning causality, then one on predictive analytics, and so on. I did a lot of that work with my colleague Eric Anderson, with whom I have now built up four days of content in our executive program called "Leading with Advanced Analytics and Artificial Intelligence," and our Executive MBA course includes similar content.

7. **What is the difference between communicating with MBA students and executives?**

The big difference, as I jokingly tell people, is that I can "torture" MBAs for six to eight weeks; as long as they like me in the last two weeks, I am fine. But that doesn't work with executives, where every hour and a half session has to be relatively self-contained and must deliver a positive experience. So I have to think of executive education as a session-by-session experience.

In an MBA course, I can tell students that for two weeks, they have to take their medicine before we can do something else. I can do something that is tedious and technical and doesn't, at that very moment, have what people see as an immediate payoff. I don't need to deliver a payoff session-to-session. I can deliver a payoff three weeks later when everything pulls together. That's a lot of freedom to be able to do things that are otherwise very difficult to pull off in an executive classroom. If I have the ability to do something that is not super fun in any one week but that builds the foundations that pay off big later, that will be overall more impactful than a positive experience every single time as in executive education, where time limitations don't make this possible.

8. **How large are your classes?**

There are sixty-five students in my MBA course. The average size of my executive education and Executive MBA courses is around fifty. My ideal is forty or forty-five students, but it works fine with sixty-five. The reason I don't like to have more than fifty is less for the actual classroom experience and more for the fact that I have trouble giving groups enough attention when they do practical exercises.

9. **How do you prepare to teach your courses?**

I swap out about 10%–20% of the course material every year, so I do have continuous change. In general, my lectures are very planned out. I know in detail what I am going to do. I use a lot of mini-cases in my class. Those are pretty structured, and I know exactly when I am going to do what and what questions to ask. I have noted that my quality of delivery is so much higher if I have completed a lecture four or five times. The first time I do anything requires a very long prep cycle. My typical amount of work to prepare a new ninety-minute lecture is somewhere around two to three weeks full-time.

I had a lecture that traditionally has worked very well on "How to Distinguish Good from Bad Analytics." I always had a nagging feeling that there was something I could do better. I spent two to three weeks just redoing this one lecture. Now it is working much better, but it took a long time to figure out how to do it. So it's a lot of work. My prep before a lecture that I have done a few times is very low. So most of the effort is in the initial preparation.

I did virtually no executive education until around three years ago. When I started this type of teaching, what I really loved about it is that it is like trying to put together an HBO special. I start with some snippet of content, say thirty minutes at a minimum, and it doesn't work very well, and I get booed out. Then I do it again with fewer boos. Then I do it again, and there is indifference. Sometimes it will take four or five or six iterations before it becomes a hit. Over this evolution of delivery, I have been able to make it much better while adding new content. Today I might have an hour of developed material, and the new content is only five minutes, so I usually don't get booed out of the room. By now, I have a pretty good sense of what is going to work.

10. **How do you manage your classes? Do you use cases? Cold calls?**
It depends on the class. I am not a traditional case teacher because most of the material I teach is analytics and quite technical in nature. My core contribution is to be able to explain difficult quantitative material that most people think is impenetrable ahead of time and do it in a way that they come out understanding. My goal is to take the magic out of what we do. I want them to feel that there is no magic left in analytics, artificial intelligence, machine learning, and so on, so that the material is transparent to them.

Although I don't do traditional long case discussions, I do use a lot of mini-cases. They are typically around two to three pages long, and the discussion lasts ten to fifteen minutes. I think very hard about where to ask questions and to ask questions that are not too trivial or undirected.

I do cold call people, but my style is warm and funny rather than being unforgiving and hard. Both styles work, but it depends on meshing with your personality. In my case, I haven't benefited from being confrontational in the classroom. I do better in an environment where people feel welcome to speak up.

11. **Has your teaching changed over the years? Do you use technology in the classroom?**
I have fallen in love with doing in-class work and exercises. I have constructed a couple of simulations for students to work on that make for really good learning. But I am skeptical about adding technology for technology's sake. I have a twelve-year-old son and have witnessed the introduction of iPads into the classroom. I see extremely little value in what that has added to the educational experience. Instead of giving a sheet of paper for their math homework, the sheet of paper is now a PDF on an iPad, which is harder to write on.

12. **Are you able to bring your research into your teaching?**
I am able to bring my research into my teaching a fair bit. Much of my research over the past few years has been about measuring the effectiveness of digital advertising, and I have done a lot of work with Facebook. That has lent itself nicely to the analytics teaching that I do. The only issue is that it covers 3%–5% of what I teach, and so there is a ton of what I teach that isn't a part of that research.

On the other hand, because I teach analytics, my experience (as somebody who was trained in econometrics and in other quantitative methods that I use all the time for my research) is 100% responsible for my having developed a roadmap about what would be useful to know as an executive to interpret evidence in the world. That is essentially what I teach: how to decide which data provides evidence for what. That has a huge overlap with my research because that is very similar to what we as researchers do. We try to investigate something and figure out whether we can tell the answer from a bunch of data that we have or from an experiment we executed.

So that's no different from what I am asking executives to learn. The research methodology and what I have learned over the years about how to do research are hugely influential in understanding what to teach. Specific topics in my research are also sometimes useful, although they are a small sliver of everything that I need to teach.

13. **How do you know whether you have been successful as a teacher?**
I evaluate success in two ways. The first is whether people have had a good experience. That is measured relatively well by teaching evaluations and also by the instant feedback one receives as a teacher.

What I am more interested in is whether people actually take away some things from it. I have had experiences in the past where I have had lectures and class materials that I know worked extremely well in that people really liked them and enjoyed what I taught them. So I ended up receiving very good feedback. But later, when I probed for the knowledge, I learned that it hadn't quite made it into their consciousness.

This is the reason I redesigned the lecture on "How to Distinguish Good from Bad Analytics." It was maybe my most successful lecture in terms of performance, and people loved it. But I realized that some of the core concepts I had been trying to teach in that lecture hadn't made it into people's consciousness and that I had failed as a teacher. Although the lecture itself was successful and they liked it, I had failed as a teacher to convincingly convey what I wanted. As a result, I totally redesigned the lecture with the question in mind of how to make this material not just fun and interesting but to make it so that people get it, it sticks, and they know how to apply it.

14. **Is teaching important in promotion and tenure decisions at Kellogg?**
Teaching is important at every business school. At Kellogg, it's hard to get tenure as a truly bad teacher. If you hit a threshold level of decent or good teaching, what you really need to be promoted is on the research side. Bad teaching can tank you; great teaching alone will never get you tenure.

15. **Do you provide teacher training for rookie professors?**
We have a lot of teacher training. First, everyone can sign up every quarter for a teaching coach. We have a wonderful coach who trained as a theater director and actor. She has also worked as a playwright. She uses the metaphor of teaching as theater, where you are a playwright in developing content, a director in the way you run the classroom, and an actor in delivering the material. She sits in on class sessions and gives feedback. She has done wonderful work with

rookies, and I and other senior people have also used her regularly to get better. For example, we shot an online course for an executive education client, and we hired her to direct the shoot to get feedback on whether we were connecting to the audience.

Second, every rookie has a teaching mentor—a senior faculty member who is a good teacher and who is basically responsible for getting them over the hump initially and who is there as a resource to give advice about classroom issues, look at the syllabus, and give them feedback after attending a lecture or two.

Third, David Besanko [IBM Professor of Regulation and Competitive Practices] is a legendary teacher at Kellogg who chairs our Teaching Excellence Project. Every semester there are two or three different talks on how to use classroom technology, how to structure a lecture, how to build a syllabus, and so on that are really useful.

Fourth, we often team teach, and we try to put junior faculty into team-taught courses. The benefit is that they have the infrastructure of someone who is teaching with them whose videos they can watch. It's pretty standard for us to record a successful senior colleague doing the course and then have the junior person watch every session before they start.

16. **What advice would you give to a rookie teacher starting at Kellogg? What was the best advice you received?**
   If you want to maximize your research time until tenure, make sure you over-invest in teaching during your first year. It is easy to get better from a decent teaching level. It is very hard to dig yourself out of a poor teaching experience because your poor reputation becomes a self-fulfilling prophecy with the students and zaps you of your needed self-confidence.
   The best advice I received: Think of the course as a story with an arc. Don't make it a series of separate topics.

17. **If you were not a professor, what profession would you choose?**
   I would probably be in the business world at a tech company or as a consultant.

18. **What profession would you least like?**
   Law. I have had some experience with being an expert in legal cases, and I've noticed that a lot of lawyers seem very unhappy. On the other hand, I have a very good friend who runs the Supreme Court practice for a large law firm. His life is not horrible at all. It is unbelievably interesting. The intellectual caliber of what he has to think about every day is spectacular.

19. **What do you do for fun outside your professional life?**
   My two main hobbies are music and woodworking. I play the viola, and right after this discussion, I am going to practice with my

nine- and twelve-year-old sons, who play violin and viola. I find building furniture to be relaxing and fun.

20. **What three individuals, living or dead, would you most like to have dinner with?**

My grandparents Ernst and Lilly, who died before I got to know them. My mother, who died before my kids got to know her really well.

21. **If there is a heaven, what would you like God to say to you when you arrive?**

"What do you want to teach?" ☺

Professor Zettelmeyer in Action

The Course: Leading with Advanced Analytics and Artificial Intelligence

I observed Professor Zettelmeyer teaching in an executive education program called "Leading with Advanced Analytics and Artificial Intelligence." He teaches this program at the James L. Allen Center on the Northwestern campus on the shore of Lake Michigan, with a view of the Chicago skyline in the distance.

Participants paid $9,800 each for this four-day program that began at noon on Monday and concluded at noon on Friday. The fee includes a private room at the Allen Center, meals, access to a fitness center, and other amenities (such as areas outside the classrooms that are well stocked with drinks, fruit, and other snacks). Kellogg offers the program twice a year on campus to around one hundred participants, but close to ten thousand participants take the program annually online or within companies.

Participants are from North America (73%), South America (11%), Asia (7%), Europe (6%), and elsewhere. The person sitting next to me in class exemplified the global nature of the class. He grew up in Venice; worked in China, Chicago, and the Netherlands; and currently lives in Vienna. Like most other participants, he held a management position in his company. Over 40% of participants were middle managers, 28% senior managers, and 24% held a top management position. They were from a variety of job functions (marketing, information systems, and so on) and industries.

This is an intense program for participants. During the four full days (Monday afternoon, Tuesday, Wednesday, Thursday, and Friday morning), the program typically begins at 8:30 a.m. and ends at 6:00 p.m., with a one-hour lunch break and three fifteen-minute breaks during the day. During the evenings, participants work on active learning projects, soak in the learning, and catch up on work from home. They can also attend optional ninety-minute evening sessions on topics such as

"Visualization Using Tableau" and "Machine Learning Deep Dive." On Thursday evening, faculty members hold office hours to meet with teams that are working on active learning projects. For example, during the week of my visit, one team was trying to figure out how to use analytics to predict no-shows for doctor visits. Another team was interested in developing a way to set up an organizational structure for an Analytics Center of Excellence within a company.

The program is also intense for Professor Zettelmeyer, who is its Academic Director along with Professor Eric Anderson. His contact time with participants is over twenty-five hours for the week, including working lunches and sessions that he co-teaches. This is his weekly schedule, including the titles of his teaching sessions. Other faculty members teach during the remaining times.

Monday

12:00–1:00 p.m.—Lunch with participants. (The daily lunches provide an opportunity for participants to ask faculty about concerns they face at work, and for faculty to learn from participants about their current challenges.)

1:00–2:00 p.m.—Welcome to the Program

2:00–3:00 p.m.—Motivation

5:00–6:00 p.m.—Integrating Analytics and AI

Tuesday

10:15–12:15 a.m.—How to Distinguish Good from Bad Analytics

12:15–1:15 p.m.—Lunch

5:00–6:00 p.m.—What to Do When True Experiments Are Not Possible

Wednesday

8:30–10:30 a.m.—Practice Case: What to Do When True Experiments Are Not Possible

12:00–1:00 p.m.—Lunch

1:00–2:30 p.m.—The Power of Predictions

7:30–9:00 p.m.—Machine Learning Deep Dive

Thursday

8:30–9:30 a.m.—Practice Case: Customer Churn

9:45–10:45 a.m.—Bridging Predictive and Causal Analytics

12:15–1:15 p.m.—Lunch

3:45–6:00 p.m.—Best Practices (Organizational Structure, People, Culture, Data, and Systems)

7:20–9:00 p.m.—Faculty Office Hours on Action Learning Projects

Friday

8:00–11:00 a.m.—Action Learning Projects

11:15–12:00 a.m.—How Organizations Succeed Using Analytics and AI

12:00–1:00 p.m.—Closing Lunch

As Academic Director, Professor Zettelmeyer (along with Co-Director Anderson) has established clear learning goals. By the time participants finish the program, they should be able to:

1. identify the business challenges that can benefit from analytics and AI,
2. distinguish between good and bad analytics,
3. learn to ask the right questions and challenge assumptions of analytics and AI,
4. utilize data, analytics, and AI to drive successful business outcomes,
5. assemble the team and resources needed to drive data analytics, and
6. gain the leadership confidence to stay ahead of a rapidly changing marketplace (Leading with advanced analytics and artificial intelligence, n.d.).

To achieve these goals, Professor Zettelmeyer strives for no less than what he calls a "transformational experience" for participants. This requires, in his words, the courage to teach managers a rigorous course, grounded in real data science.

Kellogg keeps participants focused on producing results after they return to their organizations by providing notebooks they use to reflect on their learning. Pages for each session are labeled "Key Concepts,"

"Plans for Action," and "Thoughts for Evaluation." They use the daily evaluation thoughts to note items they want to include in their end-of-program course evaluation. Given the investment that participants and their companies make in executive education programs, business schools generally respond quickly if there is any concern about program content or delivery by removing faculty members who do not meet expectations. (Some faculty members I have worked with in the past have joked somewhat nervously about a large hook in the ceiling that will yank them out of the classroom, even in mid-sentence!)

Inside Professor Zettelmeyer's Classroom

I attended a session titled "How to Distinguish Good from Bad Analytics," which focused on the second of the six learning goals. Teaching a group of seasoned managers from around the world who don't receive grades and who are paying a large fee to attend the program is a daunting experience for even veteran professors. Professor Zettelmeyer ably met the challenge, as he was a master at controlling the pace and pitching the content at the appropriate level to maximize the learning experience. Here are some details.

1. **Big-Picture Perspective**
   Professor Zettelmeyer opened the session by referring to the topics covered earlier in the program and noting how the topic for this session fit within the arc of the course.
2. **Relevance of the Learning**
   He told participants upfront why this session was important to their organizations and their careers. In short, as business leaders, they are consumers of analytics, and their ability to distinguish between good and bad analytics is a core skill. He also emphasized the importance of their role in providing an understanding of the business to data scientists.
3. **Active Learning**
   Early in the session, Professor Zettelmeyer engaged participants in a ten-minute, small-group learning activity where they discussed a case he had written called "Pentathlon." The case, which draws on the experience of several unnamed companies, involved a conflict between Quintero, the company's digital marketing director, and Cabret, the head of a business unit. Using data from a customer survey, Quintero had concluded that the company was sending out too many promotional emails to customers. Cabret disagreed based on data summarizing past consumer purchases.
   Professor Zettelmeyer asked the participant teams whether they could reconcile the conflict between Quintero's survey data and

Cabret's transactional data. Would they, as company leaders, limit the number of promotional emails? This exercise illustrated the effectiveness of active learning; the volume level in the classroom quickly increased as participants became more engaged in the discussion, much like the increase in volume at a party after people have a few drinks.

4. **Discussion Leadership**

   When the activity ended, Professor Zettelmeyer exhibited his expertise in discussion leadership. In an executive education program, where participants bring considerable knowledge and experience to the classroom, the instructor often plays the role of a conductor in orchestrating the discussion. In this role, he elicited several different reasons why the survey data might be suspect. He listened intently to questions and responded with clear answers.

   He was also able to move beyond the details to ask a big-picture question that initially puzzled many of the participants: "Are you in the business of making customers happy?" Through the discussion that followed, they realized that customer complaints about receiving company emails do not necessarily indicate that customers are unhappy with the company's products.

5. **Blending Research with Business Experience**

   During the discussion, Professor Zettelmeyer related participant comments to academic theories and research. For example, when one person suggested that some customers might receive lots of emails because they are heavy spenders, he identified this situation as a "reverse causality" problem, which he explained in detail later in the session. And when participants mentioned an academic theory ("Isn't this concern related to attribution bias?"), he responded knowledgeably while clarifying the question for the class.

   Professor Zettelmeyer was also able to link practical knowledge to a broad philosophical framework. He began a discussion of the distinction between good and bad analytics with an explanation of causality by noting a philosophical problem in analytics and in science in general. Ideally, in order to observe the impact of an ad, researchers would compare the difference between outcomes in one scenario where consumers see an ad and another scenario where they do not see an ad.

   The core philosophical problem is that consumers cannot be in both scenarios at the same time—either they see or do not see the ad. As a result, researchers must assign a group of consumers randomly to each scenario. This process goes by a variety of names, such as randomized experiments, A/B conditions, and treatment and control conditions. Professor Zettelmeyer went on to provide an example, noting the importance of assigning customers who are "probabilistically equivalent" to the two scenarios; that is, there is no systematic difference between the two groups.

The class discussion that followed produced many questions from the class. Here again, Professor Zettelmeyer listened carefully to questions and responded with clear answers that often included examples and utilized the experience and knowledge of participants. For example, when asked about sample size for experiments, he noted that it depends on the nature of the study. Using information provided by participants, he compared an experiment involving the effect of a new drug (where a small sample of twenty to thirty people might suffice) to an experiment regarding the efficacy of a Facebook ad on sales (where the study might require a sample size of millions).

He concluded the discussion by emphasizing what he considered to be the leading problem with analytics: "The #1 reason why analytics go bad is that data that were not generated as part of an experiment are presented or interpreted as if they were." He reinforced this by returning to the conflict between Quintero and Cabret in the Pentathlon case, noting that Cabret's data was suspect because it was not drawn from random transactional data.

6. Preparation and Distribution of Course Materials

Professor Zettelmeyer distributed his PowerPoint slides to the participants for use in taking notes. The slides included visualizations that helped them understand complex concepts and increased their usefulness for later reference on the job. As he noted in a Kellogg interview, because in today's world, "it's easier to visualize things, it is also easier to present such information directly to managers and directly to decision makers" (Making data work harder for you, 2015).

An example is his visualization of a causality checklist, which he explained using several examples, such as the impact of Google ads on car sales. This checklist is an especially important practical tool because of its value in diagnosing whether the analytics that a business leader receives are good or bad. The checklist has four key questions that are simplified below:

- *Is there probabilistic equivalence—that is, is there random assignment to the groups being compared?*
- *If the answer is "no," then what are the drivers that influenced the assignment to the groups?* For example, in the Google ad example, the assignment was driven by interest in buying a car. Professor Zettelmeyer suggested several questions to help participants identify the drivers.
- *Is the driver a "confound" (in my words, an additional factor that influences the outcome of a study)?* This is where analytics often go bad. In the Google example, it is important to recognize

the assignment to groups by interest in buying a car because differences among buyers, rather than Google ads, could drive the outcome.

- *Is there reverse causality, where differences in the outcome could have caused variation in a factor of interest?* For example, in the Pentathlon case, the transactional evidence analyzed by Cabret was suspect because higher sales volume could have affected the number of emails sent to customers.

7. **Session Review**

    In reviewing the session, Professor Zettelmeyer used several examples to help the participants internalize the four questions for future use when working with their data experts. He concluded with a review of the topics covered and a suggestion to the participants that they "laminate, print, and put over your desk" the four-part causality checklist.

8. **Enthusiasm**

    Throughout the session, Professor Zettelmeyer exhibited a relaxed enthusiasm. His overall demeanor was laidback; occasionally, he would sit in a chair in front of the class and casually discuss the material as if the participants were sitting in his living room. But his enthusiasm for the material was apparent and energized the participants. As he admitted to them near the end of the session, "Can you imagine someone like me getting so excited about analytics? This is about how you learn what is *true* in the world!"

Student Comments about Professor Zettelmeyer

The following quotations from his students illustrate why they value learning from Professor Zettelmeyer.

- Very engaging.
- Florian Zettelmeyer is an outstanding instructor, and one of the best in his field.
- Zettelmeyer's material was extremely interesting, important, needed, and well designed.
- Although I have been immersed in analytics for some years now, this program helped me take a step back and look at analytics from a leadership perspective. Great program and great delivery.
- This program totally opened my mind. Now I see things that I didn't before. I am ready to go back to my office and apply all this knowledge.
- I learned more from Florian's teaching than from reading four textbooks.

- The content was perfect and aligns with my job. Florian's energy and enthusiasm were infectious.
- Amazing learning.
- Great session. Good sense of humor. Good examples.
- Very impressive instructor.
- World-class presentation and insight into challenges and opportunities that big data presents for today's companies.
- Great passion and energy for the material. Packaged in a way that made it easy for managers to consume.
- Florian makes the material relevant and relatable. Not a dull moment. I feel confident that I will be able to apply the concepts to improve my business.
- Is able to effectively take real-life examples from us and marry them to the lessons. Well done!!!
- Very engaging presentations and interactions. Great mix of theory and science with pure practical application to the business.
- Excellent teacher!

Impact Beyond the Classroom

The following "Day in the Life" section provides a snapshot of the breadth of Professor Zettelmeyer's activities, including designing a new program for a global firm, preparing for and teaching in an executive education program, assisting a colleague with teaching materials, helping a company fill a vacancy, and working on next year's teaching schedules. This snapshot also illustrates how he balances his personal and professional lives.

A Day in the Life of Florian Zettelmeyer

6:00 a.m.

I wake up before my alarm sounds because I hear my kids (age ten and thirteen) going downstairs to play *Dungeons & Dragons*. I head downstairs to make myself an espresso (Peet's Arabian Mocha-Java). I sit down in our reading room, switch on the fireplace (Chicago is still cold), and open my iPad to read the *New York Times* and scan emails.

7:00 a.m.

I get started making lunch for the kids. My wife joins me in the kitchen and makes breakfast. I get dressed to teach (slacks, dress shirt, and sweater) and pack up my bag.

8:00 a.m.

I say goodbye to the kids and head off to the office about ten minutes away at Kellogg, Northwestern's business school. On the drive, I listen to "The Daily" podcast from the *New York Times*—it has quickly become my favorite podcast.

9:00 a.m.

I have a meeting with the Global Head of Learning for a multinational consulting company. My colleague Eric Anderson and I are designing a new executive education program that they want to use for all their partners and thousands of consultants. We discuss the arc for the program.

10:00 a.m.

I walk over to the Allen Center, our executive education facility, which is right next to the main Kellogg building. Eric and I are in the middle of leading a several-day executive education program called "Leading with Advanced Analytics and AI." Someone from the AV team helps me make sure that everything is ready for my upcoming session. I meet George Siedel, who is including me in a book about teaching and has come to observe me teach.

11:00 a.m.

I am in the middle of teaching a two-hour session titled "How to Distinguish Good vs. Bad Analytics" to about fifty executives. It is going well today—the participants are engaged, and there is lots of good energy in the classroom.

12:00 p.m.

Class is over, and I head with the participants to lunch in the (excellent) Allen Center dining room. I have to hurry because I have a meeting coming up in my office.

1:00 p.m.

My meeting is with a colleague who asked me to take a look at a lecture he had developed. He walks me through the syllabus so I understand where the class fits into his course. Then I ask him to role-play by delivering the lecture to me, and I take detailed notes. I give him some suggestions.

2:00 p.m.

I have a call with the CEO of a major travel company. I have been helping them find a new head of AI and Data Analytics. I hear that my favorite candidate has accepted the job, and we discuss how I can help with onboarding.

3:00 p.m.

I meet with my Associate Chair of the Marketing Department at Kellogg to talk about the current draft of next year's teaching schedule. I find out that I have to ask a few colleagues to accommodate proposed changes. It's not clear they will want to, so the Associate Chair generously leaves it to me to broach the subject with them!

4:00 p.m.

I prep for my upcoming lecture in the executive education program. Eric Anderson has been teaching the afternoon sessions so far, and I arrive in time to catch the last few minutes of his session.

5:00 p.m.

I'm up to bat again! I teach "What to Do When True Experiments Are Not Possible." I am grateful that Eric and I have kept on schedule throughout the day, and I am able to end on time. I set up the workshop the participants will do first thing tomorrow morning. I rush home.

6:00 p.m.

I take my younger son to his violin lesson at the Music Institute of Chicago and take notes so I can practice with him during the week.

7:00 p.m.

My younger son and I return home and join my older son and my wife for a dinner of homemade lentil stew. I practice with my older son, who plays viola. My kids are in the middle of a one-hundred-day practice challenge. The goal is (surprisingly!) motivating—*they* are reminding *me* that we have to practice!

8:00 p.m.

I drive back to the Music Institute of Chicago for my own viola lesson. After a long day teaching and talking about analytics, it is a great contrast to use a different part of my brain.

> **9:00 p.m.**
>
> I return home, where my wife has been helping our sons wind up the day (homework finished, iPad charging, lunchboxes ready for tomorrow). I clean up the kitchen before sitting down with a glass of wine to watch a Netflix show. My wife comes down and joins me. We catch up on the day.
>
> **10:00 p.m.**
>
> I go to bed, read a little, and fall asleep.

Professor Zettelmeyer's service in the form of leadership is especially noteworthy. Berkeley Haas recognized his leadership skills early in his career when the school named him Chair of the Marketing Group. At Haas, he also chaired or served on a number of important committees. His leadership assignments continued at Kellogg, where he serves as Chair of the Marketing Department, Director of the Program on Data Analytics, and Co-Academic Director of the "Leading with Advanced Analytics and Artificial Intelligence" executive program.

Professor Zettelmeyer has been active in service on the research front as well. He has served as Co-Editor-in-Chief of *Quantitative Marketing and Economics*, Associate Editor of *Management Science*, and on several editorial boards. The National Bureau of Economic Research appointed him as a Research Associate, and he has received research grants from the National Science Foundation. He also received the Paul E. Green Award for best article in the *Journal of Marketing Research*.

Lessons from Professor Zettelmeyer

An interview with Professor Zettelmeyer, observation of his teaching, and discussions with his students reveal the following elements that are key to his success as a teacher.

1. *Clarity in Presentations.* Early role models were Professor Ricardo Caballero at MIT and Professor Steve Tadelis at Berkeley, both of whom achieved clarity when presenting complex concepts.
2. *Ability to Structure the Course and the Accompanying Slides Using a Storytelling Format.* Professor Zettelmeyer uses a storytelling mindset when designing his courses, searching for an arc that will span the entire course. McKinsey's Gene Zelazny was especially influential in providing advice on the development of a slide structure.

3. *Focus on What Is Relevant and Important to Students.* Professor Zettelmeyer's wife, Professor Meghan Busse, helped him understand the difference between what students need to know and what they ought to know. As a result of his focus on relevance, his students praise him for the value his teaching adds to their organizations and their careers. To reinforce the emphasis on "take-home" value, participants in his executive course complete daily notebooks in which they reflect on key concepts and describe their plans for action upon completing the program.

4. *Importance of Repetition.* Professor Zettelmeyer modestly admits, "I was distinctly mediocre for a number of years." One factor in his improvement was his ability to teach the course repeatedly year after year. At the end of each iteration, he makes notes on what works and what doesn't in order to continuously improve the course.

5. *Risk Taking.* At a time when he had already achieved a reputation for excellent teaching and research, he moved into uncharted territory by agreeing to teach a rigorous program on data science to business leaders.

6. *Intense Preparation.* Professor Zettelmeyer spends around two to three weeks full-time developing a new ninety-minute lecture. He spends the same amount of time restructuring a lecture he feels is not working.

7. *Variation in Delivery.* Professor Zettelmeyer uses a combination of lectures, case studies, simulations, and group exercises. He writes many of his cases, which are shorter than traditional cases, and uses them for ten- to fifteen-minute discussions. During these discussions, he draws on the business experience of the participants through questioning and listening intently to their responses.

8. *Use of Research in Teaching.* Discussion of his specific research in class constitutes a small fraction of the class material. More important than his own research is the research mindset he brings to the classroom. Drawing on his research skills, he is able to design and deliver a learning experience that enables his students to make decisions based on data science evidence. As part of this learning experience, he matches the latest research to the participants' business experience during class discussions.

9. *Enthusiasm and Passion for the Learning Process.* Professor Zettelmeyer's enthusiasm for his material is apparent from his students' comments and from his own comment near the end of the session I attended: "Can you imagine someone like me getting so excited about analytics? This is about how you learn what is true in the world!"

The final element—Professor Zettelmeyer's enthusiasm—is the tie that binds together the other aspects that contribute to his teaching success.

As he stated to students when receiving the 2011 Kellogg award for Outstanding Professor of the Year, "I'm totally impressed with the hard work you put into the classroom. It's a huge honor to be part of that. I love teaching" (2011 professors of the year, 2011).

References

2011 professors of the year. (2011, Summer). Retrieved from Kellogg World Alumni Magazine: https://www.kellogg.northwestern.edu/kwo/sum11/brand news/2011professors.htm

Farrell, R. (2017, Spring-Summer). *Think big*. Retrieved from Kellogg Magazine: https://www.kellogg.northwestern.edu/kwo/spr14/research-initiatives/ think_big.htm

Leading with advanced analytics and artificial intelligence. (n.d.). Retrieved from Northwestern Kellogg: https://www.kellogg.northwestern.edu/ executive-education/individual-programs/executive-programs/bigdata.aspx

Making data work harder for you. (2015, July 6). Retrieved from Kellogg Insight: https://www.google.com/search?q=%22measure+things+and+it%E2 %80%99s+easier+to+visualize+things%2C+it+is+also+easier+to+present+ such+information+directly+to+managers+and+directly+to+decision+makers. %E2%80%9D&rlz=1C1GCEA_enUS794US794&oq=%22measure+ things+and

Zettelmeyer, F. (2011). Unpublished commencement address at Northwestern University.

Zettelmeyer, F. (n.d.). *Some pointers for preparing presentations*. Retrieved from Augustin Cournot Doctoral School: http://ed.ecogestion-cournot. unistra.fr/wp-content/uploads/On_presentation.pdf

Chapter 8

MIT Operations Professor Georgia Perakis

Learn How to Improve Business Operations through Innovative Research and Practice

When clothing is manufactured, a seam often appears where pieces of fabric are sewn together. The pieces of fabric that form the professional life of Professor Georgia Perakis—research, teaching, and working with practitioners—are joined in a seamless fashion that results in her remarkable accomplishments and leadership positions at MIT and elsewhere.

Professor Perakis, the William F. Pounds Professor of Operations Management and Operations Research/Statistics at MIT's Sloan School of Management, has won many research awards. One hallmark of her research is her enthusiasm for thesis supervision of students, which has resulted in lifelong relationships with many of them. When Guillaume Roels, at the time a professor at UCLA's Anderson School of Management and currently on the faculty at INSEAD, was recognized by *Poets & Quants* as one of the best young professors in the country, he singled out Professor Perakis as the professor he most admired (Carter, 2015). She has attended weddings of her former students in Casablanca, Lebanon, Prague, and elsewhere.

On the teaching front, Professor Perakis is the only professor in the history of MIT who has won the Jamieson Prize for Excellence in Teaching, the Samuel M. Seegal Faculty Prize, and the Teacher of the Year Award. The Jamieson Prize selection committee noted her "dedication, passion, and innovative thinking that have had a long-standing impact on the MIT Sloan School of Management, with exceptional contributions to the curriculum, the learning environment, and the students at Sloan" (Perakis wins MIT Sloan teaching award, 2014).

Professor Perakis' work with practitioners drives her desire to bridge the gap between academia and industry by linking theory to practice. Her goal is to address problems that are important to practice and that have academic implications. Through collaboration with practitioners, she gains access to data, tests her findings, and develops new theories that subsequently can be applied to practice. Her mantra, stated in a 2017 talk to Sloan graduates, is to "have **an impact** [her emphasis]" (Faculty session, 2017).

This work with practitioners enables her to identify problems that she can address in her research while also providing examples that enliven her teaching. As the Jamieson Prize selection committee concluded, "She has also brought research and practice into the classroom" (Perakis wins MIT Sloan teaching award, 2014). The committee mentioned one initiative where PhD students work with MBA students on company projects that, in turn, enrich the MBA and Executive MBA program curricula.

Despite her many teaching and research achievements, Professor Perakis is especially modest—a product of both her personality and her willingness to address challenging problems faced in the real world of business. As she stated in the 2017 talk to Sloan graduates,

> Professors feel that we are the smartest people in the world. Then we get humbled when we speak with practitioners and realize, actually, maybe they are not doing the optimal thing but many times they have years of experience, and that counts for **A LOT** [her emphasis].
> (Faculty session, 2017)

Professor Perakis combines modesty with a delightful sense of humor, and our conversations were punctuated with laughter. She brings subtle humor into the classroom, where she uses it to make a point. Here is an example from her 2017 talk, where she explained data analytics during a discussion of a case study: "If you torture your data enough, they will always confess to you" (Faculty session, 2017).

Meet Professor Perakis

Professor Perakis' Resume

The following resume summarizes Professor Perakis' thirty-seven-page CV.

Education

PhD in Applied Mathematics, 1993, Brown University; MS in Applied Mathematics, 1988, Brown University; BS in Mathematics, 1987, University of Athens

Appointments

MIT Sloan School of Management, 1995–present; Visiting Professor, Columbia University, 2005–2006 and 2013–2014; Visiting Associate Professor, Brown University, 1993–1995

Distinctions and Awards

Research and teaching awards include:

- INFORMS Fellow (selected for lifetime achievement)
- Presidential Early Career Award (Office of the President of the United States on Science and Technology)
- CAREER Award, National Science Foundation
- Teacher of the Year Award, MIT Sloan
- Jamieson Prize for Excellence in Teaching, MIT Sloan
- Samuel M. Seegal Award (for inspiring students to achieve excellence)
- Graduate Student Council Teaching Award (for excellence in teaching a graduate-level course)
- Production and Operations Management Society Applied Research Challenge, First Prize
- Northeast Decision Sciences Institute, Best Application of Theory Award
- INFORMS Service Science Section Best Paper Award (several times)

Subjects Taught

Courses and modules taught at MIT include:

- Data, Models and Decisions
- Leadership and Integrative Management
- Readings in Optimization (Applications of Operation Research to various topics)
- Nonlinear Programming
- Introduction to Mathematical Programming
- Decision Technologies for Managers
- Optimization Methods
- Special Seminar in Applied Probability

Thesis Supervision

Twenty-four PhD students, many of whom are professors at leading universities; over fifty Master of Science students

Leadership Positions at MIT

Served on over fifty committees at MIT and in many leadership positions, including:

- Faculty Director of Executive MBA Program
- Co-Director of the Operations Research Center
- Head of Operations Management Group
- Head of Operations Research and Statistics Group
- Faculty Director, Certificate of Analytics
- Faculty Co-Director of Leaders for Global Operations Program

Professional Activities

Many leadership positions in the Institute for Operations Research and the Management Sciences (INFORMS), and editorial positions at leading research journals.

Research

Research focuses on analytics theory and practice, with special interest in applications relating to energy, logistics, pricing, revenue management, and supply chains. Published over fifty articles in refereed journals. Over 350 research presentations at conferences and seminars. Four patents issued and filed.

Figure 8.1 Professor Georgia Perakis.

An Interview with Professor Perakis

1. What attracted you to teaching?

   I was excited about teaching and academia in general because my father always inspired us to think about academia, even though he was not a professor. I started teaching because my advisor at Brown University, where I was working on a PhD in Applied Mathematics, passed away, and I took over her classes. I completed my undergraduate degree in Greece, but for graduate school I felt that the US was the best place to be.

2. After you decided to become a teacher, did you have any role models? Were there any teachers you especially admired?

   I always admired many senior people in my field, including my two advisors at Brown University—one who passed away, Stella Dafermos, and a new one, Thomas Magnanti. I admired them a lot. But it's not that I was trying to be someone else.

3. In your YouTube videos, you seem to have a relaxed, natural, and welcoming style. As a PhD student or after you started your career, did you receive training to develop your teaching skills?

   After I became a professor, our school gave us opportunities to improve, but I didn't really have any formal training. Thank you for your comments about my style. I just try to be who I am.

4. Did anybody give you any special advice when you started your teaching career that was especially valuable to you?

   Many of my colleagues tried to help me improve my teaching over the years. One particular colleague, Robert Freund [the Theresa Seley Professor in Management Science at MIT], helped me a lot in teaching MBA students. Other professors visited my classroom and provided feedback, and at times the school has also provided specialists who came to my classroom and gave me feedback.

5. Over the years you have interacted with MBA and Executive MBA students. What are the differences you notice when teaching these different audiences?

   The Executive MBA student is typically around forty years old. They have far more experience in the real world, which enables them to engage in richer discussions. The MBA students are also smart, and in some situations technically stronger, but they don't have the same level of experience.

6. How do you prepare for class?

   I look at the student feedback from the previous year and then decide what new lectures and materials I need to introduce into the course. After I prepare my lectures, I stay home the day before class and watch videotapes of myself teaching multiple years and multiple sections. There was an improvement in the quality of my teaching after I started doing that around eight years ago.

7. Once you are in the classroom, how do you manage your class? For example, do you use cold calls?

Yes, I use cold calls and warm calls. For warm calls, I let students know before class that I am going to ask for their help. For cold calls, if students don't want to answer the question, they can pass it to another student of their choice, which I call "Phone a Friend." They can do this once during each class session.

8. You have written several cases. Do you use them in class?

Yes. I also use simulations or exercises.

9. From watching your YouTube videos I notice that you seem to be open to questions and to making the class interactive. Correct?

Yes. I hate classes that are not interactive. I need students to ask me questions so that I can understand where they are and can make adjustments. So absolutely, I do think interaction is critical.

10. How do you handle people who try to dominate the class discussion (so-called "gunners")?

I have had people like that, and I make notes during the class when I feel they dominate. To balance participation, a couple of days before each lecture, I ask my teaching assistant to give me names of people who haven't spoken, names of people who have spoken a lot, and people who have experience relevant to the material. This way, I know whom to call on.

11. Do you receive feedback from students during the course?

The Executive MBA program meets on weekends. After each week-end of class, students evaluate the lectures and give us feedback on the overall course. They provide concrete comments about what they like and what they don't like. I take that feedback seriously, and I make changes throughout the semester. For example, I received feedback on how to improve the website, and I did this during the semester. I received feedback on spending more time summarizing the material and giving them the big picture, so I did that as well.

12. What technology do you use during class?

Basically, a PowerPoint deck and also the document camera. I put selected slides on the document camera and write on them. I also occasionally use short videos.

13. Do you bring your research into teaching?

Yes, I use some of my projects and my experience to help students understand the rationale for what we are doing. I pick one company I've worked with, and I motivate the material throughout the semester using my experience with that company. And at the end of the course, I spend one lecture on a research project. Of course, I also ask students to describe their own experiences.

14. **What types of assignments do you use?**

    In courses that are more analytical and quantitative, like mine, students need to practice a bit. I use individual assignments, team projects, and team cases. The team project at the end of the course is based on one of the team member's companies. They select companies that face an important business challenge, and they use the tools learned in the class to help them improve and do things differently. The teams, typically made up of four students, decide among themselves which company to pick and what problem to select.

    Throughout the semester, students also have individual assignments that are short and that enable them to practice some mechanics and to use ideas from the course. Team cases are also assigned throughout the course.

15. **Do you use a grading curve?**

    The school requires that the class average grade should not exceed a certain number, which is a generous number. This prevents faculty from giving every single person an A.

16. **What do you like most about teaching?**

    The interaction with the students. I find teaching them fun and exciting. I also learn from them. [As she put it in a 2017 talk to Sloan graduates: "I love MIT because as a professor I keep being a student" (Faculty session, 2017).]

17. **What do you like least about teaching?**

    Obviously, it requires a lot of effort, and sometimes we are tired. [Laughter] But that's normal for anything anybody does.

18. **Can you think of a huge challenge you have had during your teaching career?**

    When I started, I was a very bad teacher, and that was a big challenge. [Laughter] It was a challenge for me to improve and to gain my confidence.

19. **How do you know when you have been successful with a course? How do you evaluate your success as a teacher?**

    By the impact on students. When students in the class have no background on the topic, and you see that they get to use what you have taught them in their businesses and in their work, you feel successful.

20. **Is teaching important at MIT for annual review purposes and for promotion and tenure?**

    Yes. If you are not a good teacher, you might not succeed. To help you succeed, the school will provide resources to help you improve. But if you don't show them that you can teach MBA students well, chances are you will not make it. So we've had cases where people were great researchers, but because they couldn't teach, they had to leave.

21. **Does MIT provide teaching support to rookie professors and to more seasoned faculty members?**
Yes. Last year, the school paid for a coach, and I had several sessions with him. He came to my classes, and he coached me on public speaking. Junior faculty also have access to the coach and to a course on how to teach the case studies. They can also have their classes videotaped.

22. **What advice on becoming a good teacher would you give to a rookie professor?**
I would advise a rookie to work hard. And to make sure that you are doing this because you like doing it. If you like doing what you're doing and you work hard, then it's going to work in the end. That is general advice, not just for teaching.

23. **What is your proudest professional achievement?**
I am proud of the awards and recognition received for research that I did with my students. Not recognition if it's just me, but when the research involved my students and me.

24. **What do you do for fun outside your professional life?**
There's no time. [Laughter] But I like going to the movies. If I can travel somewhere for a weekend, I like that. I like going to nice restaurants. My favorite vacation place is Elounda, which is in Greece, on the island of Crete. My favorite book is *The Namesake*, a novel by Jhumpa Lahiri that describes the immigrant experience (Lahiri, 2003).

25. **What profession would you choose if you were not a professor?**
This is my favorite profession. I cannot think of anything else, actually. I really love my job.

26. **What profession would you like the least if you were not a professor?**
To be honest with you, I haven't thought of this question because I never reached the stage where I was going to be something else. Since I was a kid, I wanted to be a professor, and I love my job. So I never contemplated other jobs.

27. **What general advice would you provide to students if you were asked to give a commencement address?**
I would advise them to make sure that they become principled leaders. I want to stress both "principled" and "leadership."

28. **What three individuals, living or dead, would you most like to have dinner with?**
Marie Curie, Gandhi, and my PhD students (whom I always love having dinner with, frankly!).

29. **If there is a heaven, what would you like God to say to you when you arrive?**
I hope She will not be too disappointed with how I did on earth.

Professor Perakis in Action

The Course: Data, Models, and Decisions

I visited a class taught by Professor Perakis in her course on Data, Models, and Decisions, which is a required course in the MIT Executive MBA (EMBA) program. Professor Perakis is the Faculty Director of this program.

The course introduces students to tools and techniques that are useful when they·use data to make management decisions. The course includes decision analysis, probability distributions, covariance and correlation, linear optimization, nonlinear optimization models, regression models, discrete optimization models, and dynamic programming. Everyone I talked with emphasized that the course is the most challenging in the EMBA program, and that the session I attended on discrete optimization models is an especially difficult topic. Based on my experience in the class, I have no cause to disagree with this assessment!

The EMBA program differs from a traditional MBA program in several ways. The program targets mid-career students, who face increasing professional and family responsibilities. Over a twenty-month period, they attend twenty-six weekend sessions at three-week intervals. They also attend five week-long modules, including an international project trip. The modules focus on various aspects of leadership. For example, in the final module on "Leading with Impact," the students integrate their learning from the entire program with their personal values by working with leaders in nonprofit organizations. Tuition for the program totals $178,000, not including travel to Boston and hotel costs.

In addition to active learning courses such as "Leading with Impact," students take required and elective courses clustered into three areas:

- **Business Essentials:** Competitive Strategy, Financial Accounting, Financial Management, Leading Organizations, Marketing Management, Organizational Settings, and Dynamics Change Leadership for the Rising Executive
- **Analytics Frameworks:** Applied Economics for Managers; Data, Models, and Decisions; Introduction to System Dynamics; Organizational Processes
- **Advanced Courses:** Several courses that include Law and Strategy for the Senior Executive, and Business Analyses Using Financial Statements

Students in the course I attended were in the Class of 2020. The average age of these students was forty-one, and they had an average of seventeen years of work experience. Almost 60% of them already held advanced degrees, and over 80% had a position of director level or higher. Half of them were of international origin, and two-thirds of them lived beyond driving distance of MIT. Everyone in the class was employed full-time, and they worked in a wide variety of industries.

Professor Perakis grades students in the Data, Models, and Decisions course on class participation, a final exam, team-based write-ups based on four case studies, individual homework assignments, and a team project. The individual homework assignments utilize exercises designed to help students develop technical skills that they might not have a chance to improve when working as part of a team (where they might rely on one team member with technical skills to crunch the numbers).

The team project is based on a problem that a team member addressed at work. The teams must decide how they would analyze the problem differently given what they learned in the course. One of the teams, for instance, recently worked on a project involving a snack food company that had grown rapidly and was experiencing problems with production planning and in other areas. Using the linear optimization methodology they learned in the course, team members developed a model that enabled them to calculate a production volume that optimized cost.

Students vote to determine the top four projects, and the four winning teams give a presentation during the last weekend of class. The winning team receives a large trophy; the other teams receive trophies that diminish in size depending on how each of them placed.

Given the students' demanding careers, difficult assignments, and limited time on campus, Professor Perakis and her team of four PhD students—who serve as the course's teaching assistants (TAs)—work closely with students outside class to ensure that they are maximizing their learning experience. During the weekend I visited campus, the students had a class on system dynamics from 8:30 to 11:30 a.m. on Friday. Following a lunch break that included a talk on careers, they attended the Data, Models, and Decisions class from 1:00 to 4:00 p.m. At 4:30 p.m., they could select between optional sessions—a review of accounting for an upcoming exam and a guest speaker.

Over a typical weekend, Professor Perakis teaches the same class to another section of the course on Saturday. Immediately after class ends on Saturdays, she meets with the TAs to debrief on what went well and what needs improvement. As one of her TAs (currently a professor at a leading business school) told me, she begins work on next year's class immediately after finishing her current session. On Saturday evening, she sends a wrap-up email to the class.

The TAs review the debrief information on Monday and Tuesday of the week following class, and on Tuesday evening one of them gives students a virtual one-hour presentation, called a "recitation," summarizing the class. The recitation is followed by virtual office hours. The Tuesday evening sessions are recorded for later viewing by students who cannot attend because they are in a different time zone or have a scheduling conflict. The TA team is also available for one-on-one consultations by email and when students are on campus.

During the three-week interval between on-campus classes, Professor Perakis watches videos of classes from earlier years to determine where students seem confused by the material. She uses these to improve her PowerPoint presentation. She then shares the revised presentation with the TAs so that they can suggest additional improvements.

Four days before class, Professor Perakis sends an email to students that welcomes them back to campus and covers administrative matters, such as informing them of a "before" version of the slides posted at the course website. Following class, she posts an "after" version that includes solutions to in-class exercises.

On Wednesday and Thursday before her Friday class, she blocks off time to watch the videos again and asks herself questions such as, "How can I improve?" and, "How can I answer questions better?" Before class, she also asks the TAs to identify students who are struggling with the material so that she can give them special attention during class.

Inside Professor Perakis' Classroom

Professor Perakis used a variety of teaching strategies and techniques during the class I attended.

1. **Welcoming Students**

   I arrived at the classroom at 12:45 p.m. for the 1:00 p.m. class. Professor Perakis had already set up her presentation and had spread a number of documents on a desk for use during class. This advanced preparation enabled her to focus on greeting the students as they arrived. She welcomed and talked individually with several of them.

   Professor Perakis was born in Greece, and she opened the class with a warm "Kalo Pascha" greeting—"Happy Easter" in Greek. She still has traces of a Greek accent, and one student mentioned to me that she is "proudly Greek."

2. **Clarity on Assignments**

   Professor Perakis reminded the class that they had only one more weekend on campus and discussed several assignments that were due. When covering the team project that is based on a problem faced by a team member on the job, she emphasized the real-life value of the assignment, mentioning a team that during the previous year implemented their results at work. Recognizing their busy schedules, she admonished them to be reasonable in the number of hours spent on the team project. As she noted on a slide, "Have fun! BUT don't go crazy preparing!"

3. **Big-Picture Perspective**

   Having covered what was to come, Professor Perakis provided a broad perspective on what the course had covered to date within the framework of moving from data to models to decisions—a framework reflected in the course title. She linked the framework to other courses in the program. For example, when referring to an upcoming Operations course taught during the following summer, she noted with a smile, "Remember me in the summer!" She also reminded them that "the way I see your job, you are leaders, not coders." This helped students focus on the big picture in situations where it was easy to become overwhelmed by a mass of data.

4. **Review of Previous Learning**

   Professor Perakis moved seamlessly from the big-picture perspective to a refresher on material covered in earlier sessions—with emphasis on linear optimization—and then to the topic for the day, discrete optimization. In covering these complex topics, she started with simple examples that engaged the students because they could solve them intuitively.

   Following the simple examples, the refresher covered complex situations that required a more sophisticated analysis. For instance, when reviewing linear optimization (which, in simple terms, is a method for finding optimal solutions when faced with constraints), she used as an example a seat allocation decision faced by an air carrier. The carrier must decide how many regular tickets and how many discount tickets to sell to maximize revenues. The decision is subject to constraints, such as airplane capacity and customer demand. After formulating and solving the problem, she showed how linear optimization is useful when considering changes in the constraints, such as the impact of an increase in customer demand or a change in the size of the airplanes.

   With this refresher in place, Professor Perakis paused to remind students where they were on the agenda for the day and then moved to discrete optimization—in simple terms, a method for finding optimal solutions when faced with constraints and a limited number of possibilities. As with the seat allocation problem, she started with a simple example. A company bidding for ads auctioned off by publishers must decide which of four ads to target, each with different costs and earnings. The company wants to maximize earnings but cannot bid on all four because of budget limitations. After discussing the solution, Professor Perakis quickly moved to a larger scale problem involving an increase in budget and a selection of bids from among twenty target ads.

In a 2017 talk to Sloan graduates, Professor Perakis elaborated on the challenge that professors face when trying to simplify complex models. The goal "is to try to see how I can go from the complex model to a simple model. If it's too simple, I will not capture the real complex problem, so I have to find where to be in the middle" (Faculty session, 2017). She achieved this goal in the class I attended.

5. **Encouraging Students to Co-Create the Learning Experience**
Throughout her discussion of the seat allocation and ad auction examples (along with another example involving a computer manufacturer's selection of a service center), she encouraged students to share their experiences with questions such as, "Did you find this to be true?" One of the advantages of teaching students at this level is that their experience enables them to co-create the learning environment with the instructor by learning from each other.

6. **Frequent Use of Examples**
She peppered the discussion with real-life examples, including many from her own work. At one point, she provided the class with a summary of examples of discrete optimization in practice, such as airline crew scheduling, asset management, supply chain design, and transactions in electricity markets. These examples reminded students of the relevance of the material.

7. **In-depth Case Study**
The final segment of the class focused on a case study called *International Industries, Inc.*, based on an actual company, to illustrate discrete optimization. International Industries was a large, privately held company with fifty divisions that are underperforming. Professor Perakis placed students in the position of consultants hired to advise the company whether to invest in, maintain as is, or sell each division. The goal of the advice is to maximize the net present value of the company. In discussing this goal, she reminded them of what they had learned about net present value in another course and that there were strategic and other constraints that they needed to consider during the decision-making process.

Professor Perakis started the discussion by asking the class what they would do as consultants. This question produced a variety of responses (try to understand past performance, look at efficiencies, look at the performance of each division, etc.), which spurred their interest in the formal analytics framework that she presented next.

Citing her own experience, Professor Perakis was able to emphasize that mathematical aspects are often the easiest part of the framework. Often more difficult is deciding what data is needed, available, and reliable. To make this point, Professor Perakis reviewed sample data and asked whether it made sense. When several students questioned the data, she patiently attempted to clarify their concerns: "Excuse me, I am being slow. Why are you raising this question?" She also mentioned her experience with gathering data: "For our projects it takes us around six months going back and forth to find out what is really going on. My experience is that each division has different data." She then explored reasons for the differences in data, such as situations where employees are concerned that the data might affect their job security.

Another example of putting the mathematical calculations into perspective was her discussion of strategic constraints created by company leaders—for instance, "If we sell Division 1, then we must invest in Division 2." She asked them to think about the reasons why leaders had created this so-called linkage constraint, such as the desire to maintain a presence in a particular market.

8. **Gauging Students' Understanding of the Material**

   When Professor Perakis moved to the development of a complex model, she occasionally took the pulse of the class: "Who is following me?" This was especially important as the students moved into their third hour of wrestling with complex material in class. When necessary, she slowed down and repeated the coverage. She also provided them with "cheat sheets," which were simpler, intuitive ways to look at the data.

9. **Interactive Class**

   The class was extremely interactive and students seemed eager to participate, perhaps, in part, because class participation constituted 10% of the grade. One of the TAs, who sat next to me in class, paid close attention to their participation, which he noted on a spreadsheet in binary form (that is, without commenting on the quality of participation). But the TAs do give feedback to Professor Perakis during breaks and after class about students who seem lost by the material or, at the opposite extreme, who signal that the pace of coverage is too slow.

   After asking questions, Professor Perakis did not immediately provide solutions but patiently let the discussion flow until (usually) the students reached their own conclusions. She also asked the class to help her explain the material to a student who was confused about one of the cheat sheets: "Who wants to help me?" Three students responded to her question with explanations that helped the student understand the material. Professor Perakis then thanked these students for providing her with different approaches for presenting the material in the future.

10. **Self-Deprecating Humor**

    Professor Perakis occasionally used self-deprecating humor that personalized the discussion. For example, when discussing one data set, she mentioned, "If I were selling my house, I would have to redo my kitchen, which we have unfortunately stopped using." And she poked fun at herself when she could not read one of her handouts because the print was too small. In contrast to stereotypical aloof professors, her transparency makes her approachable to students seeking advice.

11. **Closure**

At the conclusion of the class, Professor Perakis reviewed software designed to solve optimization problems and commented on the speed of optimization solvers. In her words, "An integer problem that can be solved in one second today took seven years to solve two decades ago." She then closed by reminding the students of the big-picture course focus on data, models, and decisions, and she wished them good luck on an upcoming final exam in their Accounting course. Class ended with well-earned applause from the students.

After class, Professor Perakis patiently talked with students who had questions about the class. Students told me that they also feel comfortable talking with her about topics outside of class, such as diversity and inclusion.

12. **Warm, Casual Teaching Style**

Overall, the teaching style of Professor Perakis offers an interesting contrast to her preparation for class. Her preparation is intense as she reviews every detail with her TAs and watches videos of past classes to improve her already impressive teaching style. However, in class, she has a relaxed, warm, and casual style as she moves around the front of the classroom and up and down the aisles, gesticulates frequently with arms and hands, and laughs frequently. In short, she seems to be having fun.

Student Comments about Professor Perakis

In a *Poets & Quants* interview, Executive MBA graduate Kosta Ligris mentioned that Professor Perakis was his favorite professor because "[h]er dedication to quality education and her passion and empathy for her students are remarkable" (Schmitt, 2018). Two of her former PhD students who are currently business school professors told me about her continuing support after they graduated—including help with networking, publishing, and a job search.

Here are comments from students in the class I attended:

- Engaging, lively, makes a terribly boring subject interesting.
- Has dinner with small groups of students.
- Friended us on Facebook and sent me a message on my birthday.
- Very open.
- Simplifies complex processes that we deal with on a day-to-day basis.

- She understands that our job is to make decisions based on analytics from experts.
- She puts herself into our shoes and recognizes that we are not PhDs. She brings the material to our level of understanding.
- She was the reason I enrolled in the MIT EMBA program. Having a female professor makes me feel more comfortable when speaking in class.
- She is flexible. For example, she recently changed the order of topics (by moving linear regression before optimization). She was transparent in explaining this change.
- Brings in lots of examples.
- In each new lecture she references the previous class.
- She surveys the class and discusses how she will revise her approach based on the results.
- She does a good job working with students in a class with different skill levels.
- When I read fifty pages, it is overwhelming. But after fifty minutes in class, it all clicks, especially because she uses interesting real-life cases.
- The material is applicable to my work.
- Makes the material uncomplicated and easy to digest.
- Brings in real-life examples; examples are practical.
- I have a background in financial modeling, so some of the material is familiar. But it is very useful seeing applications in other settings. This allows me to adjust my models at work.
- Her use of real-life examples makes the material digestible.
- The readings come to life when she teaches.

Impact Beyond the Classroom

A look at a typical day in the life of Professor Perakis illustrates the wide range of her teaching, research, and leadership responsibilities.

A Day in the Life of Georgia Perakis

6:00 a.m.

The alarm rings. Time to get up. Today is the day I go to the gym.

I prepare a large cup of Greek iced-coffee that I drink in the car as I quickly head to the gym to exercise for an hour with my trainer. He is strict, and I do not want to arrive there late.

7:30 a.m.

I head home and prepare another large cup of Greek iced coffee. I process and answer the mountain of emails that arrived during the night. I look at my schedule for the day and, more importantly, the "to do" list in order to be well prepared for the day and the week ahead.

8:45 a.m.

I get ready and head to the office.

10:00 a.m.

The day at MIT starts with a presentation to a research sponsor in Spain. We present what we have accomplished in the project during the past ten days and receive feedback on how our work was perceived by the industry partner. This is followed by a meeting with my PhD students on the next steps in the project. We discuss where we are stuck and where we need to go next given the discussion with the industry partner.

Noon

I head for a meeting on the EMBA program. (I serve as the Faculty Director of the program.) This meeting is with the Assistant Dean of the program and staff. We spend an hour discussing important issues and directions we need to take for the program. I am always amazed as to how well organized and well run the program is.

Afternoon

After buying my lunch from the school cafeteria, I head back to my office to eat my lunch while having back-to-back meetings with PhD students to discuss their theses, research papers, and projects.

On my way back and forth, and while in the elevator, I check social media posts and make sure I wish all my friends and students (former and current) happy birthday and see how they are doing.

6:00 p.m.

My teaching assistants arrive at my office for a meeting to discuss how the class went last weekend, the feedback we received from the students, and what needs to be done next.

7:45 p.m.

I leave the office to head home. The traffic is not as bad as earlier in the day but still surprisingly heavy.

After dinner and after cleaning the kitchen, I sit back with my laptop to process and answer several emails. I also post some material relevant to the upcoming weekend class on the course website (Canvas) and email the class on how we expect them to prepare for the next session. Although most of this plan is already in the syllabus posted at the beginning of the semester, we guide them step-by-step during the semester.

It is now rather late, and I look at my "to do" list, only to see I have an Associate Editor report due in a few days. Thankfully, there is the weekend ahead.

10:45 p.m.

I am dead tired! I wind down watching the news and falling asleep faster than I anticipate. Soon enough it will be time for a new day to start all over again.

Two aspects of Professor Perakis' activities beyond the classroom are especially notable: her leadership responsibilities and research accomplishments. On the leadership front, she serves as Faculty Director of the Executive MBA program as well as the Co-Director of the Operations Research Center. In the past, she has headed two of the most prominent faculty groups at MIT: the Operations Management Group and the Operations Research and Statistics Group. She has also served as the Faculty Director of the Certificate of Analytics, which she co-founded, and as Faculty Co-Director of the Leaders for Global Operations (LGO) program.

The LGO program enables students to develop management and technical abilities while earning an MBA and a master's degree in engineering. When Professor Perakis served as Co-Director, the program won the UPS George Smith Prize, which is awarded by INFORMS to programs for their "effective and innovative preparation of students to be good practitioners of operations research" (Waugh, 2014). The selection committee noted that:

> MIT LGO was created to bring about a renaissance in US manufacturing by developing analytically and technically sophisticated leaders to face the challenges of global competition. ... The program has developed a generation of leaders who are adept in their craft

and are innovating their operations by making operations research a core competency of their organizations.

(Waugh, 2014)

Professor Perakis has won many awards for her high-quality research. These are sandwiched between two especially notable national awards. Early in her career, the Office of the President of the United States during the Clinton administration honored her with the Presidential Early Career Award. Later in her career, in 2016, she was selected to be an INFORMS Fellow for lifetime achievement.

Lessons from Professor Perakis

Professor Perakis' professional life embodies the MIT motto, *"mens et manus"* ("mind and hand"), which symbolizes the university's goal of bringing together knowledge and practice. Her three core professional activities—research, teaching, and work with practitioners—are motivated by a desire to have an impact and to continue learning. As she put it, "I love MIT because as a professor I keep being a student." Her success on these three fronts has led her to leadership positions within her faculty groups and in the Executive MBA program.

1. *Research.* Her publication of over fifty articles in refereed journals, over 350 research presentations, patents, and Presidential and lifetime achievement awards all demonstrate the impact of Professor Perakis' research. She blends teaching and research through thesis supervision (twenty-four PhD students and over fifty Master of Science students) and the ability to bring research into the classroom through numerous examples and sessions on current research projects. She has developed lifelong friendships with many of her thesis students.
2. *Teaching.* Professor Perakis' desire to learn is an important factor in her success as a teacher. She encourages her students to provide examples from their business experience, to teach fellow students who are struggling with the material, and to provide feedback to her after every weekend of classes. She is willing to make mid-course adjustments based on their feedback. Her measure of success in the classroom is the impact the course has on students when they use the learning in their work.
3. *Work with Companies.* Professor Perakis' work with companies enables her to feed real-life problems and examples into her research and teaching, while also improving business operations. Although she finds blending theory and practice in a company setting to be a humbling experience, it is a small price to pay for the ultimate goal, which, in her words, is to "have an impact."

It might seem strange to use the word "love" in connection with a professor who teaches what many students consider to be the toughest course in the EMBA program at MIT and whose research is especially rigorous and complex. But this word permeates Professor Perakis' teaching and research relationships with her students. When I asked one student for comments about Professor Perakis, she responded simply, "I love her." And when I sent an email to Professor Perakis requesting information about her course, she asked for extra time to respond because, in the next few days, her schedule included a deadline for three paper revisions, a teaching session for prospective EMBA students, a conference at which she was chairing a competition, a talk to new faculty, and so on. Her message concluded: "I know... I work all the time. But I do LOVE my job and the students!!!"

References

Carter, A. (2015, April 16). *Guillaume Roels*. Retrieved from POETS&QUANTS: https://poetsandquants.com/2015/04/16/2015-best-40-under-40-professors-guillaume-roels-anderson-school/?pq-category=business-school-news/

Faculty session. (2017, June 27). Retrieved from YouTube: https://www.youtube.com/watch?v=iBwUmNttKCI

Lahiri, J. (2003). *The namesake*. New York: Houghton Mifflin.

Perakis wins MIT Sloan teaching award. (2014, April 3). Retrieved from SJTU China Leaders for Global Operations: https://clgo.sjtu.edu.cn/index/mits/ZHCLGO1367.html

Schmitt, J. (2018, June 20). *2018 best EMBAs*. Retrieved from POETS&QUANTS: https://poetsandquantsforexecs.com/2018/06/20/2018-best-embas-kosta-ligris-mit-sloan/

Waugh, A. (2014, April 18). *MIT LGO program wins prestigious award*. Retrieved from MIT News: https://news.mit.edu/2014/mit-lgo-program-wins-prestigious-award

Chapter 9

Harvard Strategy Professor Jan Rivkin
Develop Skills to Formulate Strategy and Gain Competitive Advantage

The leadership of faculty members like Jan Rivkin has enabled Harvard Business School (HBS) to gain an international reputation for the high quality of its MBA Program. Professor Rivkin is the C. Roland Christensen Professor of Business Administration, Senior Associate Dean, and Chair of the MBA Program at HBS. During my visit to campus to observe him in action, I was therefore dismayed to learn of disquiet in the program.

A headline in the student newspaper, *The Harbus*, noted "Rivkin Freaks Out ECs, Updates Dreaded 'Days Left at HBS' Clock." According to the article, Professor Rivkin had just sent an email to the graduating class (the so-called "ECs") reminding them that they had fewer than sixty days remaining in the program. This response from a student indicates the depth of anguish and despair caused by this message:

> "WHY ME, WHY NOW?" screamed one EC, who requested to remain anonymous. "This just is not fair. Why can I not continue to spend my time on campus building debt and reading cases forever?"
> (Rivkin freaks out ECs, 2019)

Two other articles in the newspaper mentioned additional signs of discontent. One article, titled "HBS to Remodel Case Discussion to Replicate Drunken Arguments at Bars," quoted a statement released by Professor Rivkin: "We reflected on how the real world actually works and realized that what we need most to equip our students with is the feeling that they have won every argument, similar to when they drink" (HBS to remodel case discussion to replicate drunken arguments at bars, 2019). Another article described cancellation of the HBS Field Immersion, a highlight of the first year that enables students to apply what they learn in their courses to real-world problems. The article quoted an April 1 email from Professor Rivkin: "We do not make this decision lightly" (Breaking news: FGI cancelled, 2019).

The date of Professor Rivkin's supposed email was a wake-up call that caused me to realize that it matched the date of *The Harbus* I was reading. It was the April Fool's day edition, highlighted by small headings at the top of the pages: "Bringing fake news to Harvard Business School since 1937" and "Satire—because two-thirds of HBS is BS." I had been duped! Rather than criticizing HBS, the articles offered proof that the rigors of the MBA Program had not dampened the students' sense of humor, and the frequent mention of Jan Rivkin signaled their respect for him. Professor Rivkin is also highly esteemed in the profession; in 2020 he was the first recipient of the Educational Impact Award from the Strategic Management Society, in recognition of his contributions to the teaching of strategy.

Meet Professor Rivkin

Professor Rivkin's Resume

The following resume summarizes Professor Rivkin's ten-page CV.

Education

PhD, 1997, Business Economics, Harvard University; MA, 1996, Economics, Harvard University; MSc, 1990, with distinction in Economics, London School of Economics; BSc, 1988, summa cum laude (valedictorian), Princeton University

Harvard University

Professor of Business Administration 1997–present; Senior Associate Dean and Chair of the MBA Program, 2018–present; Co-Chair, US Competitiveness Project, 2011–present; Senior Associate Dean for Research, 2015–2018; Head of Strategy Unit, 2009–2014

Principal Teaching Assignments

Required first-year course in strategy; Advanced Management Program (executive education); elective course on Advanced Competitive Strategy: Integrating the Enterprise

Non-Academic Work Experience

Strategy consultant, summer analyst, construction (in Africa)

Research

Published in leading journals, including *Management Science, Organization Science, Strategic Management Journal, Harvard Business Review,* and *Academy of Management Journal.* Two main research streams:

- Interactions among decisions: nineteen articles and book chapters; fifty-eight cases and teaching and class notes
- US competitiveness: fifteen articles and reports; nine cases and teaching notes

Other research (for example, on the roots of differences in firm performance) and course material: three articles and twenty-one cases and teaching notes.
Named one of the top thirty bestselling case authors, 2017–2018

Outside Activities

[Although not required by HBS, when he was Senior Associate Dean for Research, Professor Rivkin made available to the public a "Comprehensive Disclosure of Outside Activities" that included the following activities.]

- Consultant to companies in many different industries (but deferred consulting while Senior Associate Dean to avoid any possible conflicts of interest)
- Served on a corporate board of directors, on a fintech advisory board, and on nonprofit advisory boards

Awards and Honors

- Inaugural Educational Impact Award, Strategic Management Society
- Greenhill Award (for outstanding service to the HBS community, twice)
- Charles M. Williams Award (for outstanding teaching and contributions to the student learning experience)
- Required Curriculum Teaching Award
- Elective Curriculum Teaching Award (six times)
- Best Paper Prize, European Meeting on Applied Evolutionary Economics
- Glueck Best Paper Award (Business Policy and Strategy Division, Academy of Management)

Figure 9.1 Professor Jan Rivkin (Photograph by Russ Campbell)

An Interview with Professor Rivkin

A biography of legendary baseball player Ernie Banks quotes the president of the Chicago Blackhawks, who observed that when he asked Banks questions, "the next thing you knew, you were talking about you and not him. There never was a time where he expounded on his brilliant career" (Rapoport, 2019). I faced the same challenge when interviewing Professor Rivkin. He is extremely humble despite his many achievements and, as a veteran case teacher, he occasionally tried to flip the interview toward me. As he admitted, "I almost never have a conversation like this where I am not asking as many questions as I am answering. I feel a little self-conscious about that." When I asked him whether I could sit in on his class, he modestly replied, "The cost of admission is your feedback. You have to tell me what you think I could do differently, what I should try out."

1. **What is your family background?**

   I was born in Charleston, South Carolina, and spent my first thirteen years there. Then my nuclear family moved north when my dad's job shifted him to Maryland. So I went to high school in Ellicott City and then moved further north, ultimately following my then-girlfriend, now wife, who was in medical school in Boston. We met as undergraduates at Princeton, and after that, I went to the London

School of Economics on a Marshall Scholarship for a couple of years while she started medical school. When I finished in London, I headed back to Boston.

2. **Was your family involved in academia?**

My father was a manager of corporate engineering, and my mother was a medical technician. We were not a family of scholars or teachers. In fact, I'd say that if anything, my grandparents' generation was small Main Street business. My maternal grandfather ran a dry-cleaning plant in Charleston, and my paternal grandfather had a hardware store in Columbia, South Carolina. Although we were not from academia, there was always a discussion of ideas around the dinner table. My grandmother used to joke that the dictionary was the centerpiece of the dining room table. We were a typical multigenerational immigrant family that was blessed with people giving us some opportunity, which we then reinvested in education that brought more opportunity.

3. **Was there anything in your pre-academic career that tilted you toward teaching or sparked your interest in teaching?**

I figured out pretty early on that teaching and research would be a pretty good fit. I did a short stint in strategy consulting between my Masters and PhD, but frankly, that was intended to give me a crash course in reality as preparation for going back for my PhD. For me, the surprising thing was not that I came back to academia. The surprising thing was that I almost did not return because I enjoyed the consulting work so much.

4. **Who were your role models when you decided to become a teacher?**

I was blessed with some fantastic teachers who were inspiring. These were individuals who made it clear that they thought they had the world's greatest job, and I got the idea to teach from them. It really is an incredible profession. I am stunned that they pay us to do this. I've told the dean multiple times that I would pay him to let me do my job.

One of my role models was my fifth-grade science teacher, Mrs. Harrison. What was outstanding about Mrs. Harrison was that she always asked questions. She would never classify herself this way, but she was a case method instructor.

I recall a time when I was on the playground having a typical fifth-grade argument with my friends: if we spit from the top of the Empire State building and hit someone, would it kill them? So we ran to Mrs. Harrison and asked her. She turned to us and said, "Boys, think about rain" and walked away. Her model was always that we should experiment and ask questions and form hypotheses and test them.

One of my professors at Princeton, Bob Prud'homme [Professor of Chemical and Biological Engineering], had an intense curiosity. If you asked him, "Why is the sky blue?" he would ask you, "What if the sky were purple? How can we imagine the sky being orange?" I always loved the power of good questions.

5. **Who were your role models after you started teaching?**

At HBS there is a passion for teaching. For me, it probably starts with Michael Porter [a legendary strategy professor who is the Bishop William Lawrence Professor at HBS], who was my dissertation advisor. When I began to teach he took me into the HBS classroom and shared a half-hour of his wisdom. Three things he said stick with me to this day.

First, he conveyed the importance of what happens in our classroom. Years later, alumni will recall individual moments from their classroom experience. The character of their leadership is shaped by what they experienced in our classroom, and the decisions they make decades later will depend on them being crafted into great leaders in that setting.

Second, he emphasized that when I teach in the classroom, it is my classroom. Although the students in the section that I teach are in that room for the whole day for their entire first year, when I am in the pit I am responsible for what goes on there. [HBS classrooms are shaped in the form of a horseshoe with the instructor in the center— the pit. This layout enables students to easily maintain eye contact with the instructor and other students when they discuss the issues raised by the assigned business cases.]

Third, Mike emphasized the specialty of being a generalist. At HBS our emphasis is on developing general managers. If you want to be a fantastic financial engineer or a great quant jock on Wall Street, there are other places where you can obtain that education. HBS aims to prepare general managers—the people who set the direction for an entire organization. There are places you can go where you will dive deeper into individual functions than at HBS, but if you want to lead an entire organization, we're a pretty good place to go.

Mike also observed me teaching in the classroom. There is a strong tradition here of visiting one another and obtaining feedback. I don't know what inspired me, but early on, when teaching my first course, I decided to invite Mike to class. He arrived a few minutes before class began, and you could hear the hush all over the room and the murmurs from students: "Porter, Porter, Porter." I started the class, and everyone was afraid to speak. Finally, Mike made a joke about it, which caused the students to laugh and relax.

After class, Mike made some important comments. He suggested that I put down my notes, which I was carrying around. He also suggested, "Perhaps it would be useful if you do not appear to be in pain." This made me realize that I was not showing any joy in the classroom. I was not smiling.

The other incredible individual for me was David Garvin, who passed away in 2017. The Christensen Chair that I am honored to hold had two prior occupants: Michael Porter and David Garvin. David was quite possibly the finest teacher on this campus since Chris Christensen. Whenever the faculty got together for a case discussion, he was always the one asked to teach. He helped found the Christensen Center for Teaching and Learning and was an incredible case method instructor.

His classes would unfold magically with very little intervention by David. He had this incredible emotional range. He could be in your face asking the most aggressive question, making you think harder than you could ever think. He could also sit back and ask, "Why? Why did the managers make that decision? What was it that led them to that choice? How could the managers make such a mistake? How could they see such a brilliant move?"

There are so many other folks here who were extraordinarily helpful. When you arrive at HBS you typically teach the required first-year course. The ten sections of the course are taught by a team of six to eight individuals. Preparation for the class is through this teaching group, and in that communal activity you learn about the substance of the course, the process of teaching, and the norms of the school.

6. **What resources have you used to develop your teaching skills? Videotapes?**

Occasionally. I have viewed videotapes of myself, but that is always painful. Sometimes I spot things I would not have spotted otherwise. But I also find they make me very self-conscious. So I don't know how that nets out. One of my colleagues told me when I first started teaching that the secret of great teaching is to be "very similar to yourself." I've found that videotapes sometimes make me not be myself.

A better source of feedback that I have been blessed with is students. The students have been generous in reinforcing good things, they have been tactful but clear in telling me what wasn't working, and they have been incredibly generous and patient in being good teachers. Chris Christensen once wrote a chapter titled "Every Student Teaches and Every Teacher Learns" in his book *Education for Judgment*. (Christensen, 1992) Among the great points the reading makes is that the students themselves are great teachers for us.

7. **How do you prepare for class? Are you still nervous about entering a classroom?**

Somewhere around the third year I was teaching, I began to walk into the classroom nervous but also thinking this was going to be the best part of the day. So, no question, I still find it nerve-racking going into the classroom, but it's now become an exciting, pleasurable nerve-racking experience. I adore teaching, but I am obsessed and nervous before I do it.

I still prepare like there is no tomorrow. I don't sleep well the night before. Are you familiar with the "Snooze Alarm Test," which is used to determine whether you are doing the right thing in life? The question is: how many times do you have to hit your snooze alarm before getting out of bed? I can honestly say I have not been awakened by my alarm a single day I have taught—ever. Before the alarm, I always wake up ready to go, having thought about the case and the discussion while half asleep. [In a video titled "Inside the HBS Case Method," Professor Rivkin notes, "The morning before teaching is an important period for me. I have to go through my whole pre-teaching ritual; I have my pre-teaching trance" (Inside the HBS case method, 2009).]

When I prepare a brand-new case that I have not taught before but that is well supported by colleagues (meaning that others have shared their teaching plans or there is an official teaching note), my guess is that it requires twenty-four hours of preparation. What typically happens is that I will read the case, read the teaching plan, and think to myself, *this will never work.* Then I will think, *I cannot believe that I must do it all myself.*

I then reconstruct the case. However, when I develop an actual plan, it resembles the original teaching plan that others gave me. It is not that I have reinvented the wheel or that I have invented some brilliant insight that no one has ever thought of before. It is that I have made it my own. As part of this process, I clarify the objectives and how we might get there, look at all the ways we might go astray and how I'll pull us back on track, and decide who in the class might participate in certain ways given their pre-HBS background.

Even with an older case, I still spend hours. I am not sure exactly how many; it depends on how long it has been since I've taught the case and on how well I know the group. The tradition here is that you know your ninety students by name and are familiar with their backgrounds before you enter the classroom the first day.

8. **Are your classes interactive?**

Yes, they are interactive. They are acts of co-production. There are certain educational institutions where the faculty largely produce the experience and the students largely consume it. That is not what happens in our classrooms. It's all co-production.

[When interviewed by *Poets and Quants*, Professor Rivkin distinguished between the traditional "lean back" approach to teaching where students are passive and the "lean forward" model at HBS that involves active learning, which he described as follows:

> You're constantly on your toes; you're listening to your prof, but mostly to your peers. ... You're raising your hand and getting called on. You're speaking and trying to draw others to your point of view. You're deciding whether what others are saying is persuasive. You're deciding what you would do as a case protagonist. And then you're reflecting on what you learn. Throughout this, you are thinking for yourself. You're an active learner—and that makes all the difference, I believe. ...
>
> (Schmitt, 2018)

In a separate interview posted on the HBS website, Professor Rivkin elaborated on his role in encouraging interaction among students:

> As faculty, we push very hard to make sure that people's logic is sound, but the participants do that for each other as well. We challenge one another to bring our best thinking to the table. For example, one person might make a point, and another person will say, "I see it differently, and here's why." My job is to then go back to the first person and say, "Why does this person, who read the same case you did, see it so differently?" Through that process, everyone learns more about other points of view. Together we try to understand why people who read the same material but have diverse experiences come to very different conclusions. That's where most of the learning happens. Two individuals might start out in strong disagreement. Suddenly the light bulb goes on, and they see that they have different underlying assumptions, and that's why they disagree. I love those moments in the classroom.
>
> (Leading the enerprise as an integrated whole, n.d.)]

9. Do you cold call students?

I tend to opt for warm calls rather than cold calls, meaning that I'll let the person that I would like to start know that he or she will be the person I call on to open class that day. They can "pass" if there is a great reason why they are not prepared to do it. It is not a great thing to pass, obviously, but if the person is not prepared, I'd rather not get the whole discussion off to a bad start. If someone has arrived late on the day I was going to call on them, I might cold call them, but then [he wryly observed] they have had more time to prepare, so it seems fair.

10. **Do you use technology in the classroom?**

I show an occasional video but don't use a lot of technology. Even with PowerPoint, I try to be sparing. Some professors here think that we should not provide students with takeaways. Others think that you owe it to the students to tell them what we think they should know. I am somewhere in between. I do hand out some things in class and I'll say, "For what it's worth, this is what I think." But I'm not a big fan of using the discussion as a way to illustrate a preconceived point that I already had coming in.

11. **How do you deal with students who try to dominate the discussion (aka "gunners")?**

Our sections take care of that problem pretty effectively. If you are overly aggressive, your friends will tell you to make room for other people. When I was a PhD student and took the first-year, required MBA curriculum, I certainly benefited a lot from receiving "behavioral correction" from classmates.

On the faculty side, we try to spread participation widely and fairly. We keep careful track of who speaks. Our required courses have scribes who don't assess the comments of students but who do keep track of who says what. We have technology that will allow us to see who has spoken the most, who has spoken the least, who has gone the longest time since the last time they spoke, whether we are calling on people on the left-hand side of the classroom and on the right-hand side in equal proportions, whether we are calling on people in the top row in correct proportion to people in the bottom row, and so on. The scribe records who said what, enters this data, and the software then produces the output. That is a real gift that helps us to allocate class participation fairly.

The other thing I and many of my colleagues do if someone's hand has been up a lot is wave them off. And I may tell them after class,

> It isn't that I don't value what you say, but your hand is up all the time. If I call on you too much, we are not spreading the participation, and we are not getting the diversity of viewpoints we'd like. And if your hand has been up for a few minutes, you are probably going to comment on something that was relevant five minutes ago but not now.

12. **Do you bring your research into the classroom?**

My research focuses on this question: how should managers make decisions that don't respect organizational boundaries? To bring this question into my teaching, I often use a case about a leader who turned a business around. The leader is young, is in charge of an iconic company, and asks, "How do I set the basic direction of this company?" This is very different from "What do I need to do in marketing?" The basic direction affects everything from the factory floor to the sales force to the product designers to the relationships with retailers and so on. The whole company is involved. This type of challenge is common to many companies.

My elective course on Advanced Competitive Strategies: Integrating the Enterprise is about how you can get parts of an organization to work together better, which is one of my research interests. The course has fueled my research. The students ask questions that I have not anticipated. To some degree, we are incredibly blessed in that, if we have an idea, we can go into an MBA (or executive education) classroom and test it with ninety really smart individuals who have business experience.

[In the *Poets and Quants* interview mentioned previously, Professor Rivkin provided an example of a student who questioned why the cases they studied only involved companies that started change initiatives after they incurred losses. That question led Professor Rivkin to "look for companies that changed before they had to. Turns out, this is a very deep type of challenge and one that was largely unexplored" (Schmitt, 2018).]

13. **Do you use a grading curve?**
Yes, a grading curve is required for elective and required courses. In the MBA Program, we cannot submit our grades unless they fit the three categories of the curve. The lowest-performing 10% of students are placed in Category III, the top 15%–25% are Category I, and the remaining students are in Category II.

My interpretation of the purpose of the forced curve has evolved over my time at HBS. When I was a student, I thought the forced curve was intended to make the students work hard, but I've come to realize that the curve makes the faculty work hard too. For the students, the forced curve creates an incentive to prepare and participate, especially because half of the grade in a typical HBS course is based on class participation.

For the faculty, the forced curve makes us take grading seriously. It makes us listen carefully to our students because we know that we must explain to 10% of them why they are at the bottom of the class. It might appear to be a happy day if I could give all my students the best grade. Everyone would feel awesome. But then my incentive to really invest and figure out who is getting the material and who is struggling goes down dramatically. I've got to look 10% of my students in the eye and explain why they could be better, and this gives me a very strong incentive to pay close attention and to think about them and their individual skills in a way that I suspect that I wouldn't do if the curve wasn't there. I might be underestimating how I would behave if I didn't have the forced curve because I have only experienced the forced curve system.

14. **What do you like most about teaching?**

    I love the moment when the light bulb goes on—when a student who has been wrestling with an idea suddenly gets it. You can see the person's confidence go up. You can see them feel that they are prepared for what comes next in their career. I love it when my students stay in touch, and I adore watching how their careers and their lives unfold. I get about an email a day from a former student. In fact, as we are speaking [by phone], one just popped up. It's often my favorite email of the day. Sometimes it's just an update on how they are doing, sometimes they've got a strategy issue, sometimes they are just keeping me abreast of what's going on or letting me know when they are passing through town and want to get together.

15. **How do you know when you have been successful as a teacher?**

    Unlike some jobs where there is a clear metric that is posted on a scoreboard somewhere, here it's tougher to know when you've been successful in the short run. The good thing at HBS is that we have a very clear mission. Our job is to educate leaders who make a difference in the world. And so for me the measure of success is when I see my students years later and realize they really have made a difference in the world and they believe that the education they received in our classrooms helped them achieve that. For me, that's the metric. It doesn't show up on exams, and, in fact, some of the students on whom I feel I've had the greatest positive impact struggled in my course.

16. **What do you like least about teaching?**

    Easy—grading. If I could trade one week of my life for something in another profession, it would be the grading week. In our system, grading has to be done carefully. You can't short-change it. But it is mind numbing. And there is very little learning going on by anyone at that point. I recognize the importance of it. I take it seriously. But it's the least fun.

17. **How does HBS train rookie professors to teach?**

    Junior faculty have access to a variety of resources, including the teaching groups, classroom visits from senior faculty, and the Christensen Center for Teaching and Learning. The Christensen Center is a valuable resource for all faculty. We also have an orientation program called START for new faculty. During this program, incoming faculty have an opportunity to discuss and experience the case method and to practice case teaching. [As a Visiting Professor at HBS, I attended an earlier version of the START program. During the program, new and visiting faculty had to prepare assigned cases, and the program leaders called on us, just as they call on MBA students in a regular classroom. Being cold called in a classroom filled with faculty experts from a variety of business fields proved to be an intimidating experience, but one with enduring value because it provided me with lifelong empathy for the concerns and fears of my own students.]

18. **Is teaching important for annual reviews and promotion and tenure decisions?**

Not as much as an outside observer would think. There is sometimes a misperception that you can get tenure for teaching well at HBS. That is false. Our promotion standards go like this. We have three audiences we care about: managers, educators, and scholars. By the time you come up for tenure, you need to have had a profound impact on one of those audiences, and you need to have demonstrated the potential to have an impact on a second audience. In addition, you need to have shown competency in teaching.

Educators are one of our audiences, but influencing educators is not the same as teaching well. Instead, influencing educators involves producing teaching material that shapes how others think about problems and how they teach about those problems. In fact, in our promotion process, teaching ratings are inadmissible evidence. The only teaching evidence that is admissible is peer observations of you in your classroom. That said, the culture of HBS values good teaching. To be a real member of the community, you need to have taught well.

19. **What advice would you give to rookie professors?**

First, I would encourage them to feel a deep sense of gratitude for being in a position where they can have an impact on the world.

Second, I urge all professors, including myself, to invest deeply in their students. It's the highest-return investment I've ever made. Your students become your teachers. They help you understand the nature of business. They help you understand what knowledge you are creating is helpful for them and what knowledge you are creating is not. They continue to keep in touch with you, so you get to learn about the life of a businessperson, and they open doors for you when they are in positions to do so.

Investing in students means knowing their backgrounds before class begins and being diligent in preparation for class; it means spending time with them when they have questions or thoughts afterward. One of my students once told me, "The problem, Rivkin, is not getting into your office; the problem is getting out." I think he meant that as a compliment; at least I decided to take it that way. It also means being available to them after the course ends. I have a very clear policy: I never tell a former student that I'm too busy to talk.

20. **What is your proudest professional achievement?**
    I don't like pride. Everything my grandparents taught me about how you behave in the world says that humility is truly important. But I will say that the professional achievement that has given me the most joy was being named the C. Roland Christensen Professor of Business Administration. That meant a great deal not only because of the legend of Professor Christensen but also because of the people who held the Christensen Chair before.

21. **What do you do for fun?**
    My wife and I bicycle a lot. During the summer, we try to get in around one hundred miles a week.

22. **What profession would you choose if you were not a professor?**
    Can I be an elementary school science teacher? I have seven nieces and nephews, and I love to be the crazy science uncle. My niece will come into my house and ask, "What are we going to blow up today?" Potato cannons, super magnets, hovercrafts—we basically make stuff, much of which involves fire. I love working with kids and hands-on science projects. [Professor Rivkin's interest in science arose at an early age. A January 25, 1984 *Washington Post* article notes that, as a 17-year-old senior at Centennial High School in Ellicott City, Maryland, he was selected as one of forty students in a national scholarship program called the Westinghouse Science Talent Search. According to the article, he "investigated the role of an enzyme found in soybean nodules and bacteria that is involved in the nitrogen fixation process" (Md. school has 2 science contest winners, 1984).]

23. **What profession would you least like?**
    People at a wedding who are hired to start the dancing and celebrating. That would be the worst job in the world for me.

24. **What three individuals would you most like to have dinner with? Any from HBS?**
    I'm not sure if I could limit the dinner party to three guests, but here are three individuals who are certainly on the list.
    • Wallace Brett Donham, the second dean of HBS. Dean Donham pushed the faculty to adopt the case method in earnest; initiated genuine research at the school; moved the school to its own campus, allegedly in the face of considerable faculty resistance; led HBS to launch the *Harvard Business Review*; and inspired Elton Mayo and others to pioneer the "human relations" school of thought about management.
    • C. Roland Christensen: Professor Christensen was, by all accounts, one of the finest case method instructors in the history of HBS and the teaching profession. He not only inspired generations of MBA students, but he taught a legendary teaching

seminar that older faculty still discuss with awe. I would love to get a few tips and hope to absorb some of his magic.
- David Garvin: Professor Garvin was one of my mentors at HBS. He passed away at far too young an age. I'm sure that he would convey even more wisdom over dinner, but frankly, I'd just treasure another dinner's worth of his company.

Professor Rivkin in Action

The Course: Strategy

I attended a session in the required Strategy course that HBS students take during their first year in the MBA Program. The Strategy course has a strategic leadership focus that is important for leaders in any type of organization. A course overview describes five modules:

1. **Introduction to Strategy**: a big-picture perspective on strategy and how it is developed,
2. **Market Attractiveness**: the importance of the external environment, a framework for analyzing whether markets are attractive, and how to make a market more attractive,
3. **Competitive Advantage**: how a firm can gain competitive advantage within its own environment through making decisions on where to operate, using tools for gaining advantage in various markets, and understanding the role of innovation in transforming the nature of competition,
4. **Strategic Interactions**: making strategic decisions that take into account reactions from suppliers, customers, and rivals, and
5. **Crafting Strategy**: how strategy is developed in a variety of contexts. (Introduction to the RC Strategy Course, 2018)

I attended the final class in the "Crafting Strategy" module. The course overview notes that the sessions on crafting strategy address these questions: "What are the goals of your enterprise, what is the scope of your presence, how do you seek to build advantage, and what activities do you undertake to implement your strategy?" (Introduction to the RC Strategy Course, 2018). In the session I attended, these questions were raised in the context of a leadership change at the ice-cream company Ben & Jerry's.

Professor Rivkin bases half the grade for the course on class participation and half on a final exam (the students' analysis of a strategy case). He bases the participation grade on the quality of participation, along with a "minimum threshold of quantity" (Introduction to the RC Strategy Course, 2018). Students receive an assessment of their participation halfway through the course. To assist with the assessment, course "scribes" use computers to record participation during class.

Feedback is a two-way street, as HBS instructors ask students to provide assessments of course content and delivery. Students provide this feedback halfway through, to enable instructors to make immediate adjustments, and near the end of the course, to encourage continuous improvement of the course in the future. In addition, instructors use pre-class polls to find out where the class stands on questions that are part of the case discussion.

Students provide informal feedback directly to professors and through their "Ed-Reps." Ed-Reps are part of a student leadership team elected by students. This team meets once a week to discuss how their courses are progressing. The Ed-Rep also meets weekly with students in the class for announcements and discussion of issues affecting them.

In addition to the student-elected Ed-Rep, a research associate, a teaching fellow, and a course coordinator provide support to the course. The research associate for the course graduated from Harvard University (English with High Honors and Psychology, *cum laude*). Her role was to conduct research and interviews and to draft and update teaching materials—such as cases, teaching notes, and book chapters.

The teaching fellow was a 1994 graduate of the MBA Program who had experience as the Vice President for Global Finance and Chief Strategy Officer for a well-known global firm, as Chief Operating Officer/Chief Financial Officer for other firms, and as a strategy consultant with a leading consulting firm. She met with students two to three times a week for optional review sessions.

The course coordinator, who had a BA degree from Wheaton College and a Master of Education from Northeastern University, manages administrative projects for the Strategy Unit, including maintaining the Strategy course platform, preparing the course materials, and managing a simulation that provides students with experience in decision making related to the "Strategic Interactions" course module (number four in the list of five modules mentioned previously).

HBS divides students into "sections" of approximately ninety students each, and they take the required courses with their section in the same classroom for the entire first year. The students in the class I attended were in the class of 2020. HBS selected the 930 students in the class from over 9,800 applicants. The student mix included 41% women, 37% international students, and 26% US ethnic minorities. Students in the class of 2020 were from sixty-nine countries, and there were thirty-eight countries represented in the session I attended, as evidenced by the country flags displayed around the perimeter of the classroom.

The average age of students in the Class of 2020 was twenty-seven, and the median GMAT score was 730. Almost half of them (45%) majored in economics and business as undergraduates, 37% in STEM (science, technology, engineering, and math), and 17% in humanities and social sciences. Their most common pre-MBA experience was in one of three industries: consulting, high tech/communications, and venture capital/ private equity.

When the Class of 2020 first arrived on campus, Professor Rivkin, as Chair of the MBA program, opened an orientation meeting by removing his coat, rolling up his sleeves, and reminding the students that "637 is the number of days until graduation." After their nervous laughter subsided, he continued: "So today, we begin a 637-day journey in which every day counts" (Newsroom, 2018). He revised this metric when welcoming the Class of 2022 by noting that "we get to work together actively to create better leaders for the world" and that his "conservative estimate of the number of days of potential leadership that your class can bring" to the world's public health, economic, and social crises is 6,954,000 (A virtual welcome to the MBA class of 2022, 2020).

Professor Rivkin co-taught his section of the course with Professor Jorge Tamayo, who sat in on the class I attended. Originally from Colombia, Professor Tamayo had recently completed his PhD in Economics at the University of Southern California. He and Professor Rivkin met weekly for two hours to discuss teaching strategy with seven other professors who taught other sections of the course. Several course-planning meetings during the prior term preceded these weekly meetings.

The teaching team meetings, directed by Professor Ashish Nanda (a member of the team who serves as Faculty Chair for the course), play a key role in the success of a course. The teaching team was comprised of senior and junior faculty members and included faculty from outside the Strategy Unit. They brought a diversity of experience to the issues raised by the assigned cases. One member of the team, Professor Debora Spar, was the former president of Barnard College, and another, Professor Dennis Yao, was a former commissioner of the US Federal Trade Commission.

During the meetings, one team member presents a teaching plan for a case assigned for an upcoming class. HBS faculty write over 300 new cases every year, and it is not unusual for the author of a case to lead the discussion of the teaching plan. Teaching plans typically include a case summary, the teaching objectives, the flow of class discussion, key questions that instructors should raise in class, and a board plan for capturing information from the discussion.

Planning for case teaching is especially complex because instructors must keep one eye on the content they are delivering and the other on the process for delivering this content. An additional complication is that they deliver content through questions and discussions rather than through lectures, which requires the ability to respond to a variety of possible comments and questions that are often difficult to predict. The advice of faculty colleagues on the teaching team is especially valuable as they describe their own experiences with the case. This advice includes how to circumvent comments that might be unresponsive to the professor's question, leading the class down an unintended path. But sometimes these paths are instructive because there are no bright-line answers to many of the questions, causing members of the teaching group to engage in debate over various approaches to the business challenge presented in the case.

Just as HBS professors use teaching teams for class preparation, students create their own learning teams (also known as "discussion groups") to prepare cases for class. Over the course of the MBA Program, they will read around 500 cases that provide them with vicarious business experience. Like the professors, the students typically prepare their individual analyses of these cases before meeting with their teams and, like professors, their team meetings often engender serious debate.

Calling the faculty group a "teaching team" and the student group a "learning team" is misleading because, during their respective meetings, faculty *learn* from each other through their debates while students *teach* each other, using the considerable business experience they bring to the MBA Program. The parallel teaching and learning processes carried on by the teams continue when professors and students converge in the classroom to continue their co-creation of the learning experience.

The "Inside the HBS Case Method" video mentioned previously shows both teaching teams and learning teams in action, and it features Professor Rivkin leading a faculty team discussion and teaching a case on competitive dynamics. He captures the faculty expectations of students by noting,

> I expect students to give their heart and soul to the case. Most importantly, I expect the students to put themselves into the shoes of the protagonist of the case and ask themselves seriously, *What would I do?* I want them to think very seriously: what would they do if they had that situation in their lives?
>
> (Inside the HBS case method, 2009)

Inside Professor Rivkin's Classroom

Although I arrived at the ninety-seat classroom early, Professor Rivkin was already busy using multicolored chalk to fill three boards with data about the case. Part of the HBS culture is starting class precisely on time. In the video on the case method, Professor Rivkin commented on teaching a class that begins at noon: "As the second-hand passes the twelve on the clock, we get going" (Inside the HBS case method, 2009). [When I was a visiting professor at Harvard, I adapted quickly to the faculty suit-and-tie dress code that is part of the culture, but learned the hard way about class starting times. I decided to sit in on a leadership class taught by Professor Lynn Paine. When I returned to the classroom following a mid-class break, I was one minute late and discovered that the doors had already closed. As a result, I missed the rest of the class.]

Professor Rivkin started this class precisely on schedule by introducing me and student guests to the class. He then launched into the session, using a variety of teaching techniques.

1. **Providing a Big-Picture Perspective**

    He began by summarizing for the students where they were in the course. He did this by reviewing the five course modules and reminding them that this session was on "Crafting Strategy." He then moved to the case assigned for the day: "Ben & Jerry's: A Period of Transition."

    HBS students prepare one case per class, except for a mid-course strategy simulation. The "Ben & Jerry's" case (Ben & Jerry's Home Ice Cream, Inc.: A period of transition, 1996) is twenty pages long, including exhibits that were packed with data on the company's and its competitors' financial highlights, US per capita consumption of ice cream, ice cream market share (segmented according to butterfat content), the cost structure for ice cream consumption, total US ice cream volume by flavor, and advertising spending. A new CEO at Ben & Jerry's, Bob Holland, faced a huge challenge as he attempted to develop an explicit strategy at a time when the company was facing new competition and internal concerns.

    Professor Rivkin started the case discussion by asking the class to think broadly about the role of a strategist like the CEO. Is the role to design a strategy or to design an organization that can develop a strategy? He then moved to specific questions relating to, for example, how the CEO should address the issues that Ben & Jerry's faced, his strategic options, and the uncertainties and assumptions underlying the options that should be tested before making a decision.

2. **Active Listening Skills**

    Professor Rivkin exuded energy and enthusiasm as he ran from the board to the center of the teaching area—the "pit"—and bounded up and down the stairs to be close to the students he questioned. He frequently gesticulated with his hands and arms for emphasis, and opened his arms wide with palms up when asking questions.

    He listened carefully to student comments. He also paid close attention to their body language. ("Pete, you look skeptical. Why?") As part of the listening process, he would often list their ideas on the board and, following their comments, would clarify and confirm their thoughts. During this process, he provided positive feedback, which encouraged students to feel comfortable when contributing to the discussion.

3. **Vigorous Interaction with Students**

According to the HBS website, students do most of the talking during a case method class (The HBS case method, n.d.). Professor Rivkin's class was no exception as he peppered the students with questions that placed them in the role of the CEO ("You are Bob. Do you know why people buy Ben & Jerry's ice cream?"). He opened the class by cold calling a student, but then relied mainly on volunteer responses. He frequently scanned the horseshoe-shaped room, calling on students on all sides. Many hands shot up following each question as students competed for airtime. Their attempts to participate brought to mind basketball games where players on the bench eagerly try to establish eye contact with coaches, hoping they will send them into the game.

Once called on, the students directed their responses toward other students more often than at Professor Rivkin. Modeling themselves after the professor, the students listened intently to comments made by the other students and referred to these comments when speaking. The student interaction gave the class the feel of a corporate meeting at which the participants are discussing the direction they want to take the company, or perhaps a session at a consulting firm in which over ninety experienced consultants are debating a course of action.

While interacting with the students, Professor Rivkin liked to ask "Why?" When a student mentioned that Ben & Jerry's faced increased competition, his response was, "Why?" He encouraged debate by asking for different points of view. When he asked whether the CEO was in trouble and two students said, "Yes," he asked the class whether anyone disagreed. Eight hands shot up. At times, the debate between students was so intense that Professor Rivkin became a bystander—a participant in the learning process, observing the dialog and awaiting his turn to contribute to the discussion.

4. **Subtle Humor and Sense of Fun**

Although his approach to the case method was rigorous and challenged the students, Professor Rivkin also brought a sense of fun to the classroom, and there was frequent (occasionally nervous) laughter. He told no jokes, but he occasionally made subtle references to ice cream flavors. It took a while for the students to catch on. They missed "Why rely on Ben's taste buds in selecting flavors? That's nuts." But later on, they laughed (and groaned) at his comment about the strategy becoming more "plain vanilla."

A comment that induced laughter might carry a serious underlying message. For example, in the video on the case method, Professor

Rivkin evoked laughter when telling the class, "You never ever, ever, ever enter a price war if you don't have a credible low-cost position. If you do that, and I learn about it, I will deny that I knew you at Harvard Business School. Okay?" In the video, he also commented on the balance between fun and the challenge of learning through the case method: "It's fun, right? I mean, there's a lot of active engagement. It's hard in a lot of ways as well, though. Nothing is spoon fed to you. You've got to be prepared. You've got to come ready to play every day" (Inside the HBS case method, 2009).

5. **Clarity Where Possible: A Framework for Analysis**

   Although many of the questions raised by Professor Rivkin were subject to debate and had no clear answer, he did provide the students with a clear framework for analyzing the questions. The framework asked students to first consider their strategic objective and then explore the company's advantage and the scope of that advantage in terms of customers, products, and so on. With this advantage in mind, the framework then asked them to make decisions regarding recommended activities on several different fronts (firm infrastructure, human resources, technology development, procurement, etc.)

   At a critical juncture in the class, he compared the strategies proposed by two students by distributing copies of their frameworks, which he had selected from among several that students voluntarily submitted in advance of class. One student, "Fred," wanted to retain the social responsibility at Ben & Jerry's that was important to the founders, while the other student, "Abigail," thought that the firm needed to become more professional in order to improve financial performance. Fred described his strategy first and, after receiving applause from other students, Professor Rivkin asked the class what they liked about his plan. It was then Abigail's turn, followed by a spontaneous debate between the two students under the watchful eye of Professor Rivkin. A class vote following the debate produced a 50/50 split between those favoring Fred's approach and those favoring Abigail's.

6. **Closure**

   Case-based courses are difficult to close because, as the Ben & Jerry's case illustrates, there often are no right or wrong answers. Professor Rivkin's approach was to update the class on what happened at Ben & Jerry's following the case and to show video clips of the CEO attending a Harvard class, in which he provided an insider's perspective on his experience. These clips illustrated the importance of exercising sound judgment in the wake of uncertainty. As Professor Rivkin noted in the video "Inside the HBS Case Method," the case method "is not a passive process and, frankly, management's not a passive process. They [students] get to try out many of the component processes of management in the classroom. They need to build muscles around things like judgment" (Inside the HBS case method, 2009).

The eighty-minute class formally concluded with well-deserved applause from the students. But this did not complete the learning process, as they continued to debate several of the issues after class while clustered around Professor Rivkin.

7. **A Post-class Confession**

In the interests of full disclosure, I should make an admission. The class discussion of Ben & Jerry's—and how its early growth was fueled by the sale of its super premium ice cream that has a higher fat content and lower "overrun" (the amount of air in the ice cream) than traditional brands—triggered a craving for the product. After class, I discovered a Ben & Jerry's conveniently located near Harvard Square, a ten-minute walk from the classroom, where I indulged in a three-scoop waffle cone, which cost $9 and clocked in at an estimated 1,000 calories.

Student Comments about Professor Rivkin

- Amazing, intelligent, and engaged.
- In command of the classroom and gets everyone to participate.
- Has a wealth of knowledge and is a true master.
- Ability to step back and allow students to participate and learn from fellow students.
- He knows how to facilitate discussion and pull information out of the class.
- Professor Rivkin remembers student comments from weeks ago.
- Very familiar with the entire curriculum and references other courses.
- Very good at zooming out of a case to provide general takeaways.
- He knows all the students super well. He knows their backgrounds and uses that information in class.
- Extremely organized and prepared.
- Has a clear sense of direction but doesn't force us to follow it.
- Wants a decision and justification but doesn't force us into a decision.
- Really good at follow-up questions.
- Extremely excited about the material.
- Moves around classroom, even to the back of the class, to encourage students to talk to each other.
- Passionate.
- Pushes us if we give vague answers.
- One of the best.
- Truly cares about students.

Impact Beyond the Classroom

This snapshot of his schedule on the day I attended his class captures the wide range of Professor Rivkin's activities.

A Day in the Life of Jan Rivkin

6:05 a.m.

Wake up a little before my alarm. On class days, I never sleep until my alarm goes off. I'm always excited and eager to go.

Exercise on the stationary bike (because the roads are wet), shower, dress.

7:20 a.m.

Commute to work.

7:45 a.m.

"Walk the perimeter." Since becoming Chair of the MBA Program, I have made a point of walking the campus, especially the student gathering places, every day. This almost always leads to interesting conversations.

8:15 a.m.

Prepare some materials for class, but especially prepare for the 9 a.m. task.

9:00 a.m.

Meet with corporate recruiters who have gathered on campus for the day to discuss the latest innovations in our MBA Program. What are our current curricular priorities?

10:00 a.m.

Meet with a colleague about an administrative matter that is brewing in the MBA Program.

10:30 a.m.

Complete my class preparation (which began several days earlier). For the Ben & Jerry's class, I especially want to dive into the strategic options volunteered by my students.

1:00 p.m.

Set up the classroom, especially the chalkboards.

1:25 p.m.

Teach—my favorite part of the day.

2:45 p.m.

Debrief with students and then with my co-teacher, Jorge Tamayo.

3:30 p.m.

Meet with a student about class participation and career aspirations.

4:00 p.m.

Walk the campus and talk with a colleague from another business school who is thinking about moving to HBS.

4:30 p.m.

Meet with two former HBS students, now accomplished professionals, who have founded an organization that aims to revive democracy in the United States. We discuss their strategy.

5:30 p.m.

Commute home, listening to an audiobook that is pertinent to my role as MBA Chair.

6:00 p.m.

Make and eat dinner with my wonderful wife. Catch up with her.

7:30 p.m.

Catch up on email (thirty-two outbound messages) and work a bit on a new case that is in-progress.

11:00 p.m.

Head to bed.

Professor Rivkin is well known for his work beyond the classroom, which blends his research skills with a passion for service to the country and the business community. With Co-Chair Michael Porter, he leads the US Competitiveness Project that HBS launched in 2011. Professor Rivkin and others have produced several reports based on surveys of HBS alumni and the public.

The 2016 report, "Problems Unsolved and a Nation Divided," defines competitiveness as follows:

> A nation is competitive if it creates the conditions where two things occur simultaneously: businesses operating in the nation can (1) compete successfully in domestic and international markets, while (2) maintaining and improving the wages and living standards of the average citizen.
>
> (Porter et al., 2016)

The report diagnoses the decline in US competitiveness and identifies weaknesses in the tax law, educational system, transportation infrastructure, healthcare system, and political system.

While the project has identified strengths in the US economy, such as the communications infrastructure and capital markets, it has also highlighted the fact that these strengths do not benefit everyone. Weaknesses in the system have been especially harmful to American workers. Not content with analysis alone, Professor Rivkin and his co-authors have developed a plan that includes specific, realistic actions that government can undertake to improve competitiveness and enable workers and small business owners to share in the country's prosperity.

Business leaders also play an important role in achieving shared prosperity. In an article published in *Fortune,* Professor Rivkin and his co-author Michael Porter conclude that business leaders must recognize that weaknesses in the economic system represent a

> tragedy of the commons [that] is destined to become their tragedy. Collectively, they must recognize that the long-term health of their businesses is tied inextricably to the health of their communities, the local business environment, and the education and skills of their workers.
>
> (Porter & Rivkin, 2015)

Not satisfied with encouraging others to take action, Professor Rivkin has devoted his own time and effort to educating civic leaders. When working on the Competitiveness Project, he learned about exciting initiatives in cities where young leaders from various sectors were working together to improve the "commons." For instance, business leaders were working with community colleges to train workers, and universities were working with local governments to enable startups to use lab research. Realizing that their work related to his own teaching and research on cross-boundary collaboration within companies, he welcomed the opportunity to teach in two leadership development programs.

First, he has participated in the Bloomberg Harvard City Leadership Initiative, in which HBS partners with Harvard's Kennedy School and Bloomberg Philanthropies to provide leadership and management training to city mayors and senior officials. The mayors meet for in-person classes, followed by one year of virtual learning sessions. In an article in *The Harvard Gazette*, Mayor Rosalynn Bliss of Grand Rapids, Michigan noted, "In addition to the talented professors who challenged us to think differently about how best to solve community problems, we had the opportunity to connect with and learn from other mayors" (Mayoral initiative heads for year two, 2018).

Second, Professor Rivkin is active in the Young American Leaders Program (YALP). Leaders of the Competitiveness Project created YALP after they recognized the importance of educational and infrastructure resources for local workers. HBS has developed a partnership with fourteen cities where senior leaders have identified young individuals whom they believe will be next-generation leaders. These young leaders come from a variety of organizations—government, business, nonprofit, educational, faith-based, labor unions, and so on. The leaders are invited to campus, where they participate in a boot camp on cross-sector collaboration targeted toward shared prosperity. After returning home, they have achieved impressive collaborative results in a number of cities (Bridging the gap, 2019).

Lessons from Professor Rivkin

Professor Rivkin's teaching and research accomplishments are instructive for leaders and teachers at all levels. As the quintessential case method teacher, he exhibits a number of skills that create a learning environment in a classroom or boardroom. Key among them are the ability to:

- place the specific issue under discussion in context by looking at the big picture,
- exercise the power of good questions by identifying the most important questions that are essential to the success of an enterprise and to the specific challenge at hand,
- ask these questions in a manner that encourages decision makers to think deeply about the rationales for their initial responses,
- engage all decision makers and encourage them to voice conflicting points of view, and
- listen carefully to responses to the questions and encourage others to do likewise.

The utilization of these skills and the passion Professor Rivkin brings to the learning process enable him to create an active learning environment in which he and his students are co-producers of the learning experience. As summarized by one student on *Quora*:

> Rivkin possesses a dedication to subject matter expertise and classroom engagement that keeps case discussions suspenseful, riveting, and thought provoking. Rivkin understands classroom dynamics, personalities, and how to meaningfully engage … dozens of students in each class.
>
> (What is the best class you've taken at HBS? 2012)

Professor Rivkin's unbridled enthusiasm bleeds into his work beyond the classroom, where he combines his research skills with a commitment to making America more competitive. This enthusiasm is based on an optimistic outlook that became apparent when I asked him about YALP:

> I'm sorry, but this is like asking someone, "How is your golf game" or "Tell me about your grandkids." I'll tell you more about this than you'll ever want to know. I've got to tell you that if you want to be optimistic about the future of America, turn off the news and spend a week in the classroom with these young leaders. You will feel like we are in good shape. We are going to be fine.

The country owes a debt of gratitude to talented individuals like Professor Rivkin for developing a new generation of leaders who will have a positive impact on society. His efforts inspire and encourage them to recognize the importance of improving the commons—the resources that benefit all Americans—so that people at all levels will be able to share in the country's prosperity.

References

A virtual welcome to the MBA class of 2022. (2020, September 3). Retrieved from YouTube: https://www.youtube.com/watch?v=U-3jgc_1jMU

Ben & Jerry's Home Ice Cream, Inc.: A period of transition, Harvard Business School Case 796-109 (January 1996).

Breaking news: FGI cancelled. (2019, April 1). *The Harbus*, p. 1.

Bridging the gap. (2019, December 1). Retrieved from Harvard Busines School: https://www.alumni.hbs.edu/stories/Pages/story-bulletin.aspx?num=7182

Christensen, R. (Ed.) (1992). Every student teaches and every teacher learns. In *Education for judgment* (pp. 99–119). Boston: Harvard Business Review Press.

HBS to remodel case discussion to replicate drunken arguments at bars. (2019, April 1). *The Harbus*, p. 2.

Inside the HBS case method. (2009, April 10). Retrieved from YouTube: https://www.youtube.com/watch?v=eA5R41F7d9Q

Introduction to the RC Strategy Course, Harvard Business School Course Overview Note 719-447 (December 2018). Retrieved from Harvard Business Review Store.

Leading the enerprise as an integrated whole. (n.d.). Retrieved from Harvard Business School: https://www.exed.hbs.edu/insights/advanced-management-program-jan-rivkin

Mayoral initiative heads for year two. (2018, July 20). Retrieved from The Harvard Gazette: https://news.harvard.edu/gazette/story/2018/07/bloomberg-program-at-kennedy-school-helps-mayors-govern-more-creatively-effectively/

Md. school has 2 science contest winners. (1984, January 25). Retrieved from The Washington Post: https://www.washingtonpost.com/archive/local/1984/01/25/md-school-has-2-science-contest-winners/65fd5f75-1f9c-4894-811a-a7da46df0ea4/

Newsroom. (2018, August 31). Retrieved from Harvard Business School: https://www.hbs.edu/news/articles/Pages/welcome-class-2020.aspx

Porter, M. E. & Rivkin, J. W. (2015, March 26). A wake-up call for tomorrow's top 1 percent. *Fortune.* Retrieved from https://fortune.com/2015/03/26/a-wake-up-call-for-tomorrows-top-1-percent-rebuild-americas-middle-class/

Porter, M. E. et al. (2016). *Problems unsolved and a nation divided.* Harvard Business School. Retrieved from https://www.hbs.edu/competitiveness/Documents/problems-unsolved-and-a-nation-divided.pdf

Rapoport, R. (2019). *Let's play two.* New York: Hachette Book Group.

Rivkin freaks out ECs. (2019, April 1). *The Harbus,* p. 3.

Schmitt, J. (2018, March 10). *B-schools with the best teaching faculty.* Retrieved from POETS&QUANTS: https://poetsandquants.com/2018/03/10/business-schools-with-the-best-teaching-faculty/

The HBS case method. (n.d.). Retrieved from Harvard Business School: https://www.hbs.edu/mba/academic-experience/Pages/the-hbs-case-method.aspx

What is the best class you've taken at HBS? (2012, November 24). Retrieved from Quora: https://www.quora.com/Harvard-Business-School/What-is-the-best-class-youve-taken-at-HBS

Chapter 10

Lessons for Leaders and Teachers

The Teaching Process and the Power of Authenticity

"What qualities do you value most in a professor?" I send this question to my University of Michigan students at the beginning of every course. When you think about a favorite teacher (or leader who has great teaching skills), how would you respond to my question?

The results from a most recent course are typical of responses I have received over the years. I taught two sections of the course Negotiation and Dispute Resolution, one to MBA students and one to undergraduates, during the 2019–2020 academic year. One hundred students enrolled in the two sections—fifty-eight undergraduate students and forty-two graduate students. They were from twelve countries, and the students from the United States were from sixteen states. Eighty-three students completed the questionnaire, which was voluntary.

As you might anticipate, most students focused their comments on course content and delivery. These students value professors who combine academic theory with real-life examples, establish clear expectations, provide timely feedback, use an interactive approach in the classroom, teach well-structured classes, present material that challenges them, are prepared for class, communicate clearly, are accessible outside of class, understand student needs, have a deep understanding of the course material, are open to questions, use clear and concise explanations, and provide practical suggestions.

What you might not expect—and what surprised me when I first used the questionnaire several years ago—are the large number of comments that mention qualities that are more elusive. Almost 60% of the students used these words when describing what they value most in a professor: authentic, empathetic, passionate, love of teaching, humility, interest in and respect for students, fair, transparent, enthusiastic, friendly, approachable, kind, lack of ego, curious, understanding, candid, energetic, patient, committed, available, and honest.

At first blush, it might appear that teachers (and leaders in their teaching role) need superhero powers to achieve these elusive qualities, not to mention the skills necessary for the effective development and delivery of course content. However, Chapters 3–9 contain abundant evidence that these qualities are attainable in courses that span a variety of disciplines in undergraduate, MBA, Executive MBA, and executive education programs.

Drawing on Chapters 3–9, this chapter first highlights how the professors profiled in this book manage the teaching process to achieve student expectations relating to course content and delivery. The chapter then, under the heading of "authenticity," turns to the more elusive qualities that—in the words of profound educator Parker Palmer—are more important than teaching techniques. In his essay titled "The Heart of a Teacher," Palmer observes (italics in the original) that this is the "secret hidden in plain sight: *good teaching cannot be reduced to technique: good teaching comes from the identity and integrity of the teacher*" (Palmer, n.d.).

These two sections—on the teaching process and authenticity—provide a menu of suggestions for teachers and for leaders in their teaching role. Not all the selections in the menu will be of interest to everyone, but I hope that at least a subset will enrich your experience as a teacher and leader.

The Teaching Process

Six themes relating to the teaching process emerge from the faculty profiles in Chapters 3–9.

"Prepare, Prepare, Prepare"

When asked about the advice he would give to a classroom teacher or a manager in a teaching role, Professor Shell's response was clear: "Prepare, prepare, prepare." While important for both new and experienced teachers, this advice is especially daunting for rookie professors, who must establish their research chops while at the same time achieving satisfactory performance in the classroom. What to do?

Although it might sound counterintuitive for rookies faced with tremendous pressure to publish their research within a limited time-frame, perhaps the best advice came from Professor Zettelmeyer, who recommended an overinvestment in teaching early on:

> If you want to maximize your research time until tenure, make sure you over-invest in teaching during your first year. ... It is very hard to dig yourself out of a poor teaching experience because your poor reputation becomes a self-fulfilling prophecy with the students and zaps you of your self-confidence.

Professor Kaplan agreed, noting,

> I recommend putting in extra work the first time that you teach to make yourself a better teacher. ... The first time you teach, you will be spending a lot of time anyway, which will take you somewhat away from your research. So you should go all in to develop these tools. This will pay dividends for a long time.

Preparation to become a teacher. Preparation is a double-edged sword. First, it is necessary to become an effective teacher, covered in this section. Second, preparation is required to design and deliver specific courses, covered in the next section.

The preparation process used by the seven professors to become effective teachers is characterized by their willingness to ask for help. Most of their schools provided very little teacher training in the past. As Professor Spreitzer noted, she had no training when, as a PhD student, she was asked to teach a Human Resources course. She was instructed to "just do it ... it was sink or swim." Even at Harvard Business School (HBS), which has had an orientation program for new faculty in place for many years, Professor Rivkin benefitted from asking legendary professor Michael Porter to observe him in class.

Two types of "asks" are especially important. First, ask an experienced professor for teaching advice. For example, Professor Lee asked colleague Carlton Griffin (former chair of the Board at Deloitte), "How do you do this? I don't think I am ready." The key piece of advice he received, by the way, was, "Charles, it's preparation, preparation."

Second, ask for an opportunity to observe experienced professors in class, but make this a two-way mirror by also asking them to observe you. Professor Lee summarized the benefits of sitting in on sessions taught by veteran professor David Wright:

> I started to realize that understanding accounting is really very different from teaching accounting. I knew the technical aspects of accounting, but I didn't know how to convey the material in a way that would matter to the students. Sitting in on Professor Wright's class was eye-opening.

When Professor Rivkin invited Michael Porter to sit in on his class, he learned some valuable lessons:

> He suggested that I put down my notes, which I was carrying around. He also mentioned that "Perhaps it would be useful if you do not appear to be in pain." This made me realize that I was not showing any joy in the classroom. I was not smiling.

Both Professor Rivkin and Professor Kaplan availed themselves of MBA courses while enrolled in the PhD program at Harvard. And Professors Kaplan and Shell benefited greatly from taking executive education courses.

The benefits from observing an outstanding teacher (or, in the business world, an outstanding leader) come with one important caveat mentioned by several of the professors: Be yourself. Do not try to imitate someone else's teaching style. As Professor Spreitzer noted:

> If I tried to be a Bob Quinn, I would be a pretty mediocre Bob Quinn. If I try to adopt the style of Jane Dutton, it wouldn't work. But I can observe pieces from each of them that I can use.

In a presentation to new faculty members, Professor Lee put it this way:

> I tell them that the intimidating part about watching good teachers is that you'll say, "I'll never be like that." You might not be able to be someone who starts each class with a joke or someone who walks into the room like a talk show host and interviews students. Maybe *you* can do this, but I can't. But it isn't necessary to imitate the style of another teacher.

In sharp contrast to the past, today the seven business schools where the professors teach offer teacher development opportunities for both rookie and experienced professors. Professor Zettelmeyer described four types of opportunities available at Northwestern Kellogg. First, anyone can sign up for a teaching coach, who will visit classes and provide feedback. Second, Kellogg assigns a senior faculty member who is a successful teacher as a mentor to rookie professors. The mentor provides advice about teaching concerns, reviews the course syllabus, and attends classes. Third, a Teaching Excellence Project schedules regular talks on issues relating to teaching. Finally, the school assigns junior faculty to courses that are team-taught so that they can benefit from the experience of having a senior faculty member on the team.

HBS uses teaching teams that include senior and junior faculty members and also has an orientation program called START, in which new faculty have an opportunity to discuss the case method, experience it from a student perspective, and practice case teaching.

Preparation to teach a course. The seven professors provided many useful suggestions relating to the design and delivery of a specific course.

a. *Think of the Course as a Story.* The teaching coach at Northwestern Kellogg trained as a theater director and actor. She uses the metaphor of teaching as theater, where the teacher takes on the role of a playwright in developing course content, as a director in organizing the class, and as an actor in delivering the material.

In developing and organizing the content, Professor Zettelmeyer uses a disciplined approach that he learned when working for the consulting firm McKinsey. The core idea, he explains in Chapter 7, is to use "the structure of slides to force yourself to be very systematic about generating the story you are telling and in uncovering the weaknesses in that story." In addition to its use in developing specific classes, this story structure could extend to an entire course. Professor Zettelmeyer realized that he "should tell a story in an arc that would span the whole semester."

Referring to a framework from Aristotle, Professor Lee observed that logos—that is, content development—"begins with the development of a central theme or idea for each lecture and for the course as a whole. This theme is akin to the trunk of a tree," with each lecture conveying the leaves and branches that can encompass that trunk.

b. *Identify Best Practices.* You do not have to reinvent the wheel when developing a new course. Try to find colleagues at your school or elsewhere who have taught courses similar to the one you are developing and seek their advice on best practices. For example, when developing her course titled "Navigating Change," Professor Spreitzer "went to people in the field whom I respected and who taught change. I asked them about the most powerful exercises, cases, readings, and modules they used."

c. *Develop Your Own Materials.* All the professors include their own cases in their course materials. This adds to their credibility when teaching the cases. For example, they can describe the origins of a case during class discussion. In a 2021 interview, Professor Rivkin mentioned that case writing is also a wonderful faculty development vehicle because it gets faculty members "out in the field, interacting with managers, figuring out what the biggest problems they face are, what the biggest challenges are" (Crafting, studying, and teaching strategy in a volatile world, 2021).

d. *Create a Detailed Game Plan.* As discussed later in this chapter, each professor uses a highly interactive approach in the classroom. This creates the risk that the discussion will go astray and that the key learning points of the class will not receive sufficient attention. One antidote to this is to develop a detailed plan for each session. Professor Shell, for example, walks

> into class with a one-page, minute-by-minute game plan of exactly what we are going to do, in what order, and how we are going to do it. The class may not always follow that flow, but it gives me a baseline I can go back to.

e. *Video recording your class.* The professors provided mixed advice on recording their own classes. Professor Rivkin noted that while recordings are sometimes useful, they also make him feel self-conscious: "One of my colleagues told me when I first started teaching that the secret of great teaching is to be 'very similar to yourself.' I've found that videotapes sometimes make me not be myself."

However, Professor Perakis finds the use of video recordings helpful in preparing for class. She blocks off time before class to watch herself teaching over multiple years while she asks, "How can I improve?" and "How can I answer questions better?" She also uses videos to identify areas where students are confused by the material. Her conclusion: "There was an improvement in the quality of my teaching after I started doing that [watching videos] around eight years ago." And Professor Kaplan was able to use recordings to identify "quirks" in his teaching: "I would talk with a cup of coffee in my mouth. I decided that I needed to stop doing that!"

f. *Prepare After Class.* In my own teaching, I find that the best time to prepare for a future class is immediately after finishing a class, while the experience is still fresh in mind. This practice was affirmed by Professor Perakis, who conducts a debrief immediately after class ends to determine what went well and what needs improvement. Using this information, she immediately begins to work on next year's class. And Professor Kaplan conducts a supplementary evaluation in which he asks students to rate his assigned cases. Using this information, he evaluates each case at the end of the term to decide which ones need rewriting or replacement.

Build a Learning Community

In her chapter in the book *Education for Judgment*, Laura Nash compares a good discussion class to raising a barn: "Everybody participates and contributes to the knowledge process, whatever his or her level of skill. People have to work together to get the job done." She concludes that "learning how to learn together [is] an important skill for any field requiring teamwork and complex analysis" and cites Plato's notion that truth can "be discovered only through the discourse of friends" (Nash, 1991, p. 231).

The seven professors use the following approaches to create learning communities where learning takes place through the "discourse of friends." Leaders of organizations who want to encourage teamwork can also use several of these approaches.

Match the classroom with the class size. Engaging students in the learning process can be difficult when teaching a small number of them in a large classroom. Recognizing the importance of what he calls "social energy" in establishing a community relationship among students, Professor Shell tries, whenever possible, to teach a packed classroom. He cites the philosophy of Italian physician and educator Maria Montessori, who started Montessori schools in which class sizes are larger than traditional classrooms.

Use frequent interaction with students. Professor Lee emphasized the importance of frequent interactions with students during and outside class. For example, he noted several guidelines for in-class interactions, including sharing your teaching philosophy with the class, establishing expectations through a learning contract, providing highlights from future lectures, and summarizing key concepts at the end of each class.

Professor Perakis offered several examples of interaction outside of class. Four days before each weekend class taught to her Executive MBA students, she emails them a reminder of administrative matters, such as how to access the slides for the class. After class, she sends a wrap-up email and solicits feedback on the class. She also arranges for her teaching assistants to provide a one-hour virtual presentation that summarizes the class.

Interacting with students when courses went online during the COVID-19 pandemic created new challenges—and opportunities. For example, Professor Kaplan noted that

> I met in small Zoom groups—5 or 6 students—for a breakfast or lunch with most of the students in my course. With 200 students, this meant 35 of these sessions. I found them very valuable in getting to know the students and showing the students that I was a person and not just a face on a screen.

Know your students' names and backgrounds. In an article in *The Chronicle of Higher Education*, veteran University of Kansas professor Carol Holstead notes one of the key lessons she has learned: "Show students you are invested in them, and they will feel a lot more invested in the work they do for your course." What makes them feel that a professor has invested in them? Here is the top response in a survey she conducted: "When the professor learned their names" (Holstead, 2019).

Learning student names in large classes is challenging. Professor Kaplan begins to memorize the names of the two hundred-plus students in his three sections early in September for a course that begins at the end of the month. This enables him to greet students using their first names when they enter class for the first time. As one former student noted, "On day one of class, Kaplan showed up having memorized everyone's names and random facts about our backgrounds."

Apart from showing students you have invested in them, knowing their names and backgrounds helps professors ease opening-day jitters. Professor Spreitzer uses LinkedIn to research her students. As a result,

> I feel that I know the students as human beings rather than just a name on a piece of paper. I also use LinkedIn to connect with them, and they realize that I am doing my homework. This pre-class connection with the students reduces the butterflies.

An additional benefit of her LinkedIn research is that she learns about the employment history of her students, which she uses when teaching a case involving companies where they have worked.

Decide whether to use cold calls or warm calls—and how to handle gunners. A cold call occurs when a professor calls on a student without advance warning. The most memorable example of cold calling was by the rude and arrogant Professor Kingsfield in the movie *The Paper Chase*, a portrayal for which actor John Houseman won an Oscar. A friend of mine who taught at the University of Michigan Law School once invited Houseman to his class without advance warning to his students. When Houseman walked to the front of the class in place of the professor, several students were terrified, thinking that they had crossed the line from reality into fiction.

Perhaps aware of the chilling effect of cold calling on the learning process, the professors profiled here use a kindlier version of cold calling, and balance cold calls with what they call "warm calls." As Professor Zettelmeyer put it, "In my case, I haven't benefited from being confrontational in the classroom. I do better in an environment where people feel welcome to speak up." Professor Spreitzer apparently agrees, as she uses cold calls for positive purposes to encourage students to participate in class discussions and to share their experiences that relate to cases under discussion.

Other professors soften the use of cold calls. Professor Perakis allows students to pass a question to another student, which she calls "Phone a Friend." Professor Rivkin gives students advance warning when he decides to call on them to open a class. And he allows them to pass if they have a great explanation for why they are not prepared because he would "rather not get the whole discussion off to a bad start."

One reason why professors do not use cold calling more is that there are so many student volunteers in courses where class participation is factored into their grades. Even Professor Kaplan, who is reputedly one of the toughest professors at Chicago Booth, uses cold calls selectively. As he puts it,

Because so much of the grade is class participation, plenty of students raise their hands. But I would use a cold call if someone has not spoken after the first two or three weeks of the course. After that, some of them start participating more. Others don't. If they want 40% of the grade to be an 'F,' that is their decision.

Enthusiastic student volunteers raise the question of how to handle "gunners"—students who attempt to dominate class discussion. Professor Rivkin observed that sometimes this situation is resolved when a gunner receives a "behavioral correction" from classmates. He also occasionally explains to a gunner after class that he wants to spread participation among the class and obtain a diversity of opinions. Professor Spreitzer sometimes interrupts a long-winded gunner by saying, "That's helpful. Let's pause for a second and get a different point of view."

Team assignments. Team assignments can be useful in building a learning community. However, these assignments are challenging when students in a course have different levels of experience. For example, Professor Lee's course mixes students with significant investing experience with those he calls "newbies." His solution is to use both individual assignments, where students can build on their various levels of experience, and team assignments where he uses an "adopt a newbie" policy to create teams where at least one-third of each team must be newbies.

Co-create the learning experience. Building a learning community encourages students to participate in the design and delivery of courses. An example is the session on "Gratitude" in Professor Spreitzer's course. Gratitude was the topic of choice from the prior year's class. Her development of a session on this topic uncovered a rich vein of academic research and business experience that resulted in resources and tools for students to use after graduation.

Professor Perakis used feedback that students provided after each session to make immediate improvements in course design. In the course I attended, she used their feedback to make mid-course changes in the website and in the way she summarized material. As one student noted, "She surveys the class and discusses how she will revise her approach based on the results."

When teaching the course, Professor Perakis and others encourage students to share their experiences, using questions such as, "Did you find this to be true?" She also asked for suggestions from the class ("Who wants to help me?") when attempting to help a confused student. When several students responded with explanations that enabled the student to better understand the material, she thanked them for providing an alternative pedagogical approach.

Emphasize the Big Picture

Our seven professors are adept at emphasizing the big picture. Professor Rivkin began the session I attended by reminding students where they were in the course through a review of the five course modules. He then kicked off discussion with a big-picture question: Is the role of a strategist like the CEO to design a strategy or to design an organization that can develop strategy?

In a similar approach, Professor Perakis reminded her students of the broad framework of the course, which moved from data to models to decisions. She depicted the framework on a slide that included each of these three elements in a box and observed with a smile, "By now you are probably sick of these boxes." Throughout the session, she continued to emphasize the big picture: "The way I see your job, you are leaders, not coders."

There are three specific "big-picture" elements to keep in mind.

Go beyond your course when discussing the big picture. Encourage students to think beyond the boundaries of the course. Professor Perakis reminds her students of how her course relates to other courses in the Executive MBA program. Professor Lee takes care to mention current research he is working on, even when it does not relate specifically to the course topics.

Other professors occasionally inject broad philosophical questions into their courses. Professor Shell at one point asked the class, "What is ownership?" This led to a debate that focused on the role of property rights in a capitalist society. Professor Zettelmeyer asked his class, "Are you in the business of making customers happy?" Though the question initially produced puzzled looks, the participants soon realized how it related to analytics.

Review material from prior sessions. The professors used different approaches when reviewing material from earlier sessions. In Professor Spreitzer's course on thriving in the new world of work, a speaker in the prior session (a recent graduate who was not much older than students in the class) discussed the coping strategies he used after he was blindsided by a layoff. Framing the review of the prior session as a "Gift of Feedback" to the speaker, she encouraged students to think about how they would handle a layoff early in their careers.

Professor Perakis provided a detailed refresher of earlier coverage of linear optimization before moving on to the topic for the day—discrete optimization. In her refresher, she started with simple examples that students could solve intuitively before moving to more complex situations.

Professor Shell used a novel approach when he asked two students who were taking the course, designated as "TAs-for-the-day" (volunteer teaching assistants), to summarize the prior class. In doing so, they developed a sophisticated 360-degree perspective of the material that, in addition to providing continuity from one class to the next, provided him with feedback on how students were processing the material.

Provide an end-of-class summary. The professors differed in their opinions about end-of-session reviews. Professor Rivkin, cognizant that case-based courses like those at HBS are difficult to summarize because there are often no right or wrong answers, closed the class on the assigned Ben & Jerry's case by showing video clips of the company's CEO. In the clips, the CEO provided an insider's perspective on his experience. However, Professor Kaplan, also trained at HBS, used a different approach by taking a few minutes at the end of class to explain the key learning points from the case, including the strategic rationale for an acquisition, the parties' incentives, valuation methods, and implementation concerns.

"Simplify, Simplify"

Henry David Thoreau's plea in *Walden* to "simplify, simplify" is valuable advice for teachers and business leaders. The dilemma is that, while complexity enriches course content, too much complexity impedes learning. As Albert Einstein noted, "Everything should be made as simple as possible, but not simpler" (In honor of Albert Einstein's birthday, n.d.). Reducing complexity can be a special challenge for rookie professors, who are too often tempted to teach the last thing they learned in a PhD program as the first thing in an introductory course.

Professor Lee cited Oliver Wendell Holmes when describing this dilemma:

> Simplicity does not mean being shallow in covering the material. Instead, it requires what Oliver Wendell Holmes called "the simplicity on the other side of complexity." This is a simplicity that arises from understanding the material so completely that you are able to simplify it for others to learn.

Stated another way by Professor Perakis, the goal

> is to try to see how I can go from the complex model to a simple model. If it's too simple, I will not capture the real complex problem, so I have to find where to be in the middle.

Attempting to learn from someone who uses unduly complex explanations can be a challenging experience even for professors as talented as the ones profiled in this book. When he was a PhD student, as a result of an encounter with a famous professor who was especially confusing,

Professor Zettelmeyer was intimidated and thought that he might be an admissions error. After learning that the professor was indeed a bad teacher, Professor Zettelmeyer developed the confidence to state, "I don't get it. Could you please explain?"

Here are some approaches to simplification mentioned in Chapters 3–9.

Use visualization. Influenced by designers, visualization is becoming more popular in the business world, where it is even used to improve wordy contracts and other legal documents. The professors' PowerPoint slides included many examples of visualization, such as Professor Zettelmeyer's causality checklist, which he recommended that participants should "laminate, print, and put over your desk." However, visualizations were also more informal, as when Professor Kaplan diagrammed on the board the relationship between Viacom and Paramount when discussing revenue and cost synergies that might result if they combined.

Use a clear framework to guide discussion. Although Professor Rivkin raised questions that had no clear answer, he was able to provide students with a clear framework for analyzing these questions. Using this framework enabled them to clarify their thoughts about a company's strategic objective, the scope of its advantages (relating to customers, products, etc.), and decisions relating to human resources, technology development, procurement, and so on.

Consider using "cheat sheets." Moving into the third hour in a session on the difficult topic of discrete optimization (in a course considered to be the most challenging in the MIT Sloan Executive MBA program), Professor Perakis found it useful to provide students with comfort food in the form of "cheat sheets." These sheets gave them simpler, more intuitive ways to consider the data.

Use everyday language. Professor Lee was especially adept at using everyday language to explain complex concepts. For example, he used a "can opener" analogy to explain an assumption of investment success that raises complex questions. He also noted that a beta approach to investing is cheap, like orange juice, because investors can simply invest in a low-cost mutual fund, while an alpha approach (based on a forecast of a stock's potential to appreciate) is more expensive, like vodka.

Slow the pace. Professor Lee also uses two approaches that, while not exactly examples of simplification, do help students understand the material by slowing the pace. First, he assigns pre-class recorded lectures in which he explains background material. Having access to the videos enables students to slow down the speed and watch the lectures more than once, both of which are especially useful when English is not their first language. Second, when taping the lectures he writes comments in the margin of his slides, which sets a measured pace for students to take notes. He also used this approach in class.

Make the Learning as Interactive as Possible

Influential educational reformer John Dewey once observed, "Only in education, never in the life of a farmer, sailor, merchant, physician, or laboratory experimenter, does knowledge mean primarily a store of information aloof from doing" (Dewey, 1922, p. 218). According to studies mentioned by David Garvin in *Education for Judgment*, in a traditional classroom, teachers spend as much as 80% of the time "telling" (Garvin, 1991, p. 3).

The "aloof from doing" and "telling" model has at least two potentially negative consequences. First, this model might encourage a performance mentality, especially among new professors. As noted by Jane Tompkins (1996) in *A Life in School*:

> What I had actually been concerned with was showing the students how smart I was, how knowledgeable I was, and how well prepared I was for class. I had been putting on a performance whose true goal was not to help the students learn, as I had thought, but to perform before them in such a way that they would have a good opinion of me.
> (p. 119)

Second, the "telling" model might lead, at least in professional education, to an overemphasis on what Donald Schon (1987) has called the "high ground" in an essay reprinted in *Teaching and the Case Method*:

> On the high ground, manageable problems lend themselves to solution through the use of research-based theory and technique. In the swampy lowlands, problems are messy and confusing and incapable of technical solution. The irony of this situation is that the problems of the high ground tend to be relatively unimportant to individuals or to society at large—however great their technical interest may be—while in the swamp lie the problems of greatest human concern.
> (p. 246)

While a performance mentality and overemphasis on the high ground are possible even in classrooms that are highly interactive, the professors highlighted in this book use a variety of interactive approaches to focus the spotlight on their students' engagement rather than on their own "performances" and to balance the high ground with the realities of the swamp. As Professor Shell describes his belief in student engagement,

> Overall, my teaching philosophy closely tracks a Chinese Confucian aphorism: "Tell me and I'll forget, show me and I might remember, involve me and I will learn." ... I follow this rule of thumb: every moment students are engaged by participation is good.

Here are some approaches to encourage active participation by students in the learning process.

Use a variety of learning experiences. Professor Spreitzer uses a variety of experiences to prevent becoming what she calls a "talking head":

> I try to break [the class] up into several different parts—some parts lecture, some parts group discussion, some parts that use an exercise so that students do something active and I am not a talking head. I walk into class with the times all plotted out.

Flip the learning experience. In a traditional class, professors use the classroom to provide content to students via lectures, and students engage in active learning through homework assignments outside of class. With a flipped classroom, professors provide more content outside of class—for example, through recorded lectures—and this increases the time available for active learning in class.

Professor Lee used a formal flipped classroom model. As noted previously, the class I observed was preceded by a forty-minute recorded lecture that provided background information and enabled him to devote more class time to active learning. As he described his use of a flipped classroom:

> For me, the preparation for class is really making sure I am delivering something that is alive and hot instead of something heated up in a microwave. ... So I figured out that if I outsourced some material to the pre-class videos, then I can do other things in class that are more live and keep me in the moment.

Although they did not use a formal version of a flipped classroom with pre-class videos, the other professors engaged their students in active learning. Professor Rivkin noted, "There are certain educational institutions where the faculty largely produce the experience and the students largely consume it. That is not what happens in our classrooms." He contrasted the "lean forward" model with the traditional "lean back" approach where students are passive learners, noting that if you are a student in a "lean forward" classroom,

> [y]ou're raising your hand and getting called on. You're speaking and trying to draw others to your point of view. You're deciding whether what others are saying is persuasive. You're deciding what you would do as a case protagonist. And then you're reflecting on what you learn. Throughout this, you are thinking for yourself. You're an active learner—and that makes all the difference, I believe. ...
>
> (Schmitt, 2018)

Decide whether and how to factor class participation into the course grade. On the high end among the seven professors, Professor Rivkin bases 50% of the grade on class participation, which is common at HBS. A "scribe" in his course keeps track of student participation. After the scribe enters this data, software enables Professor Rivkin to analyze not only the level of participation but also whether he is favoring a certain part of the class, such as the right-hand versus the left-hand side of the classroom or the top rows versus the bottom rows.

Professor Kaplan also allocates a high percentage of the grade to class participation. After each class, he reviews student performance. Students who did not talk in class receive a zero, while others receive a grade ranging from one to ten. Professor Shell uses a Peer Rating system where students can confidentially indicate whether participation by their peers enhanced or reduced the value of the course.

Be creative in developing new models of active learning. Professor Spreitzer was especially creative in developing active learning exercises related to gratitude, the topic in the class I attended. For example, at one point she asked students to express gratitude to others by immediately sending them a text or email. At the end of class, she asked students to share the replies they received. The replies—for example, "made my day" and a return expression of gratitude—illustrated the power and importance of expressing gratitude. She also gave students time to write journal entries on the best expression of gratitude they had ever received and on an expression of gratitude that did not work. She used the results when discussing current research on gratitude.

Professor Shell has developed a unique "call and response" technique to help students internalize the elements necessary for the legal analysis of a business opportunity or challenge. Through this approach, he imprinted in his students the sequential analysis that lawyers use when providing advice on legal aspects of business decision making.

Extend active learning beyond the classroom. Students especially appreciate the willingness of professors to work with them one-on-one after class. In every classroom I visited, students swarmed the professors during breaks and after class. The professors also conveyed to students their interest in working with them during office hours. As Professor Kaplan noted on his syllabus, "I enjoy talking with students. I am happy to talk about the course, your career, current events, etc." According to one of his former students, he is serious about this commitment: "As intimidating as he may appear in the classroom, he made time to meet with students to go over concepts or discuss their career interests and business ideas."

Professor Rivkin kiddingly observed that "one of my students once told me, 'the problem, Rivkin, is not getting into your office; the problem is getting out.' I think he meant that as a compliment; at least, I decided to take it that way." Professor Rivkin also, in effect, offers lifelong office hours:

> I love it when my students stay in touch, and I adore watching how their careers and their lives unfold. I get about an email a day from a former student. In fact, as we are speaking [by phone], one just popped up. It's often my favorite email of the day. Sometimes it's just an update on how they are doing, sometimes they've got a strategy issue, sometimes they are just keeping me abreast of what's going on or letting me know when they are passing through town and want to get together.

Ask small teams to work on active learning projects during class. Several of the professors incorporated small-team assignments into class. For example, both Professors Shell and Zettelmeyer asked small teams to discuss short cases that they wrote. These discussions energized the students.

Develop your ability to ask questions and to listen carefully to the answers. Especially important among the skills necessary to run an interactive class are the abilities to ask questions and listen carefully to the responses—two skills that stand in contrast to the "telling" skills noted previously. Listening is a special challenge because it involves complex multitasking, as described by Chris Christensen:

> You're listening to a comment about geographically decentralized companies, and you have to recall and link it to previous points made by individuals using particular words. At the same time, you're thinking about your next decision, the next person to call on. You have to determine if the discussion is building a path and whether it connects to a path that was built last week. And all this time, you have to listen to the comment as intently as you can.
>
> (Maas, 1991)

Several of the professors used what is known as "active listening." For example, Professor Spreitzer summarizes student comments to make sure that she has understood them correctly. She also encourages their comments through non-confrontational, supportive statements such as, "I think you are on to something, but I want you to take one more step."

Professor Lee was also positive in responding to comments, even when they missed the mark, by saying, "That's a pretty good guess." His listening skills were evident when he referred to comments made by students in earlier classes.

The professors were also adept at following up a student's answer with another question. For example, when a student commented that a company was a takeover target because it was undermanaged, Professor Kaplan used questions to elicit how the student had reached this conclusion. And Professor Perakis patiently attempted to clarify student comments by asking, "Excuse me, I am being slow. Why are you raising this question?" She, like other professors, did not provide quick solutions when students were off the mark, but instead (perhaps reflecting her Greek origins) used the Socratic method to let the discussion flow until they reached their own conclusions. Even during the COVID-19 pandemic when her course went online, use of the Zoom chat function encouraged class participation by shy students.

Active listening involves more than listening to comments, as illustrated by Professor Rivkin's remark on body language: "Pete, you look skeptical. Why?" His overall listening skills served as a model for students, who listened intently to comments made by their classmates.

Emphasize Why the Course Is Important

When discussing the importance of course content development, Professor Lee emphasized,

> You want students to see why the course is important to them. I once heard that the main goal of teaching is not to feed students but to make them hungry. When we dump everything from our brain into their brain, that's not teaching. Teaching is asking them to look at the world and say, "Isn't that cool? And why is it cool? Why is it like that?"

Professor Shell agreed and mentioned William James, the "Father of American Psychology," who emphasized the importance of motivating students by gaining their attention and then directing them to what is important.

The professors used a number of approaches to emphasize why their courses are important.

Open the class with a discussion of why the material is important. Professor Zettelmeyer opened class with a discussion of why analytics is important to business leaders who, as "consumers of analytics ... [must be able] to distinguish between good and bad analytics." Professor Shell opened his class with a review of the day's *Wall Street Journal*, which included numerous features on why it is important for business leaders to understand legal concepts.

Use real-life examples and stories. Students in my pre-course surveys especially value a professor's ability to provide examples, and Professor Lee explained an important reason why:

> The examples, to some extent, are more important than the structure because you can find the structure in many places, but it's the

examples that bring it to life. ... So you spend a lot of time gathering good illustrations. I *lovingly* collect them.

Professor Shell added that "nobody learns anything except on the foundation of what they already know. So your selection of examples, images, stories, and metaphors is crucial."

The professors used examples from a variety of sources that include their own research and their own experiences with business leaders. They also used examples provided by colleagues, such as Professor Spreitzer's description of a retreat that her colleagues from the Center for Positive Organizations conducted for the University of Michigan basketball coaches and team at the beginning of a season in which they later played in the national championship game.

All the professors mined the experiences of their students and related these to in-class discussion and current research. As Professor Shell noted, some of "the most powerful moments in class come from these stories of conflicts at work, with family, in a particular culture, and so on. After they have shared their experiences, we tie the stories to the course themes." Sometimes professors bake student experiences into class assignments, as when Professor Perakis assigned team projects based on challenges that team members faced at work.

If you cannot find useful examples from your own experience and research, from your colleagues, or from your students, you should question whether the topic needs to be in the course at all, noted Professor Zettelmeyer. He mentioned the experience of his wife (who is also a professor at Northwestern Kellogg) in teaching the income substitution effect in a microeconomics course. When she could not provide an example of what the effect was useful for, she eliminated it from the course.

Professor Shell noted a couple of caveats about using examples. First, make sure that you understand your audience: "Don't use a sports example in a class where students are unfamiliar with that sport. Think about your audience's common experience and then seek examples, stories, and images they can identify with." Second, he noted, "uncontrolled use of [student] stories might be risky." But he felt that this risk is worthwhile because of the importance of encouraging a truthful sharing of their life experiences.

Keep students focused on how they will use the learning. Professor Zettelmeyer, for example, provided participants in his Executive Education course with notebooks that included pages for each session labeled "Key Concepts," "Plans for Action," and "Thoughts for Evaluation." The notebooks caused the participants to reflect daily on the value of the learning and to think about how they would apply the learning after returning to their organizations.

Invite visitors who can share their real-world experiences. Professor Kaplan invited a prominent corporate attorney to class. He sat in the first row and provided candid, unscripted answers to student questions such as, "Does anyone do this type of valuation?"

Authenticity

Chapters 3–9 contain abundant examples of the six key themes relating to the teaching process that are used by the extraordinary professors profiled in this book. But the profiles of these professors evidence something greater than mere teaching skills. To repeat the words of Parker Palmer from earlier in this chapter, "[G]ood teaching cannot be reduced to technique: *good teaching comes from the identity and integrity of the teacher*" (Palmer, n.d.). In other words, a sound teaching process is necessary for great teaching, but on its own is not sufficient. In addition, great teachers exhibit an identity and integrity that are best captured in the word "authenticity."

What is authenticity? The quality of authenticity is based on being "authentic," which is defined by Merriam-Webster as "based on fact," "not false," and "true to one's own personality, spirit, or character" (Authentic, n.d.). However, these definitions are vague, and the word might have different connotations depending on whether the subject is business, psychology, leadership, philosophy, food, history, art, music, biology, or basketball shoes. Given this definitional challenge, I will fall back on US Supreme Court Justice Potter Stewart's oft-cited expression: "I know it when I see it" (Jacobellis v. Ohio, 1964) by using examples to illustrate what the word might mean in the teaching context. I hope that these examples will be useful in measuring your own authenticity, regardless of whether you are the leader of an organization or a traditional classroom instructor.

You might notice that "content expertise" is missing from the examples of authenticity that follow. While the seven profiled professors are certainly experts in their respective fields, many other teachers with similar expertise lack authenticity. As education professor Selma Wasserman (1987) put it bluntly (in an essay reproduced in *Teaching and the Case Method*), a teacher "who has acquired knowledge, but behaves in ways that are churlish, hostile, or morally repugnant does not earn our esteem." An admired teacher, on the other hand, has "a consistency about him that is clearly observable … [a consistency] between what he says and what he does. Some call this congruence—the quality of authenticity. He is no phony" (p. 181).

In another comment from *Teaching and the Case Method*, education professor Neil Postman notes that "one simple fact" is most important in education: "[W]hen a student perceives a teacher to be an authentic, warm, and curious person, the student learns. When the student does not perceive the teacher as such a person, the student does not learn" (Ginott, p. 84). As Chris Christensen reminds us in *Education for Judgment*, "[M]ost students want to know how much you care before they care how much you know" (p. 111).

The examples of authenticity from the profiles of the seven professors fall within three clusters: passion for the material and concern for students, dedication to continuous learning, and a higher purpose that has a positive impact beyond the classroom.

Passion for the Material and Concern for Students: Pathos and Ethos

At the outset of my research, I anticipated that these award-winning professors would be entertainers, with a flair for drama and humor. What I discovered instead was that they are best characterized by the intersection of passion for their material and concern for their students. In short, they love both their subject matter and their students. Professor Lee used the Aristotelian concept of "pathos" to describe passion for the material, which he concluded is a key element in motivating students. In his words, if "you are not excited about what you are doing and you cannot see a reason for it, there is not a chance that you are going to succeed as a teacher."

He notes that another important element in the Aristotelian framework is "ethos," which he considers to be

> the speaker's character as determined by the perceived concern the speaker has for the well-being of the students. Does it really matter to you who they are and how their life is going? Are they important to you? If you get this one right, everything else follows along. ... The key takeaway is to love your subject and love your students.

Professor Perakis put it more simply in an email in which she asked for extra time to respond to one of my requests: "I know ... I work all the time. But I do LOVE my job and the students!!!"

Like Professor Perakis, the other professors exhibited their love for both their subjects and students. Professor Rivkin is so enthusiastic about this duality that on teaching days he always passes the "Snooze Alarm Test" by waking up before his alarm rings. As he enters the classroom, he thinks to himself that this is "going to be the best part of the day." Professor Zettelmeyer also passes the test. As he stated to his class at the end of the session I attended, "Can you imagine someone like me getting so excited about analytics? This is about how you learn what is true in the world!"

The professors' strong concern for and interest in their students is illustrated by many examples from the Teaching Process section of this chapter. These examples include intense preparation, warm greetings to students as they enter the classroom, attempting to build a learning community, an interactive learning process that extends beyond the classroom, co-creation of courses with students, and active listening. In the words of Professor Rivkin, "Investing in students means knowing their backgrounds before class begins and being diligent in preparation for class; it means spending time with them when they have questions or thoughts afterward." Professor Spreitzer's advice for rookie professors is: "Try to love your students. Look for the bright spots. Try to see the best in them as learners and future leaders."

Although the wellspring of the professors' love for their subject matter and students is subject to speculation, it is clear that they all have a strong sense of self. As Parker Palmer notes in the *Change* article cited earlier, "[W]e teach who we are." While teachers use a variety of techniques, "good teachers share one trait: a strong sense of personal identity infuses their work" (Palmer, n.d.). Professors Shell and Spreitzer both quoted Apple's co-founder Steve Jobs, who died of pancreatic cancer at the age of fifty-six: "Your time is limited, so don't waste it living someone else's life. ... And, most important, have the courage to follow your heart and intuition. They somehow already know what you truly want to become" (You've got to find what you love, Jobs says, 2005)

Professor Spreitzer elaborated on this in a speech she gave at a University of Michigan graduation ceremony. Great teachers, she concluded, find meaning in their everyday work. Aware of the difference between what David Brooks calls "resume virtues" and "eulogy virtues," they "keep their hearts open" through interest in their students that extends beyond the classroom. And great teachers "find their own path" while avoiding, in the words of Steve Jobs, letting "the noise of others' opinions drown out your own inner voice" (Spreitzer, 2015).

Dedication to Continuous Learning

One of the strongest commonalities shared by the seven professors is their love of learning. They are lifelong students. As Professor Perakis put it, "I love MIT because as a professor I keep being a student." They manifest their enthusiasm for learning—an important aspect of their authenticity and credibility—in two ways: in class (where they learn from students) and through their research.

Learning from students. The professors treat classrooms as laboratories for learning where, in the words of John Bonsignore, teaching lies "at the edge of understanding rather than safely within zones where there is confidence" (Bonsignore et al., 1996). In these laboratories, their students play a teaching role. As Professor Rivkin put it: "[My] students have been generous in reinforcing good things, they have been tactful but clear in telling me what wasn't working, and they have been incredibly generous and patient in being good teachers." He agrees wholeheartedly with the title of a chapter by Chris Christensen in *Education for Judgment*: "Every Student Teaches and Every Teacher Learns" (Christensen, 1991).

Professor Rivkin elaborated on why the teaching role played by students is so important:

> They help you understand the nature of business. They help you understand what knowledge you are creating is helpful for them and what knowledge you are creating is not. They continue to be in touch with you, so you get to learn about the life of a businessperson, and they open doors for you when they are in positions to do so.

One of the reasons that he and other professors dislike grading, he adds, is that "it is mind-numbing. And there is very little learning going on by anyone at that point."

I have encountered professors who complain that they become bored when required to teach the same course year after year. But when the classroom becomes a learning experience for professors as well as students, that boredom vanishes, and a concomitant opportunity to improve the course appears. As Professor Zettelmeyer put it: "The process of repeating the course made an enormous difference in my ability to get the course right. I would make improvements from year to year by writing down in great detail what worked and what didn't work."

Learning from research. Their research interests and productivity, along with the honors they have received for the high quality of their publications, evidence the seven professors' love of learning. Their research skills are an important factor in classroom success because business school courses, unlike those offered by commercial providers with little or no research capability, benefit from research that looks beyond current practices. The synergy between research and teaching is multifaceted and characterized by the following elements:

a. *Preparing teaching material for use in the classroom.* All seven professors have written case studies and other materials designed for use in class. While not considered traditional academic research, this pedagogical research can play an influential role in business school education. Not surprisingly, given his position in the home of the case method, HBS Professor Rivkin is an especially prolific case writer. At last count, he has written over eighty cases and teaching notes, and in 2017–2018 he was named one of the bestselling case authors. His oeuvre reflects the fact that the development of cases for use at other business schools is an important part of the HBS mission. When making tenure decisions, for instance, Harvard looks at a candidate's impact on three audiences—managers, educators, and scholars—and Professor Rivkin notes that the impact on educators "involves producing teaching material that shapes how others think about problems and how they teach about those problems."

b. *Using academic research in the classroom.* The professors assign their own research in their classes. Sometimes it relates to only a few of the issues covered in a course, while in other courses there might be significant overlap between their academic research and the course content. Professor Kaplan observed that

> virtually every paper I write is of interest to both academics and practitioners. If research isn't relevant, why do it? So my research is about private equity and venture capital, and when I do that research, I immediately teach it to the MBAs, along with other people's research.

Professor Spreitzer publishes companion pieces that are useful for class assignments: "When I publish my research in an academic journal, I often try to publish a companion piece in a journal that is more accessible to the business community like the *Harvard Business Review* or the *Sloan Management Review.*"

Professor Lee finds that "my research and teaching are very synergistic, so I can apply findings from my papers when I show students how to predict stock returns, etc." However, he occasionally will also "briefly share with students some research I am working on that doesn't have anything to do with our class but that I think is exciting." When he started doing this while teaching at Michigan Ross, he told his students that

> one of the reasons you pay high tuition to attend a leading MBA program is that professors are doing research most of the time. It would be a waste of your money if you left the program without knowing about our research.

c. *Using the classroom experience to develop research ideas.* This theme is best illustrated by Professor Shell's comment: "I think of myself as a teacher who writes. This is not a part of our common identity in academic life. My books have all been about courses I have taught. Teaching is my source code."

Professor Spreitzer elaborated on teaching as a source of research: "I like learning from the students. Sometimes I have not thought about some of the questions that students raise or the insights that they bring to the classroom and their questions might stimulate a research idea." Professor Kaplan noted that because of his course on entrepreneurial finance, he "ended up doing research on venture capital, and one of the papers that came out of the teaching is one of my most cited papers, which Oliver Hart mentioned in his Nobel Prize lecture."

In addition to generating research ideas, classrooms provide laboratories for testing them. Professor Rivkin noted that "we are incredibly blessed in that if we have an idea, we can go into an MBA (or executive education) classroom and test it with ninety really smart individuals who have business experience."

d. *Course design and the research mindset.* An often-overlooked benefit of research is that it can provide a methodology for deciding what to include in a course. As Professor Zettelmeyer put it, "The research methodology and what I have learned over the years about how to do research are hugely influential in understanding what to teach." Having a research mindset is also useful in being able to evaluate and select articles from research produced by others for student assignments.

A Higher Purpose That Has a Positive Impact Beyond the Classroom

In recent years, there has been increasing interest in the impact that business schools have in improving organizations and society. The Association to Advance Collegiate Schools of Business (AACSB International) is the world's leading business school accreditation organization, accrediting only the top 5% of the world's business schools. The introduction to AACSB accreditation standards emphasizes that "business schools are a force for good, contributing to the world's economy and to society" (2020 guiding principles and standards for business accreditation, 2020).

The professors profiled in this book provide many examples of the positive impact on society that is encouraged by the AACSB. They manifest this impact in their classrooms, as described previously in the section on the teaching process. But their authenticity is also a product of a sense of purpose that extends well beyond the classroom and that benefits future leaders, organizations, and society at large. Here are some examples.

The Veritas Forum. Professor Lee is the faculty sponsor of the Veritas Forum at Stanford, which encourages students to think about, in his words, the questions a security guard might ask "when he sees you late at night: 'Who are you? What are you doing here? Where are you going?'" In forums at Harvard, Berkeley, Brown, Cornell, and elsewhere,

Professor Lee has engaged in dialog with university leaders to encourage students to think about these questions.

The Purpose, Passion, and Principles Program. Professor Shell co-founded and serves as the faculty advisor of the "Purpose, Passion, and Principles" (P3) Program at Wharton. During this eight-week, student-run program, students reflect on how they define success and happiness. As one student noted, "At a crossroads in my life, P3 has proven to be an important forum to slow down for introspection, to reflect on my values, to recalibrate my compass, and to anchor my actions with integrity" (P3: Purpose, passion, and principles at Wharton).

The New Venture Challenge. Professor Kaplan started the "Edward L. Kaplan, '71, New Venture Challenge," which enables students at Chicago Booth to develop business plans and receive funding for their startup companies. According to the Challenge website, the program has resulted in "more than 330 startup companies and created thousands of jobs for the economy" (Edward L. Kaplan, '71, New Venture Challenge, n.d.).

Center for Positive Organizations. In recent years, a new management research field has emerged, called "Positive Organizational Scholarship." According to the Center for Positive Organizations, this field focuses on the creation of positive work environments that enable leaders to "enhance engagement and performance and inspire their employees to innovate, find opportunity, and strive for excellence" (Positive organizational scholarship, n.d.). Professor Spreitzer has played a leadership role in the field through her service as co-director of the Center, her publications, and her advancement of positive leadership principles in her work with business leaders.

Program on Data Analytics. Concerned that business schools were not doing enough to educate MBA students and business leaders about analytics, Professor Zettelmeyer agreed to serve as director of a new program on data analytics. Armed with a firm belief that understanding this area is a leadership issue, he reached out to the business community by developing a series of lectures that evolved into one of the most popular executive programs in the world. In his words, "At its core, analytics is a leadership problem. The hardest part of making analytics work is not the data science or technology. All the major challenges are ones that leaders must solve" (Data analytics at Kellogg, n.d.).

Leaders for Global Operations Program. Professor Perakis has served in many leadership roles at MIT Sloan, but her work as Faculty Co-Director of the Leaders for Global Operations (LGO) program perhaps best symbolizes her passion for blending teaching and research with the real-life problems faced by companies. When the LGO program received the George Smith Prize from INFORMS, the selection committee noted that the program "was created to bring about a renaissance in US manufacturing" and that it had succeeded in developing "a generation of leaders who are adept in their craft and are innovating their operations" (Waugh, n.d.). Professor Perakis summarized her mantra in a 2017 talk to Sloan graduates: "Have **an impact**" (her emphasis) (Faculty session, 2017).

The US Competitiveness Project. With Co-Chair Michael Porter, Professor Rivkin leads the US Competitiveness Project, which is designed to "improve the competitiveness of the United States—that is, the ability of firms operating in the US to compete successfully in the global economy while supporting high and rising living standards for Americans" (U.S. competitiveness, n.d.). He also plays an active role in the Young American Leaders Program—an offshoot of the Competitiveness Project that provides next-generation leaders with the tools they need to develop the cross-sector collaboration that is required to enable people across all segments to share in the country's prosperity.

These high-impact activities bring to mind the words ascribed to aviator and author Antoine de Saint-Exupery: "If you want to build a ship, don't drum up people to collect wood and don't assign them tasks and work, but rather teach them to long for the endless immensity of the sea" (BookBrowse's favorite quotes, n.d.). Through the positive impact of their work, the seven professors serve as role models, inspiring their students to consider goals that extend beyond developing skills for business success and that reflect the need for business leaders to address societal challenges not unlike "the endless immensity of the sea."

Conclusion

As a result of their authenticity—measured by their passion for the material they teach, concern for their students, love of learning, and engagement in high-impact activities that extend beyond the classroom—the seven professors profiled in this book serve as role models for their students. Recent years have witnessed an increase in the number of business education programs offered by commercial organizations that hire practitioners to teach their courses. Practitioners have a tendency to emphasize current practices—in effect, using de Saint-Exupery's words, how to "drum up people to collect wood" and how to "assign them tasks." These seven professors move beyond current practice in both their teaching and actions. In the words of one student, Professor Spreitzer "exemplifies the transformative leader and is a teacher of good people, not just good students." Professor Shell, says another student, is one of "those rare people you meet who appears to walk the talk."

An underlying trait shared by these professors is a sense of empowerment. As noted in Chapter 6, Professor Spreitzer, one of the world's leading experts on the subject, has identified four dimensions that define empowered individuals. These dimensions are especially applicable to the seven professors profiled here:

- *Sense of Meaning*: Driven by their sense of meaning, they are passionate about their initiatives that benefit students, organizations, and society.
- *Sense of Competence*: Although they are all modest, through creativity and hard work in preparing to teach, they have developed extraordinary teaching skills. Confidence in their proven abilities has resulted in their appointment to leadership positions at their respective universities.
- *Sense of Self-Determination*: They have the freedom to propose and develop courses that they feel are the most important to their students. Administrators at their schools do not micromanage their decisions; on the contrary, the seven professors receive strong support for their innovations.
- *Sense of Impact*: As discussed in the prior section, the impact of their work extends well beyond the classroom.

The empowerment exhibited by these professors can have a ripple effect that results in the empowerment of students. Teachers can empower students even in organizations where empowerment is not encouraged. Professor Spreitzer uses a clip from *Dead Poets Society* to illustrate this. In that film, John Keating (played by Robin Williams) is a new English teacher at conformity-bound Welton Academy. Despite the oppressive environment at Welton, he empowers himself to do what he thinks is best for his students. During one scene, for example, he instructs students to rip out a book's preface that recommends a mathematical approach to understanding poetry. This action symbolizes his encouragement of students to think for themselves. As he says elsewhere in the film, "*Carpe diem*. Seize the day, boys. Make your lives extraordinary." At the close of the film, the students honor Keating with the salute, "O Captain! My Captain!" while standing on their desks—as the conservative headmaster looks on in dismay (O captain, my captain!, 2014).

Walt Whitman wrote the poem "O Captain! My Captain!" as an elegy in honor of Abraham Lincoln following his assassination. The poem is a reminder that the adoration of Lincoln was temporal: "[F]or you the shores a-crowding; for you they call, the swaying mass, their eager faces turning. ... It is some dream that on the deck, you've fallen cold and dead" (Whitman, n.d.).

The poem cautions us that, all too often, in the words of John Dewey, "[t]he successes of [great teachers] tend to be born and to die with them" (Dewey, 2008). I hope that this book will enable the teaching successes of these seven professors to live on, just as the wisdom of Chris Christensen, to whom this book is dedicated, has continued to inspire teachers and leaders. As Chris once noted, "Teaching is the greatest of all vocations because it allows you to combine the momentary and the infinite" (The art of discussion leading, n.d.).

This book's dedication mentions a seminar of his that influenced my decision to write this book. Chris liked to close his seminars with this reference to the poet Amy Lowell: "Teaching, Ms. Lowell said, is like dropping letters into the postbox of the unconscious. You never know whether they have been posted, delivered, or read." He concluded with this wish that I now pass on to you: "May your letters be well posted, studied, read, and acted upon in the coming years" (The art of discussion leading, n.d.).

References

2020 guiding principles and standards for business accreditation. (2020, July 28). Retrieved from AACSB: https://www.aacsb.edu/-/media/aacsb/docs/accreditation/business/standards-and-tables/2020%20business%20accreditation%20standards.ashx?la=en&hash=E4B7D8348A6860B3AA9804567F02C68960281DA2

Authentic. (n.d.). Retrieved from Merrian-Webster: https://www.merriam-webster.com/dictionary/authentic

Bonsignore, J. et al. (1996). Toward the definition of a great teacher. *Journal of Legal Studies Education*, 14, 103–132.

BookBrowse's favorite quotes. (n.d.). Retrieved from BookBrowse: https://www.bookbrowse.com/quotes/detail/index.cfm/quote_number/401/if-you-want-to-build-a-ship-dont-drum-up-people-but-rather-teach-them-to-long-for-the-endless-immensity-of-the-sea

Christensen, R. (1991). Every student teaches and every teacher learns. In R. Christensen et al. (Eds.), *Education for judgment* (pp. 99–119). Boston, MA: Harvard Business School Press.

Crafting, studying, and teaching strategy in a volatile world. (2021, January 7). *YouTube.* Retrieved from https://www.youtube.com/watch?v=FHtSklBAaxU

Data analytics at Kellogg. (n.d.). Retrieved from Northwesterm Kellogg: https://www.kellogg.northwestern.edu/data-analytics.aspx

Dewey, J. (1922). *Democracy and education.* New York: The Macmillan Company.

Dewey, J. (2008). Sources of a science of education. In A. Boydston (Ed.), *The later works of John Dewey, Volume 5* (p. 4). Carbondale, IL: University of Southern Illinois Press.

Edward L. Kaplan, '71, New Venture Challenge. (n.d.). Retrieved from Polsky: https://polsky.uchicago.edu/programs-events/new-venture-challenge/nvc/

Faculty session. (2017, June 27). Retrieved from YouTube: https://www.youtube.com/watch?v=iBwUmNttKCI

Garvin, D. (1991). Barriers and gateways to learning. In R. Christensen et al. (Eds.), *Education for judgment* (pp. 3–14). Boston: Harvard Business School Press.

Ginott, H. G., et al. (1987). Teaching and teachers: Three views. In R. Christensen (Ed.), *Teaching and the case method* (pp. 83–84). Boston: Harvard Business School.

Holstead, C. (2019, September 11). *Want to improve your teaching? Start with the basics: Learn your students' names.* Retrieved from The Chronicle of Higher Education: https://www.chronicle.com/article/want-to-improve-your-teaching-start-with-the-basics-learn-students-names/?cid2=gen_login_refresh&cid=gen_sign_in

In honor of Albert Einstein's birthday. (n.d.). Retrieved from Championing Science: https://championingscience.com/2019/03/15/everything-should-be-made-as-simple-as-possible-but-no-simpler/

Jacobellis v. Ohio, 378 U.S. 184 (1964).

Maas, J. (1991, Fall). Reflections on discussion teaching. *Harvard Business School Publications Newsletter*, p. 4.

Nash, L. (1991). Discovering the Semester. In R. Christensen et al. (Eds.), *Education for Judgment* (pp. 231–248). Boston: Harvard Business School Press.

O captain, my captain! (2014, August 13). Retrieved from YouTube: https://www.youtube.com/watch?v=j64SctPKmqk

P3: Purpose, passion, and principles at Wharton. (n.d.). Retrieved from Wharton: https://www.wharton.upenn.edu/story/p3-purpose-passion-principles-wharton/

Palmer, P. (n.d.). *The heart of a teacher.* Retrieved from Center for Courage & Renewal: http://www.couragerenewal.org/parker/writings/heart-of-a-teacher/

Positive organizational scholarship. (n.d.). Retrieved from Center for Positive Organizations: https://positiveorgs.bus.umich.edu/an-introduction/

Schmitt, J. (2018, March 10). *B-schools with the best teachng faculty.* Retrieved from POETS&QUANTS: https://poetsandquants.com/2018/03/10/business-schools-with-the-best-teaching-faculty/

Schon, D. (1987). The crisis of professional knowledge and the pursuit of an epistemology of practice. In R. Christensen (Ed.), *Teaching and the Case Method* (pp. 241–253). Boston: Harvard Business School.

Spreitzer, G. (2015, May 1). Becoming the best in you. Unpublished Graduation Address at the University of Michigan.

The art of discussion leading. (n.d.). Retrieved from Vimeo: https://vimeo.com/104311202

Tompkins, J. (1996). *A life in school.* New York: Perseus Books.

U.S. competitiveness. (n.d.). Retrieved from Harvard Business School: https://www.hbs.edu/competitiveness/about/Pages/default.aspx

Wassermann, S. (1987). How I taught myself how to teach. In R. Christensen (Ed.), *Teaching and the case method* (pp. 175–183). Boston: Harvard Business School.

Waugh, A. (n.d.). *MIT LGO program wins prestigious award.* Retrieved from MIT News: https://news.mit.edu/2014/mit-lgo-program-wins-prestigious-award

Whitman, W. (n.d.). *O captain! My captain!* Retrieved from Poetry Foundation: https://www.poetryfoundation.org/poems/45474/o-captain-my-captain

You've got to find what you love, Jobs says. (2005, June 12). Retrieved from Stanford News: https://news.stanford.edu/2005/06/14/jobs-061505/

Appendix A

Zoom Lessons for Leaders

Author's note: The following 2021 article is adapted from my post on *AACSB Insights* (Siedel, 2021). In addition to the lessons in the article, the professors profiled in this book have expressed their own views about teaching via Zoom. According to Professor Rivkin, "We can only deliver about seventy percent as much content per class session. [When teaching via Zoom], we need new ways to keep students engaged" (Crafting, studying, and teaching strategy in a volatile world, 2021). One innovative way to keep students engaged is to connect with them before class. For instance, Professor Kaplan advised me that

> [t]he more connection you can create ahead of time, the better. I met in small Zoom groups—5 or 6 students—for a breakfast or lunch with most of the students in my course. With 200 students, this meant 35 of these sessions. I found them very valuable in getting to know the students and showing the students that I was a person and not just a face on a screen.

In this article, you will find other advice for leaders engaged in remote teaching. While these lessons are based on experience during the pandemic, I hope that they will be useful to leaders in any scenario where people work and learn remotely.

5 Zoom Lessons for Leaders

In the title of his landmark 2018 article in the *Harvard Business Review*, Sydney Finkelstein of Dartmouth College notes that "The Best Leaders Are Great Teachers." He takes this idea one step further, concluding that "if you're not teaching, you're not really leading" (Finkelstein, 2018).

Noel Tichy of the University of Michigan makes a similar argument in his book *The Cycle of Leadership: How Great Leaders Teach Their Companies to Win*, where he notes that "the essence of leading is not commanding, but teaching" (p. 74). Average leaders set goals for their teams, but great leaders, Tichy explains, also provide teams with the motivation and knowledge necessary to achieve those goals.

Not surprisingly, the pandemic has placed business leaders at the same disadvantage as other educators. They have had to use still-developing video communication technology to engage employees scattered around the world—at a time when employee engagement is of utmost importance. A survey of 9,000 managers and employees commissioned by Microsoft and the Boston Consulting Group and supervised by Michael Parke of the Wharton School (Microsoft, 2020) indicated that they lose a sense of purpose when they work remotely.

That raises the question: What can CEOs and managers learn from instructors who have gained substantial experience teaching courses remotely over video conferencing platforms?

During the pandemic, I started using Zoom to teach negotiation courses to MBA and undergraduate students, some of whom were stranded by lockdowns around the world. I've recently used other video conferencing platforms to present webinars to professional groups in the United States, Asia, and South America. I want to share the following five lessons, based on my experiences so far.

Select Video Features Intentionally

The good news is that a video conferencing platform like Zoom includes features that meet a variety of teaching needs—you can chat, conduct a poll, share screens, record, use breakout rooms, annotate materials, or add captions. The bad news is that using too many of these features at one time can complicate and dilute the learning experience. When designing learning experiences, take to heart Thoreau's plea in *Walden* to "Simplify, simplify."

For example, I do not direct participants to use Zoom's chat function because I don't want my students to multitask during class. I also do not use the polling feature extensively, so that I do not distract them from the main discussion.

But I do use the features in ways that serve my intentions. Instead of setting up my iPad or other device as a whiteboard, I find it simpler to use the platform's annotation feature. And because I appreciate the ability of polls to keep students engaged, I use the voting feature that allows students to respond to questions with a simple "yes" or "no." In a post-course evaluation, one student noted, "I liked the 'yes or no' voting feature that was utilized a lot by the professor because it helped make me feel more engaged in class."

Solve the "Eye Contact" Dilemma

In their June 2020 *Harvard Business Review* article, "You Might Not Be Hearing Your Team's Best Ideas" (Parke and Sherf, 2020), Michael

Parke of the Wharton School and Elad Sherf of the University of North Carolina, Chapel Hill, highlight skills leaders can use to bring out the best in others. These include asking questions, inviting ideas, following up, and creating a sense of psychological safety.

These skills are easier to apply during in-person meetings, where you can maintain eye contact and scan participants' facial expressions to gauge whether they understand the material or need encouragement to speak up.

In Zoom interactions, such skills are far more difficult to practice. The "Hollywood Squares"-type boxes that display participants' faces are small, and everyone present might not fit on one screen. Noticing when someone wants to make a comment or respond to a question can be difficult.

When I first started teaching over Zoom, I tried to scan my students' faces as I would in a physical classroom, but this distracted me from maintaining eye contact with the camera. I finally stuck a Post-it Note near my camera with "Look here" written on it as a reminder. I also take advantage of the "Raise Hand" icon, which allows me to call on students in the order that they volunteer.

This solution is not perfect, as some students are so enthusiastic about participating that they click the icon before I can complete my questions. As a student noted in an email, "The raise hand feature was helpful but it can lead to the fastest person who clicks the button getting chosen each time." To prevent "quick-draw" students from dominating class discussion, I occasionally skip them, noting that "I want to give Sue a rest by calling on Pete." In this way, I still can make sure that everyone is heard.

Improve the 70% Expectation

Video conferencing platforms present a number of technology challenges, from video freezing to students forgetting to unmute. Because of such interruptions, there is a consensus among faculty that they should expect to cover only around 70% of the material online that they would typically cover in a traditional in-person course.

To increase this percentage, I have worked to make my own presentation more efficient. Students complete a larger percentage of the coursework before class. And instead of the 90 minutes I normally would set aside for team-based discussion of a case on negotiation ethics, I ask the entire class to discuss a shorter scenario. Then I have them watch "The Burger Murders" (Ethical dilemma, 2020), a five-minute video of the shorter case that Christine Ladwig of Southeast Missouri State University and I developed for TED in July 2020.

Address Zoom Fatigue

As one of my students recently put it, "I don't think I would've felt the same level of fatigue from an all-day class if we had been in person."

So-called "Zoom fatigue" is exacerbated by the fact that a course that begins at 8 a.m. in Michigan starts at 5 a.m. for students in California and at 9 p.m. for students in China. A course that ends at 5:30 p.m. Eastern time finishes at 4:00 a.m. the next morning in India.

To address this fatigue, I continually engage students with different activities, including lectures, team-based breakout sessions, videos, and interactive case discussions. I also stand as I teach, which students say increases their energy levels.

When I mentioned this approach to a colleague, he gave me a puzzled look before asking, "If you stand, wouldn't the camera be aimed at your belt buckle?" My desk is adjustable, so the camera rises with it when I adjust its height to stand.

Embrace Flexibility—and Humility

Teaching from my home study has presented problems that I had never faced with in-person learning. Would I have to manage a hardware failure or a power outage during class? Would the video platform crash? What lighting adjustments should I make —for example, to minimize an unwanted halo effect on my balding head caused by an overhead light? How do I minimize outside noise such as the loud hum of my neighbor's lawnmower? How would I respond if Zoombombers hacked into the course?

The students also encountered unique challenges. One student was forced to drop my course after contracting COVID-19; another missed class because of contact tracing. One student had Wi-Fi problems when he had to move into isolation after his girlfriend contracted COVID-19; another lost his broadband connection when he and his ten roommates streamed at the same time. A new mother had to turn off her camera periodically when pumping breast milk for her son; others coped with distractions from family members or family pets.

That's why we all must embrace flexibility. When one student lost Wi-Fi twice during a key negotiation exercise, she called in on her phone. I also established a chain of communication to reach students if the internet connection failed, and I kept my laptop turned on and ready to go in case my desktop computer failed.

As it turned out, I lost connection with students only once, and the lapse lasted only for a few seconds. A class recording captured the reactions of two students who forgot they were being recorded. "Did we lose him?" asked Student A. To which Student B responded, "Yeah, awesome."

This exchange offers a final lesson for leaders: Maintain a touch of humility as you navigate this technology. Every moment is an opportunity to learn and refine your teaching skills.

References

Crafting, studying, and teaching strategy in a volatile world. (2021). Retrieved from YouTube: https://www.youtube.com/watch?v=FHtSklBAaxU.

Ethical dilemma: The burger murders. (2020). TEDEd. Retrieved from https://ed.ted.com/lessons/ethical-dilemma-the-burger-murders-george-siedel-and-christine-ladwig.

Finkelstein, S. (2018). The best leaders are great teachers. *Harvard Business Review*, pp. 142–145.

Microsoft (2020). *Building resilience & maintaining innovation in a hybrid world*. Retrieved from http://d1c25a6gwz7q5e.cloudfront.net/reports/2020-11-09-workplace-whitepaper-FINAL.pdf.

Parke, M. and Sherf, E. (2020, June 4). *You might not be hearing your team's best ideas. Harvard Business Review*. Retrieved from https://hbr.org/2020/06/you-might-not-be-hearing-your-teams-best-ideas.

Siedel, G. (2021, January 5). 5 zoom lessons for leaders. AACSB Insights. Retrieved from https://www.aacsb.edu/insights/2021/january/5-zoom-lessons-for-leaders.

Tichy, N. (2009). *The cycle of leadership: How great leaders teach their companies to win*. New York: HarperCollins.

Business School Rankings and the Methodology for Business School Selection

The seven professors highlighted in this book teach at leading business schools. Selection of the seven schools required reliance on one of the most controversial words in the business school world: rankings. Because they think of rankings as a report card, business school deans love them when their schools do well and dislike them (and criticize their "suspect" methodologies) when their schools do less well. Regardless of how their schools are ranked, deans cannot ignore rankings because prospective MBA students and recruiters use them for school selection and hiring decisions.

The History of Business School Rankings

The practice of publishing business school rankings on a regular basis using a consistent methodology originated in 1988 through the efforts of John Byrne, at that time the management editor and later Editor-in-Chief of *Business Week* (now *Bloomberg Businessweek*) magazine. Because of his pioneering work on rankings and his creation in 2010 of *Poets and Quants*, the premier source of information about business schools, Byrne has become an influential presence in the business school world. I first met Byrne in 1991 when he visited the Ross School of Business. Later, when I was Associate Dean at Ross, he interviewed me for an article on virtual business schools.

As Byrne later recounted (Byrne, 2014), in 1988 he sat down at his Macintosh computer at home and created a survey of MBA students. His family helped him stuff around 3,000 surveys into envelopes, and he later personally summarized the results from the responses. His work resulted in a *Business Week* cover story (one of his fifty-eight cover stories) and one of its bestselling issues ever. Byrne's efforts launched regular *Business Week* MBA rankings. *US News* began publishing annual rankings two years later (in 1990), followed still later by other publications, notably *The Economist*, *The Financial Times*, and *Forbes*.

In a podcast from his home during the 2020 coronavirus pandemic, Byrne confessed that he felt "a little bit like Dr. Frankenstein. I created this monster. This monster roams the earth wreaking havoc in the offices of one dean after another" (Our love-hate relationship with MBA rankings, n.d.) While admitting that there are flaws in ranking methodologies, he also noted that his intentions were good in that he hoped that rankings would make business schools more responsive to their students and recruiters.

The Decision to Use an MBA Ranking

Before selecting a specific ranking to identify the seven leading business schools, I first had to decide whether to use an MBA ranking or rankings of other business school programs such as undergraduate, Executive MBA, and executive education programs. I went with rankings of MBA programs, which are the flagship programs in business schools. In addition, rankings of other programs are based on incomplete data as all schools do not have undergraduate or Executive MBA programs.

For example, using 2020 rankings, *US News* ranks the leading undergraduate programs as follows (Allen, No surprise: Wharton tops U.S. News' undergrad biz rankings again, 2019):

1. Wharton
2. MIT Sloan
3. Berkeley Haas and Michigan Ross (tie)
5. Carnegie Mellon Tepper, New York University Stern, and University of Texas-Austin McCombs (tie)
8. North Carolina Kenan-Flagler and Virginia Darden (tie)
10. Cornell Johnson and Indiana Kelley

Notably missing are Harvard, Stanford, Chicago, and Northwestern—because they do not have undergraduate programs. These schools are also missing from the other leading 2020 rankings of undergraduate programs, developed by *Poets and Quants* (Allen, Wharton again tops P&Q's best undergraduate b-Schools of 2020, 2019):

1. Wharton
2. Michigan Ross
3. Virginia Darden
4. New York University Stern
5. Georgetown McDonough
6. Notre Dame Mendoza
7. Washington University Olin

8. Cornell Johnson
9. North Carolina Kenan-Flagler
10. Carnegie Mellon Tepper

The same problem arises with combined rankings of graduate programs. *The Financial Times* uses a methodology that combines graduate and postgraduate business education: MBA, Executive MBA, and executive education programs. Like the undergraduate rankings, this ranking is misleading because some schools do not offer a full array of programs. For instance, in a recent ranking of graduate programs based in the Americas (Moules, 2018), Harvard and Stanford ranked lower than usual because they do not have Executive MBA programs.

1. Wharton
2. MIT Sloan
3. Columbia
4. Chicago Booth and Michigan Ross (tie)
6. UCLA Anderson
7. Duke Fuqua
8. Washington University Olin
9. Stanford Graduate School of Business
10. Harvard Business School

Selecting a Specific MBA Ranking. After deciding to use an MBA program ranking, the next step was to select seven schools from the fifteen or so "top ten" schools that appear in the popular rankings mentioned earlier. From these, I initially focused on *Bloomberg Businessweek* because of its long history, and *US News* and *The Financial Times* because their rankings include the seven essential areas of business.

I decided to select *US News* for several reasons. First, it includes the most complete rankings of the seven essential areas of business. Second, it was the most current ranking. *US News* published what it calls its 2019 ranking in March 2018, shortly before I began my research.

Third, *US News* is, in the words of John Byrne in an article in *Poets and Quants*, "arguably the most watched and followed of all the MBA rankings" (Byrne, 2020). According to a survey of Harvard MBA students, *US News* was the most read ranking and the one that most influenced their choice of school (Cautela, 2020).

Finally—and most importantly, given the general criticism of rankings—*US News* is highly regarded for its methodology. In 2013, distinguished marketing researcher Dawn Iacobucci of Vanderbilt published an article in the *Journal of Marketing Education* with the cumbersome title: "A Psychometric Assessment of the *Businessweek, US News & World Report*, and *Financial Times* Rankings of Business Schools'

MBA Programs." The article investigates the reliability and variability of these three leading rankings (Iacobucci, 2013). In an interview published in *Poets and Quants*, Professor Iacobucci concludes that, based on this research, she prefers the *US News* ranking, mentioning the "objectivity of the measures and components that go into the ranking. They are less easily gamed" (Byrne, 2013).

The 2019 *US News* Ranking. Based on a peer assessment, success in placing graduates, and student selectivity, the top seven business schools in the 2019 ranking (Byrne, 2018) are:

1. Chicago Booth and Harvard Business School (tie)
3. Wharton
4. Stanford Graduate School of Business
5. MIT Sloan
6. Northwestern Kellogg
7. Berkeley Haas and Michigan Ross (tie)

Although the actual rank of each school on the 2019 list varies from year to year, these schools constitute the top seven in an average of historical rankings by *Bloomberg Businessweek* (the ranking with the greatest longevity) from 1988 to the date my research began in 2018, with three exceptions. Duke is included in the historical averages, and MIT Sloan and Berkeley Haas are missing. The schools on the 2019 list are also on the "top seven" list in the original *US News* annual ranking from 1990—except that Dartmouth Tuck was on the original list, not Chicago Booth and Berkeley Haas. ·

Because of the tie at #7 in the 2019 *US News* ranking, I had to choose between Berkeley Haas and Michigan Ross. This was a difficult decision because I have connections with, and deeply admire, both schools. I spent most of my teaching career at Ross, apart from years when I was a visiting professor (at Harvard and Stanford), a visiting fellow (three times at Cambridge University), and a Fulbright Scholar. Later, my position as a visiting scholar at Berkeley and close ties to the Bay Area increased my appreciation of the outstanding Haas MBA program and the Berkeley campus in general.

Because this book focuses on the seven essential areas of business, I used the *US News* 2019 ranking of these areas as the tiebreaker. *US News* asked the deans of business schools and MBA program directors to rate these areas, which the magazine calls "specialties." The publication ranked five of the seven essential areas in 2019 and had previously ranked a sixth area, Business Law. (The *Financial Times* also periodically ranks Business Law, with Wharton and Michigan Ross among the top ten in 2016 and 2017.) Michigan Ross ranked among the top five schools in five of the six areas, while Berkeley Haas did not have a top-five ranking (Ethier, 2018). Based on these results, I selected Ross as the seventh school.

Matching the Top Seven Schools with the Seven Essential Areas

When matching the top seven schools with the seven essential areas, I started with the *US News* rankings for each area. However, because *US News* does not rank Strategy, I used recent *Financial Times* rankings for this area. Harvard Business School was an easy match with Strategy because it ranked either #1 or #2 in the world for four of the five years preceding my research.

For the remaining six areas, I attempted to select the top school in the *US News* specialty rankings whenever possible. This resulted in pairing Wharton with Business Law, Kellogg with Marketing, and MIT with Operations. The remaining three pairings were problematic because schools that had already been paired claimed the top spot for two of the areas—Wharton for Finance and Harvard for Management—while the top place in Accounting was held by the University of Texas McCombs School of Business, which was not one of the top seven schools. For these three areas, I went further down the list of in the specialty rankings to pair Chicago Booth with Finance, Michigan Ross with Management, and Stanford with Accounting.

References

Allen, N. (2019, September 10). *No surprise: Wharton tops U.S. News' undergrad biz rankings again.* Retrieved from POETS&QUANTS: https://poetsandquantsforundergrads.com/2019/09/10/no-surprise-wharton-tops-u-s-news-undergrad-biz-rankings-again/

Allen, N. (2019, December 20). *Wharton again tops P&Q's best undergraduate b-Schools of 2020.* Retrieved from POETS&QUANTS: https://poetsandquantsforundergrads.com/2019/12/20/wharton-again-tops-pqs-best-undergraduate-b-schools-of-2020/

Byrne, J. (2013, June 10). *Mostly reliable & valid MBA rankings?* Retrieved from POETS&QUANTS: https://poetsandquants.com/2013/06/10/which-mba-ranking-is-best/

Byrne, J. (2014, May 14). *Confessions of an MBA ranking guru.* Retrieved from POETS&QUANTS: https://poetsandquants.com/2014/05/14/confessions-of-ranking-guru/

Byrne, J. (2018, March 19). *Ten surprises in U.S. News' MBA ranking.* Retrieved from POETS&QUANTS: https://poetsandquants.com/2018/03/19/ten-biggest-surprises-in-u-s-news-mba-ranking/

Byrne, J. (2020, February 25). *U.S. News ranking due out March 17th*. Retrieved from POETS&QUANTS: https://poetsandquants.com/2020/02/25/u-s-news-ranking-due-out-march-17th/?pq-category=business-school-news/

Cautela, M. (2020, February 6). *HBS analyzes data from student-wide survey on MBA rankings*. Retrieved from THE HARBUS: https://harbus.org/2020/hbs-analyzes-data-from-student-wide-survey-on-mba-rankings/

Ethier, M. (2018, March 26). *How business schools rank by specialization*. Retrieved from POETS&QUANTS: https://poetsandquants.com/2018/03/26/how-business-schools-rank-by-specialization/

Iacobucci, D. (2013). A psychometric Assessment of the Businessweek, U.S. News & World Report, and Financial Times rankings of business schools' MBA programs. *Journal of Marketing Education, 35*(3), 204–219.

Moules, J. (2018, December 2). *FT 2018 Americas and Asia-Pacific top 25 business school rankings*. Retrieved from Financial Times: https://www.ft.com/content/14221926-e9bb-11e8-94da-a6478f64c783

Our love-hate relationship with MBA rankings. (n.d.). Retrieved from SOUNDCLOUD: https://soundcloud.com/poetsandquants/our-love-hate-relationship-with-mba-rankings

Index

Note: *Italics* page numbers refer to figures.

accounting 10; Stanford Graduate School of Business 17–18
after-class session 44
ambiguity 83
authenticity 203–210

best practices 189
big-picture perspective 83, 89, 127, 148, 175, 194–195
Bonsignore, John 205–206
Brooks, David 205
business law: in large organization 12; in start-up 10; at Wharton School of University of Pennsylvania 18–20
business school education: content of 7–8; seven essentials in 13
business school rankings 220–224
Byrne, John 220–221

call and response 62
case studies, in class 43, 149–150
character 48
"cheat sheets" 196
Christensen, Chris 200, 204, 206
clarity: analysis and 177; on assignments 147–148; in presentations 134
closure 151, 177–178
cold calling 98, 165, 192–193
Coles, Robert 29
community, learning 190–193
companies, working with 155
competence, sense of 109
content 47–48; relevant 82, 88; thoughtful organization of 68
conversational style 43

course materials 129–130, 189
COVID-19 pandemic 47, 201; *see also* Zoom lessons

discussion framework 196
discussion leadership 128

end-of-class summary 44, 84, 89, 195
energy 43
enthusiasm 43, 130, 135
ethics, business 19–20
examples: interesting 61; real-world 43; relevant 61
experience: real-life 104–105; research and, blending 128–129
eye contact, in Zoom 216–217

finance 10; at University of Chicago Booth School of Business 20–21
Finkelstein, Sydney 215
flipped classroom 77
fun 176–177

game plan 189
Garvin, David 197
grading curve 143, 167–168
Griffin, Carlton 187

Harvard Business School: Professor Jan Rivkin at 157–183, *160*; strategy at 25–26
holistic approach 69
HRM *see* human resources management (HRM)

human resources management
(HRM): in start-up 10
humor 150–151, 176–177

impact, sense of 109
interactive class 43–44, 88, 150,
164–165, 197–201
interactive teaching style 82–83,
105–106

Jobs, Steve 205

Kaplan, Steven 71–89, 73, 188, 191,
199, 201, 209

language, everyday 42–43, 196
leadership: discussion 128; role of
teachers 5–8
learning: action 199–200; active
61–62, 68, 105, 127–128, 199;
continuous 205–208; relevance of
127; from research 206–208; from
students 69
Lee, Charles 29–49, 31, 187, 189,
195–196, 198, 200, 207–209
legal studies 19–20; see also business
law
listening skills 88, 175–176

management: in large organization
12; in start-up 10; at University of
Michigan Ross School of Business
21–22
marketing: in large organization 12; at
Northwestern Kellogg
School of Management 22–24; in
start-up 10
meaning: sense of 109; in teaching
110–111
MIT Sloan School of Management:
operations at 24–25; Professor
Georgia Perakis at 137–156, 140

Nash, Laura 190
Northwestern Kellogg School of
Management: marketing at 22–24;
Professor Florian Zettelmeyer at
113–136, 115

operations: in large organization
12; at MIT Sloan School of
Management 24–25; in start-up 11

pace, in classroom 42, 196
Palmer, Parker 186, 203, 205
participation: evaluation of 77; in
grading 98–99, 199
passion 48, 135, 204–205
Perakis, Georgia 137–156, 140, 191,
193–195, 201, 204, 209–210
perspective, big-picture 61
Porter, Michael 187, 210
Postman, Neil 203–204
preparation 68, 135, 163–164,
186–190

rankings, business school 220–224
repetition 135
research, synergy of teaching and 88
review, of prior session 104, 130,
148–149
rigor, support and 83
risk taking 135
Rivkin, Jan 157–183, 160, 187–188,
196, 198–200, 204–207, 210

Schon, Donald 197
self-determination 109
seven essential areas: in business
schools 13; in large organization
11–12; in start-up 9–11
Shell, Richard 50–70, 53, 186,
194–195, 197, 202, 209
simplification 195–196
Spreitzer, Gretchen 90–111, 94, 187–
188, 192, 198, 200, 205, 207–208
Stanford Graduate School of Business:
accounting at 17–18; Professor
Charles Lee at 29–49, 31
start-up: seven essentials in 9–11
storytelling 134, 188–189
strategy: at Harvard Business School
25–26; in large organization 12; in
start-up 11
students: backgrounds of 191–192;
co-creation of learning experience
by 104, 149, 193; dealing with
ambiguity 83; feedback from 142;
gauging understanding of 150;
interaction with 176, 191; learning
from 69, 205–206; personal
interest in 82, 88; relevance to 135;
welcoming 147; who dominate
discussion 99, 142, 166, 192–193
support network 111

teachers: as leaders 7; leadership role
    of 5–8
teaching process 186–203
team assignments 193
Tichy, Noel 215
Tompkins, Jane 197
transparency, in sharing
    experiences 69

University of Chicago Booth School
    of Business: finance at 20–21;
    Professor Steven Kaplan at
    71–89, 73
University of Michigan Ross School
    of Business: management at 21–22;
    Professor Gretchen Spreitzer at
    90–111, 94

variation, in delivery 135
Veritas Forum 208–209
video recording 190
visitors 203
visualization 196

welcome, classroom 42
Wharton School of University of
    Pennsylvania: business law at
    18–20; Professor Richard Shell at
    50–70, 53
Wright, David 187

Zettelmeyer, Florian 113–136, 115,
    186, 188–189, 194, 196, 201–202,
    204, 208–209
Zoom lessons 215–218

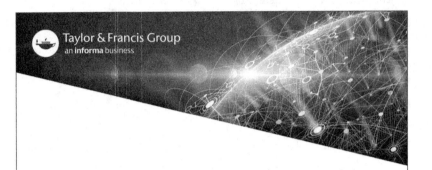

Printed in the United States
by Baker & Taylor Publisher Services